Using Psychology: Principles of Behavior and Your Life

Using Psychology

Principles of Behavior and Your Life

Second Edition

Morris Holland University of California, Los Angeles

Gerald Tarlow University of California, Los Angeles

Little, Brown and Company

Boston   Toronto

Library of Congress Catalog Card No. 79-64317

First Printing

Publishing simultaneously in Canada
by Little, Brown & Company (Canada) Limited.

Printed in the United States of America.

Acknowledgments

The authors gratefully acknowledge permission to use excerpts from the following works:

Beck, Aaron T. From *Depression* (Harper & Row), pp. 333–335. Copyright © 1967 by Aaron T. Beck, M.D. Reprinted by permission.
Christie, Richard. From "The Machiavelli Among Us," *Psychology Today* 6:4 (1970). Reprinted by permission of Academic Press, Inc.
Ebert, Alan. From "Fears of the Famous." Reprinted by permission from the May 1973 issue of *Good Housekeeping Magazine*. © 1973 by the Hearst Corporation.
Huxley, Aldous. Abridged from pp. 20–24 *Brave New World*. Copyright 1932, 1960 by Aldous Huxley. Reprinted by permission of Harper & Row, Publishers, Inc., Mrs. Laura Huxley, and Chatto and Windux Ltd.
Laing, R. D., and Esterson, A. From *Sanity, Madness, and the Family,* © 1964 by The Tavistock Institute of Human Relations, Basic Books, Inc., Publishers, New York. Reprinted by permission.
Luria, A. R. From *The Mind of a Mnemonist,* © 1968 by Basic Books, Inc., Publishers, New York. Reprinted by permission.
Stuart, R. B. and Davis, B. From *Slim Chance in a Fat World: Behavioral Control of Obesity* (Champaign, Ill.: Research Press, 1972). Compiled from Durnin, J. V. G. A., and Passmore, R., *Energy, Work and Leisure* (London: Heinemann Educational Books Ltd, 1967); Passmore, R., and Durnin, J. V. G. A., "Human Energy Expenditure," *Physiological Reviews* 35 (1955); and Consolazio, C. F., Johnson, R. E., and Pecora, L. J., *Psychological Measurements of Metabolic Functions in Man* (New York: McGraw-Hill, 1963).
Watson, D., and Friend, R. From "Measurement of Social-Evaluative Anxiety," *Journal of Consulting and Clinical Psychology* 33 (1969). Copyright 1969 by the American Psychological Association. Reprinted by permission.
Wolberg, L. R. From "Hypnotic Experiments in Psychosomatic Medicine," *Psychosomatic Medicine* 9 (1947). Reprinted by permission of Elsevier North Holland, Inc.

To our parents—Wilber and Ada, Saul and Mildred

Preface

The goal of *Using Psychology* is to teach the principles and methods of psychology and demonstrate how they can be used in everyday life. Our desire is to make these methods and principles available to all who face difficulties in some area of life and are eager to make changes for themselves. In the classroom, this text is designed to supplement and enrich courses in introductory and general psychology, psychology of personal development, applied psychology, and other courses in the social sciences.

The approach is to show how situations in life can be altered through direct application of the principles of psychology to life situations, without professional training or diagnostic tests. Each chapter presents a brief study, drawn from a case history or scientific research, of a situation similar to one that a student may have experienced. The psychological principles that apply are described, with supporting research, and followed by a discussion of how application of the principle can bring about change. Step-by-step explanation enables students to integrate these new principles into their own experience.

The psychological principles are drawn from recent research, and their application to the studies is discussed and evaluated in depth. Checklists and exercises help students to locate areas that present difficulties to them, and to evaluate their understanding of the material.

This second edition of *Using Psychology* represents many significant revisions. We have added three new chapters on anger, repression, and shyness—areas that represent problems for many people and to which recent research has made some important contributions. In addition, most of the remaining chapters have been edited and revised. The readable style, clear explanations combined with concrete examples, firm foundation in research, and step-by-step detailing of how to apply the principles, all part of the first edition, remain unchanged.

We would like to thank Kent Butzine, Jim Hail, Harry Keenan, and Clair Wiederholt for their helpful comments and suggestions. We have benefited from the thoughtful reactions of many instructors and their students who read and used the first edition. With this new edition, we remain interested in your personal experiences and welcome your comments.

Morris K. Holland
Department of Psychology
University of California,
  Los Angeles

Gerald Tarlow
Department of Psychiatry
University of California,
  Los Angeles

Contents

List of Psychological Principles

List of Exercises

Using Psychology: Principles of Behavior and Your Life

Chapter One

I THINK PSYCHOLOGY IS A TOOL.

LIKE A WRENCH?

NO, MORE LIKE A SCREWDRIVER. IT SEEMS LIKE I HAVE A FEW LOOSE SCREWS RATHER THAN A LEAKY FAUCET.

Written by Stephanie Crane/Drawn by Ben Black

Using Psychology

Ben was worried. He was thinking of dropping out. The old dream of getting a college degree was all but gone.

He had done well in high school, but this was his first year of college, and he was lost. Nothing seemed to be going right. He used to make A's and B's; now he made C's and D's. He used to have a few friends; now he was alone and feeling blue. He began to think that he didn't really belong in college after all.

Studying never used to be much of a problem, but now he recognized that his way of studying just was not adequate at the college level. He was becoming increasingly worried about his grades and was approaching each exam with such anxiety and nervousness that his mind would just "go blank" when the test was passed out. He tried to avoid speaking in his classes, but sometimes he could not avoid it; whenever he had to speak in a class, his heart would pound, his mouth would go dry, he would sweat profusely, and he would have difficulty getting his thoughts expressed. He was "on edge" much of the time and couldn't seem to relax. His discussions with his parents alternated between long silences and angry arguments. They were disappointed in his college performance and didn't understand why he was doing so poorly. For his part, Ben did not seem to be able to carry on a respectful conversation with his father; he always wound up making sarcastic remarks and getting into a yelling match. All of his problems were weighing him down. What could he do?

What do you do when you feel the way Ben feels? Does psychology offer any help for Ben's problems?

Two Psychologies

The psychology that you know now and practice in your daily affairs is *public psychology*. Every day you must be concerned with understanding

3

yourself and other people, and predicting how others will behave. You control your own behavior and influence the behavior and feelings of others. You practice public psychology. The discipline which incorporates a century of systematic inquiry and observation dedicated to understanding the principles of human behavior is *scientific psychology.* Scientific psychology does not necessarily contradict public psychology — it rather contributes detail, depth, and specificity to common understanding.

Scientific psychology consists of a method of inquiry, a body of accumulated principles of behavior, and a set of techniques for producing change.

Scientific psychology's method of inquiry is systematic observation. Using scientific controls, often under careful laboratory conditions, research psychologists determine what conditions affect behavior. Measurements are made, so that conclusions are often quantitative as well as qualitative. For example, a psychologist might examine the effectiveness of a particular method of reducing fear — "desensitization" (see Chapter Seven) — by comparing two groups of people who suffered from a mild snake phobia: the technique would be applied to those in one group but not to those in the other. Afterwards, a physiological measure of anxiety — the galvanic skin response — would be taken for each person in the presence of a snake. If the "desensitization" technique was successful, it should significantly reduce the average level of anxiety for those who applied it. (As a matter of fact, desensitization has been shown to work in reducing fear.)

Studies such as this one have built up a large body of knowledge about what is and what is not true for people, knowledge slowly accumulated over the history of the science of psychology. Through asking relevant questions about human behavior and systematically investigating those questions, psychologists have gathered empirical data. In this way they have determined some of the fundamental principles governing the nervous system, simple learning, visual and auditory perception, memory, personality development, group dynamics and other areas of human behavior. These fundamental principles are called "empirical generalizations" — empirical because they come from observation and experience; generalizations because they hold for most people under most circumstances. This does not mean that there are no exceptions to these rules; there are many. But the principles nevertheless are generally true, and their discovery has been a major achievement of the science of psychology.

Psychologists have developed ways to apply these principles to change behavior. These techniques are ways of influencing what people do and how they feel. Psychologists have learned how to reduce fear and anxiety, how to gain self-control over brain waves, how to induce deep relaxation, how to change attitudes and beliefs, how to improve memory, and how to break undesirable personal habits of long standing. Applying some of the tools of psychology requires complex instruments and professional training; but many can be applied by anyone, and these are the tools described here.

Psychology and Human Nature

The study of human behavior must deal with the fundamental issue of human nature. What are your views of human nature? Do you judge people as being basically good, or basically bad? Rational or irrational? Trustworthy or untrustworthy? Independent or conforming? Selfish or unselfish? Fixed or modifiable? Unique or alike? The answers you give to these questions depend, in some cases, upon your personal beliefs and values; people with different values would answer them differently. Value judgments about human nature form an important basis of public psychology.

Certain questions about human nature also can be answered scientifically: for example, it is an empirical fact that people are to some extent modifiable — they change with experience. The variables which produce change in human behavior are the object of much study by psychologists. It is also an empirical fact that people are different from each other, but to some extent consistent over time; you are different from me and you are about the same today as you were yesterday. Some of these fundamental generalizations about people can be called "metaprinciples" — superordinate principles about human behavior. These metaprinciples form an important basis for scientific psychology. For example:

The principle of individual differences: each person is physically and psychologically unique. Your uniqueness begins with your genetic uniqueness, the pool of genes inherited from your parents. Unless you are an identical twin, no one else has your genetic structure. Even identical twins — those growing from a single fertilized egg — grow to be physically and psychologically different. In the womb itself, one identical twin may rob the other of blood through a placental transfusion, so that one twin winds up anemic. From birth onward, experience shapes each twin differently: no one takes the same path through life and collects the same history of experiences as another person; our lives are unique. Although identical twins are more alike than any other two people, many identical twins eat differently, sleep differently, and differ in their personalities.

The principle of behavior consistency: a person behaves relatively consistently over time and in different situations, as a consequence of genetic, environmental, and behavioral determinants. You do not randomly change from day to day; you are more or less the same person today that you were yesterday, last year, and even a decade ago. You carry with you a psychological identity: dispositions to behave in certain consistent ways. These dispositions comprise what psychologists call your personality. Of course people grow and change over time; but they do not change completely. One aspect of personality that is particularly stable over time is the extent to which you are active and outgoing versus inactive and withdrawn.[1] If you are active and outgoing now, chances are you were the same as a young child.

The principle of biological determination: behavior is influenced by the chemical, electrical, and structural properties of the body. The most significant bodily influence on behavior comes from the nervous system and its most complex organ, the brain. However, certain chemicals can profoundly affect the way the brain functions. For example, one researcher reported the following experience after taking LSD:

Six hours after the ingestion of LSD . . . all objects appeared in unpleasant, constantly changing colors, the predominant shades being sickly green and blue. With closed eyes multihued, metamorphizing fantastic images overwhelmed me. Especially noteworthy was the fact that sounds were transposed into visual sensations so that from each tone or noise a comparable colored picture was evoked, changing in form and color kaleidoscopically.[2]

Damage to specific structures in the brain also causes fairly specific behavioral changes. There is a "speech area" in the left hemisphere of the brain that is centrally involved in the production of speech; temporal lobe areas on the sides of the brain apparently control memory; and the occipital lobe at the back of the brain does visual processing. Aggressive behavior can be strongly influenced by damaging certain hypothalamic brain structures through a brain operation; aggression can also be affected by chemical and electrical stimulation.

The principle of environmental determination: behavior is influenced by the physical and social environment, both present and past. There is no doubt that you are influenced by the immediate physical environment: your visual and auditory sensations guide you through the maze of the world. It is perhaps more interesting that you are strongly influenced by what happened in the past, your early experiences in childhood and your experiences gained since then from your interactions with the world and with other people. Usually, the people around you in early life are supportive and loving and encourage your growth toward independence and competence; they foster the development of strengths you will draw on throughout the remainder of your life. Occasionally, early experiences with other people can be traumatic, as in the following case of a boy who became schizophrenic (lost contact with the world as we know it) as a consequence of his experiences:

When the younger boy was not yet three years old, the older brother and some of his friends had played a hanging game with the boy as victim. The rope had cut off the child's breathing and he was only revived after artificial respiration had been applied. Dreading that the boy might tell, the older ones established a regime of terror. Repeatedly and severely they beat up this youngster, threatening even worse tortures if he should ever reveal the story. In order to make the threat more effective, they repeatedly locked him up in a dark and inaccessible excavation and kept him there for prolonged periods despite his terrified screaming.[3]

The principle of self-determination: behavior is influenced by personal choices, intentions, needs, beliefs, and feelings. We are not robots, inflexibly determined by our anatomical mechanisms and the present state of the physical environment: we are conscious, we think, we feel, and we choose. Passionate beliefs motivate and energize many arduous tasks; many have died for their beliefs concerning freedom or nationalism. Passionate feelings motivate and energize extreme actions; for love or for hate, men and women have built monuments and destroyed monuments, written poems and burned books.

This book attempts to take the principles and tools of scientific psychology and make them available to public psychology. Throughout the book, selected principles and supporting data are clearly identified for you and set off from the text.

Understanding human problems is an important goal of the science of psychology. For a century scientists have struggled to discover the basic principles underlying human behavior and have attempted to apply these principles to promote human welfare. The number of professional psychologists, however, is not enough to serve all people with problems; consequently many psychologists focus their efforts on the most severe difficulties, such as neurosis, drug addiction, mental retardation, or schizophrenia.

Some metaprinciples:

1. *The principle of individual differences: Each person is physically and psychologically unique.*
2. *The principle of behavior consistency: A person behaves relatively consistently over time and in different situations, as a consequence of genetic, environmental, and behavioral determinants.*
3. *The principle of biological determination: Behavior is influenced by the chemical, electrical, and structural properties of the body.*
4. *The principle of environmental determination: Behavior is influenced by the physical and social environment, both present and past.*
5. *The principle of self-determination: Behavior is influenced by personal choices, intentions, needs, beliefs, and feelings.*

But psychology can be applied by everyone. You can be a psychologist. In fact, you already are. You are now applying psychology in your life. You have lived a long time and have learned a great deal about human behavior, and much of what you have learned is true. The science of psychology extends, corrects, and deepens the understanding of human behavior gained from living intimately with yourself and with others. When you apply scientific principles of psychology, it is like using tools that are finer and sharper. This book attempts to sharpen some of your old tools and to provide you with some new ones as well.

Do-It-Yourself Psychology

Psychological principles can be applied by everyone. You can learn to use scientific psychology to help solve your own problems. There are a number of important advantages of do-it-yourself psychology. One factor is manpower. For most people, the major problem a few generations ago was physical survival: now it is psychological survival. We seem to be tense, alienated, confused. Suicide, addiction, violence, apathy, neurosis — are all problems of the modern world. Psychological problems are accelerating and there are not enough professional psychologists to go around. Nonpsychologists *must* practice psychology if psychology is to be applied to our problems.

A second advantage of do-it-yourself psychology is the factor of closeness. Professional psychologists must always operate after the fact and at a distance. You know your own problem most intimately; other people—even professional psychologists—are on the outside. You experience it; they listen to you talk about it. You know how it feels; they can know it only verbally. Furthermore, you are there when the problem occurs; a professional psychologist hears about it afterwards. If you are afraid of heights, if you can't concentrate on studying, if you sometimes have difficulty relaxing and going to sleep—you experience these problems more intimately than anyone else can. You are closer to them.

A third advantage of do-it-yourself psychology is the factor of power. If you can acquire the competence to cope with your own problems, to implement your own solutions, you are far better off. Psychological principles are powerful tools for change; the one who actually wields these tools exercises great power. Who is to use that power and for what ends? How will you be changed? Professional psychologists follow a strict code of ethics and do not use psychological tools to change people for selfish or personal reasons; nevertheless, if you take responsibility for your own change, the direction of that change will more likely correspond to *your* goals, rather than someone else's. Self-control and self-responsibility can be gained through do-it-yourself psychology.

A fourth advantage of do-it-yourself psychology is the factor of immunization. During the past few decades many people have become sophisticated in the use of psychological principles in business, advertising, education, and politics. With the spread of psychological knowledge among the elite, the danger of psychological manipulation of the many by the few has emerged as a serious potential problem. There are now other people using psychology against you for their own ends; for example, to manipulate you into buying their product or voting for their candidate. You can resist psychological manipulation far better when you understand the techniques being applied. Only when the general public is aware of the principles and tools being applied will the danger of covert control subside. Knowledge of these principles, in effect, helps to immunize you against covert psychological manipulation.

You can use psychology to help solve your problems, to feel better, to change your behavior, to expand your potential, and to enrich your life.

Let's return to Ben's problems and see if psychology can help.

Using Psychology: Some Examples

Learning to Relax

Ben found it very difficult to get to sleep the night before a big test at school. He would go to bed but stay awake for hours worrying about the exam. The next day he would be tired from lack of sleep. After learning about the progressive relaxation technique, he was able to ease his tension and get more rest. (See Chapter Six for the steps of this procedure.)

Studying Effectively

Ben read all the assigned material for his classes but had a hard time remembering the material for a test. He often got material from one class confused with reading from another class. He solved these problems by applying the "SQ3R" method. (See Chapter Three for additional information.)

Coping with Depression

Like many people, Ben began to feel depressed when he thought of his problems. He never seemed to smile much and couldn't find anything that interested him. One day Ben began to change some of the thoughts he had about himself and began to identify experiences that made him feel good. Gradually he started to feel less depressed. (See Chapter Thirteen for more details.)

Overcoming Shyness

Ben had trouble meeting new people. He was living away from home for the first time in his life and didn't know anyone in his dormitory. After learning about assertiveness training, he began to approach people and slowly started making new friends. (See Chapter Eleven for more details.)

Improving Personal Relationships

Whenever Ben communicated with his father, he was either angry or silent. He never really listened to what his father said and never felt he could accept his father as a person. After learning to disclose feelings and express acceptance, Ben began to communicate with his father. (See Chapter Ten for details.)

Using the Exercises

Throughout the book there are simple exercises that help to demonstrate the various techniques discussed. Most of the exercises involve either one person (you) or two (you and one other person). No expensive equipment is needed to do these exercises, and most can be completed within a short time. It might be fun to try even those exercises that deal with problems you feel you don't have.

Using the Suggested Readings

At the end of each chapter, there is a list of several books and articles which you might wish to read if you are interested in the content of the chapter.

There are also many good introductory psychology textbooks that contain detailed information about the topics discussed in this book. Your instructor should be able to recommend an appropriate textbook.

There are many scientific journals available in the library that deal with specific uses of psychology. *Psychology Today* is a good popular magazine that discusses the uses of psychology.

Summary

Scientific psychology is the study of human behavior using the method of systematic observation. The fundamental principles of psychology are called empirical generalizations, and these principles can be applied to change behavior. There are superordinate principles called metaprinciples which form a basis for scientific psychology.

Psychological principles can be applied to solve your own problems. The remainder of this book will deal with the application of these principles to some common problems.

Notes

1. Freedman, D. G., Loring, C. B., and Martin, R. M. Emotional behavior and personality development. In Y. Brackbill (ed.), *Infancy and early childhood*. New York: The Free Press, 1967.

2. Brecher, E. M. *Licit and illicit drugs*. Boston: Little, Brown, 1972.

3. Bettelheim, B. Schizophrenia as a reaction to extreme situations. *American Journal of Orthopsychiatry*, 1956, **26,** 507–518.

Chapter Two

Written by Stephanie Crane/Drawn by Ben Black

Recognizing Serious Problems

It was just like I was petrified with fear. If I were to meet a lion face to face, I couldn't be more scared. Everything got black, and I felt I would faint, but I didn't. I thought, "I won't be able to hold on." I think sometimes I will just go crazy. My heart was beating so hard and fast it would jump out and hit my hand. I felt like I couldn't stand up, that my legs wouldn't support me. My hands got icy and my feet stung. There were horrible shooting pains in my forehead. My head felt tight, like someone had pulled the skin down too tight, and I wanted to pull it away. I couldn't breathe. I was short of breath. I literally get out of breath and pant just like I had run an eight mile race. I couldn't do anything. I felt all in, weak, no strength. I can't even dial a telephone. Even then I can't be still when I'm like this. I am restless, and I pace up and down. I feel I am just not responsible. I don't know what I'll do. These things are terrible. I can go along calmly for a while, and without any warning, this happens. I just blow my top.[1]

What is your behavior problem? And how do you know if a problem really exists? There are, in fact, no clear-cut rules for determining this. A behavior such as shyness may or may not be classified as a problem, depending on where and when it occurs. However, there are a few guidelines that may help you to determine whether you have a problem.

A behavior that is socially inappropriate might be called a problem. A socially inappropriate behavior is one that occurs at the wrong time, or in the wrong setting. For example, it may be okay to express your anger at home, but this behavior may be a problem if you get angry at work and yell at your boss.

Any behavior that is unpleasant enough for someone to want to change may be considered a problem. It might be that you want to change the behavior of overeating. Perhaps a member of your family wants to change one of your behaviors, such as your angry outbursts at home. There may even be some other person, a schoolteacher or your employer, who feels that your behavior is disturbing enough to want to change it. In most instances, if your behavior does not affect an individual, that individual is not likely to do anything about it.

A third type of behavior that might be a problem that is senseless or "self-defeating." A self-defeating behavior is one that does you more harm than good. If you don't study for your exams, you're engaging in self-defeating behavior. Some problems, such as the anxiety attack described at the beginning of the chapter, are obviously more serious than others and should not be handled using do-it-yourself psychology.

How can you tell whether your problems are "serious"? No sure rule can be given, but here is a guide: If your problems significantly interfere with your ability to function in life, have continued for some time, and are causing you considerable distress, and if you have been unable to solve them on your own — then you should seek professional help. These are some of the problems for which professional help is desirable:

Intense depression, with feelings of worthlessness and suicidal thoughts

Unwanted, intrusive thoughts and frightening, irresistible impulses

Auditory or visual hallucinations in the absence of drugs

Recurrent periods of blanking out

Fears of objects, people, or situations so severe that you alter your life to avoid them

Prolonged intense anxiety for no apparent reason, accompanied by such physical symptoms as chronic headaches, stomach upsets, or muscular tremors

Sexual problems that are recurrent, severe, and distressing

The Need for Professionals

The problems with do-it-yourself psychology are very real and should not be dismissed. One problem is the factor of closeness — closeness is both an advantage and a disadvantage. When you are very close to a problem, you sometimes cannot see it very well; because you are involved, you cannot be objective. Is objectivity desirable? Sometimes it is desirable and necessary. You may have friends whose problems you — but not they —

are able to see clearly. When do-it-yourself psychology fails, one reason may be this failure to see your own problems with clarity. A professional psychologist can help with this.

A second problem with do-it-yourself psychology is implementation. Many of us can analyze our problems and identify possible solutions, but lack the push and determination to implement the solutions. Or, we want to grow, to gain self-understanding, to become more confident, to become better able to meet our own needs — but feel we need a guide for that journey. Knowing what to do is one thing, actually doing it is another. This book contains numerous tools, psychological techniques that you can apply in your own life; but you must make your own implementations. A professional, on the other hand, can implement these for you.

A third problem with do-it-yourself psychology is that some problems are serious enough to require professional help. There is a difference between the understanding of psychology gained from one book and the understanding gained from years of professional study and experience. The professional's depth of understanding is a necessity for dealing with serious psychological problems. Serious problems should be taken to a professional in private practice, in a clinic, or in a college counseling center. Your teacher, minister, or family doctor may be able to advise you about nearby sources of psychological help. Community mental health clinics offer inexpensive counseling and therapy and some large cities have help available in free clinics. Self-help groups — such as Alcoholics Anonymous or Weight Watchers — offer support and help for special problems.

What kind of a person will you want to ask for help? The way you feel about this person is important, and you should trust your own feelings. You should pick someone you can trust and with whom you can feel comfortable. You should pick someone whose basic values seem similar to yours. And you should pick someone whom you perceive as warm, genuine, and empathic.

Classifying Mental Disorders

Classifying serious problems, or mental disorders, is a task very different from that of classifying rocks or insects or physical disease. Rocks and insects are objects with physically distinguishable features; physical disease is usually classified according to some observable physical cause, such as a particular variety of virus. By contrast, so-called mental disorders are observable only in behavior. A person behaves strangely — shows certain behavioral "symptoms" — and is thereby classified as suf-

fering from a particular variety of mental disorder, for example, schizophrenia. The definitions of the different diagnostic classifications for mental disorders are therefore clusters of particular behavioral symptoms:
lists of unusual ways of behaving.

Definitions of terms describing selected mental disorders:

*Anxiety disorder: A condition marked by intense periods of apprehen-
sion or fearfulness. Symptoms may include sweating, trembling,
faintness, chest pain, or a fear of dying or going crazy. The problem
described at the beginning of the chapter could be called an anxiety
disorder.*

*Obsessive-compulsive disorder: A condition characterized by obsessions
(unwanted, recurring ideas) or compulsions (repetitive, intrusive
urges to perform some act), or both.*

*Conversion disorder: A condition marked by physical symptoms —
such as paralysis or blindness — in the absence of any physical disease
or injury.*

*Bipolar affective disorder (manic-depressive psychosis): A severe
mental disturbance characterized by extreme elation and depression;
the condition cycles from one extreme of mood to the other.*

*Paranoid disorder: A rare disorder marked by systematized, unshaka-
ble delusions of grandeur and persecution.*

*Schizophrenic disorder: A group of disorders marked by a retreat from
reality characterized by disturbances in language and communication
(making up new phrases); thinking (delusions), preception (hallucinations), mood (inappropriate emotional reactions or a total lack of
feeling), sense of self (confusion about identity), volition (reduction
in self-initiated activity), relationships to external world (withdrawal), and motor behavior (rigid or bizarre postures).*

*Antisocial personality disorder: A condition that is associated with
persistent violation of the rights of others. This may include repetitive
lying, stealing, fighting, and sexual promiscuity.*

The modern system of classifying mental disorders is based on the
work of Emil Kraepelin, who published his diagnostic scheme in 1907

after carefully observing the behavior of thousands of disturbed individuals. Kraepelin grouped mental disorders into two major types: what are now called "affective disorders," such as bipolar affective disorder, and what is now called "schizophrenia." Affective disorders are marked by disturbances in affect, or states of feeling; the classic "raving maniac" — a wildly excited and incoherent individual — may be classified as having an affective disorder. Schizophrenia refers to a loosely defined group of disorders marked by thought disturbances, perceptual disturbances, or social withdrawal. A schizophrenic may hallucinate by hearing voices or may withdraw totally from all contact with the world.

In an effort to clarify the descriptions of the various categories of mental disorders, the American Psychiatric Association has developed a diagnostic and statistical manual of mental disorders.[2] The third edition is the most comprehensive attempt yet to classify mental disorders. With this revision some very common descriptive terms such as "neuroses" have been virtually abandoned as diagnostic classifications. What previously was called anxiety neurosis would now probably be called an anxiety disorder. Because the classification system is so new, it is difficult to determine if it is, in fact, more precise and accurate than the old system.

The Limitation of Labels

Even with the new classification system, people that are classified with a "disorder" will still be described as "mentally ill" by the general public. What does it mean to call someone mentally ill, to refer to someone as suffering from a "nervous disease"? Such terms imply the existence of an illness or disease affecting the brain or nervous system. In fact, however, the majority of cases of "mental illness" may have no discernible physical cause whatsoever.

Psychiatrist Thomas Szasz argues that "mental illness" is a social judgment; it refers to behavior that deviates from acceptable social standards, not to some medical problem or disease. According to Szasz, people are labeled mentally ill when they fail to conform to psychosocial and ethical standards or norms.[3] Scheff, a sociologist, asserts that a person is called mentally ill who "offends the public order" by violating the standards of behavior in a particular culture.[4] There are two kinds of standards or norms, Scheff writes, the explicit — those clearly stated and perhaps written in law; and the implicit — those unwritten understandings or agreements among ourselves to behave in certain ways. According to Scheff, the symptoms of mental illness are violations of these subtle understandings:

The medical model of disease refers to culture-free processes that are independent of the public order; a case of pneumonia or syphilis is pretty much the same in New York or New Caledonia.

Most of the "symptoms" of mental illness, however, are of an entirely different nature. Far from being culture-free, such "symptoms" are themselves offenses against implicit understandings of particular cultures. "Everyone knows," for example, that during a conversation one looks at the other's eyes or mouth, but not at his ear. For the convenience of the society, offenses against these unnamed understandings are usually lumped together in a miscellaneous, catchall category. . . . In earlier societies, the residual [catchall] category was witchcraft, spirit possession, or possession by the devil; today it is mental illness.[4]

The term "schizophrenia" is a label for people who are abnormal in certain respects. Labels are sometimes used too lightly or even misused by untrained persons, but the problems of mental disorders are very real. The psychological state called "schizophrenia" is typically a joyless experience full of anxiety, apathy, terror, or dread.

Assessing Problem Behaviors

At times it is very difficult to assess problem behaviors, that is, to determine if a problem exists and, if so, how serious it is. For many behaviors, such as cigarette smoking, you can simply count the number of times the problem behavior occurs. Other behaviors, like depression, are more difficult to define and quantify.

Psychologists use interviews, tests, rating scales, and questionnaires to assess problems. A new alternative to traditional psychological assessment is behavioral assessment, which focuses on recording observable behaviors. Throughout this book there are many questionnaires and rating scales that will help you identify problem behaviors. Using the assessment scales, however, is only one step in identifying how serious a problem is and what behaviors need changing.

Exercise — Assessment

Counting and recording behavior is often a helpful way to determine if a problem exists. Before a problem behavior can be observed and recorded, however, it must be behaviorally defined, that is, defined in terms of the specific behaviors that are associated with it. This exercise will give you some practice in thinking about your behavior. Depression, for example,

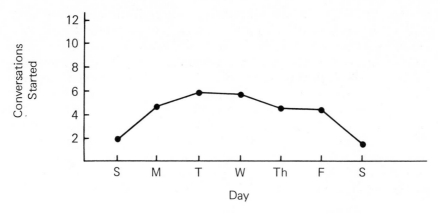

Figure 2.1 *Number of Conversations Started per Day*

could be defined behaviorally by the occurrence of certain symptoms: sleep problems, poor appetite, loss of energy, and suicidal thoughts. How might some of the following problems be defined behaviorally?

1. Uncontrolled temper
2. Shyness
3. Nervousness
4. Stubbornness
5. Procrastination

Now choose one of the problems listed above and, using your definition, record how often the behavior occurs daily for a one-week period. This information can easily be summarized on a graph. For example, Figure 2.1 is Debbie's graph for the number of conversations she initiated each day.

According to the graph, Debbie initiated fewer conversations on the weekend than during the week. What did you find out about your problem when you started to observe and record it?

Why should you record a problem before you start to do something about it? How can you account for the intensity of a problem using this type of assessment?

Summary

It is difficult to determine what types of behavior are problems. Generally, socially inappropriate behavior, behavior that someone wants changed, and self-defeating behavior are classified as problems. Problems that interfere with your ability to function may be serious and require psychological help. This help is available from many different agencies.

Classifying mental disorders is a difficult task. Kraepelin was the first person to devise a classification system. These labels for mental disorders are often misused by mental health people and the general public.

The various methods of assessing problems include interviews, tests, questionnaires, and rating scales. Behavioral assessment, which utilizes objective observations, is a new alternative to traditional psychological assessment.

Notes

1. Laughlin, H. T. *The neuroses in clinical practice.* Philadelphia: Saunders, 1956.

2. American Psychiatric Association. *Diagnostic and statistical manual of mental disorders* (Third edition). Washington, D.C.: 1980.

3. Szasz, T. The myth of mental illness. *American Psychologist,* 1960, **15,** 113–118.

4. Scheff, T. J. Schizophrenia as ideology. *Schizophrenia Bulletin,* 1970, **2,** 15–19.

Suggested Readings

Coleman, J. C. *Abnormal psychology and modern life.* Glenview, Ill.: Scott Foresman, 1976.

Kesey, K. *One flew over the cuckoo's nest.* New York: Viking Press, 1962.

Scheff, T. J. *Labeling madness.* Englewood Cliffs, N.J.: Prentice-Hall, 1975.

Stuart, R. B. *Trick or treatment: How and when psychotherapy fails.* Champaign, Ill.: Research Press, 1970.

Szasz, T. *The myth of mental illness.* New York: Dell, 1961.

Chapter Three

Written by Stephanie Crane/Drawn by Ben Black

Studying Effectively

Ann was a sophomore who had not decided on a major. She was a very quiet and soft-spoken person but she had many friends. She dated frequently and had recently started dating someone she really liked.

She described her parents as "middle-class" people who were very concerned about her education. They had paid her tuition and had given her enough spending money so that she would not have to get a job that would take away valuable study time. She felt very close to her parents and would occasionally spend the weekends at home.

Last week, Ann was placed on probation because of her low grades. She had a 1.00 (D) grade-point average and was in danger of flunking out of school, since she had been on probation during her freshman year.

When Ann was first seen at the counseling center she appeared very depressed and frustrated. She often stated that she "studied a lot, but didn't seem to do well," and that perhaps she was "not smart enough." She claimed to study about fourteen hours a week but had a hard time concentrating. She didn't take notes during lectures and often did not understand the professors. She thought that her study habits were good but that "there must be some other problem getting in the way of her doing well."

Ann stated her goal was to "get off of probation." We agreed on a contract to change her study habits that included changes in the way she read her books, the effective use of her time and preparing for examinations. She had some resistance to the program, but finally agreed to try it.

Your motive to study can come from passion or from punishment; it can be a pleasure or a pain. It is certain that it has been both for you.

Sometimes you study — not just for a test — but for yourself, because you want to know. Sometimes studying is more than a means to a grade—it is a way of growth. You have felt the quiet satisfaction gained from mastering difficult concepts and perhaps even experienced what has been called the "unspeakable pleasure" of studying. But the requirements and pressures of school often preclude studying for its own sake. Instead, you study to pass a test and work to achieve distant goals only remotely related to the material you must learn. Rather than studying because you are curious and want to understand, you study because you want to avoid the consequences of failure.

Studying can be a "weariness of the flesh." Do you remember when you studied something and felt only confusion and self-doubt? Do you remember how you felt when—after studying diligently—you scored poorly on a test?

Studying does not have to be punishing. There are ways to study more effectively than you do now; and if you can learn to study more effectively you can reduce the pain and the punishment now accompanying the process. You can study more successfully; studying is a skill that, like other skills, you can learn how to do.

Identifying Study Problems

Before continuing, you may want to identify your specific study problems by using the following checklist.

_____ I'm too tired to study. When I try to read my assignments, I feel sleepy and sometimes find myself dozing. Then I wake up and force myself to go on.

_____ I try to study, but I can't seem to concentrate on the material. I'll be reading along and before I know it I'm daydreaming; my mind will be miles away.

_____ I never have enough time to do the studying I need in order to keep up. Before exams I find myself behind schedule, with not enough hours left to learn what I need. The only time I have free time is when I don't need it.

_____ I feel totally lost in some of my classes. I can't seem to understand what I read or what I hear in lecture. Even after I've reread a paragraph two or three times, it still doesn't make sense to me.

_____ I read my books and take down everything that's said in lectures, but I never know what's important. The tests are always on something I didn't study very well.

_____ I read everything that I'm supposed to read for a course, but I just can't remember it. After I read a chapter I try to remember it, but it's gone, just as though I had never seen it at all.

_____ I can't keep the material from one class separate from the material for another. The classes get all mixed up in my mind, and I'm never sure whether what I'm remembering is for the right class or not.

_____ I learn a lot, but it's all just isolated bits of facts that don't fit together. Nothing I'm learning relates to anything else I already know. I feel like an encyclopedia of trivia.

_____ I'm never able to determine what questions will be on an exam. I always seem to guess wrong.

_____ I don't know whether I should change my answers on a multiple choice test.

_____ I never do well on essay exams. I always leave out important points I have learned.

_____ I have no trouble studying for exams, but I always put off term papers until the last minute.

_____ I can remember things fine for an exam, but once the exam is over, I've forgotten it all. What's my education for if I don't know anything when it's all over?

How You Study

Let's return to Ann's study problems.

At one session Ann was feeling panicked because finals were coming up in a few days and she felt completely unprepared for them. In high school she had to study very little to make good grades, but in college she had begun to feel unintelligent and incapable of handling the course assignments. She was accustomed to making a big push right before the exams, reading the material that was assigned previously, and staying up all night to do it, if necessary.

Ann has not learned how to study. She, like many other college students, has some bad habits — habits that could be changed. A common misconception about studying is that you should be able to learn the material in your textbook after reading it once or twice — but almost nobody is able to do this; you would have to have a photographic memory in order to recall material you had read only once. For most people — even geniuses — learning requires considerable *practice:* reading the material several times, and often, in addition, writing it down on paper in summary form or rehearsing it out loud. Many experimental studies in human memory have shown that your ability to reproduce material after you have read it only once is quite poor; you must actively practice or rehearse material in order to place it with some permanence in your memory. If you were to try to learn the names of all the presidents of the United States, for example, you would not be able to learn such a list after only one reading; you would have to practice it several times. However, you should not practice it only until you can repeat the entire list; you should continue to practice it for a while after that point. Continuing to practice after you have learned the list is called *overlearning,* and material that has been overlearned is remembered longer than material that has not. The mind is not a camera or a tape recorder; seeing or listening to something once is typically not sufficient for retention. The idea is that "practice makes perfect," and this is expressed in *the rehearsal principle: practice improves retention and performance.*

The rehearsal principle: Practice improves retention and performance.

Peterson and Peterson presented subjects with nonsense syllables (such as LEK or MIV) and sometime later asked the subjects to recall them. Remembering three letters is normally not at all difficult; anybody can remember three letters — all you have to do is repeat them to yourself (rehearse them) a few times. But what if you can't rehearse them? To prevent the subjects from rehearsing the nonsense syllables, the Petersons required them, after hearing the nonsense syllable, to count backwards rapidly by threes from a certain number. The results showed the subjects' recall began to deteriorate after a few seconds, and was very poor after as little as fifteen seconds. Most subjects completely forgot the three letters after twenty seconds. Without practice the memory was lost. Practice, or rehearsal, is also essential in learning perceptual motor skills.

Glanzer, M., and Meinzer, A. The effects of intralist activity on free recall. *Journal of Verbal Learning and Verbal Behavior,* 1967, **6,** 928–935.

Keller, F. S. The phantom plateau. *Journal of the Experimental Analysis of Behavior,* 1958, **1,** 1–13.

Peterson, L. R., and Peterson, M. J. Short-term retention of individual verbal items. *Journal of Experimental Psychology,* 1950, **58,** 193–198.

Most people know that studying requires some effort, that you have to work at it; but they typically put it off until the last minute and then "cram." Suppose that you have only four hours to devote to studying chemistry. Consider two different ways to distribute your study time: you either study one hour a week for four weeks, or you study four hours immediately before the exam. Which is better? Although there are some exceptions, spaced — or distributed — practice almost always works out better than massed practice, or cramming. For studying, you should plan, not cram. This follows from *the distribution of practice principle: for most skills, massed practice does not work as well as spaced practice.* Cramming can actually be very useful, but only when it is used as a reminder of what has been previously studied through spaced or distributed study sessions; that is, cramming at the last minute should not substitute for other study, but it can serve as an appropriate adjunct.

The distribution of practice principle: For most skills, massed practice does not work as well as spaced practice.

It is usually better to practice a little on each of several days than to practice a lot in a single session. Lorge asked subjects to write while watching the hand in a mirror. This task is difficult because the apparent movement of their hand is reversed. Some subjects learned the task with no breaks in the practice; others had the same amount of practice but had breaks of either a minute or a day during their practice. Lorge found that even breaks as short as a minute improved performance on this and other tasks. This effect is strongest and most clear-cut for tasks involving motor skills, especially complex motor skills.

Kientzle, M. J. Properties of learning curves under varied distributions of practice. *Journal of Experimental Psychology,* 1946, **39,** 187–211.

Lorge, I. Influence of regularly interpolated time intervals upon subsequent learning. *Teachers College Contributions to Education,* 1930, No. 438.

Underwood, B. J. Ten years of massed practice on distributed practice. *Psychological Review,* 1961, **68,** 229–247.

What You Study

The key to study is active practice — but what do you practice? Deciding what to study — what is important and what is not — is often very difficult.

Most textbook authors provide many hints as to what the key ideas are in their chapters. Key ideas are often emphasized by headings, by using boldface or italics, and by inclusion in a chapter summary. Many textbooks come with workbooks and study guides that are also helpful in emphasizing what to study. Instructors often repeat key ideas in lectures. Taking notes — outlining lectures and reading assignments — is a useful skill. However, taking down everything that you hear or read is not efficient; you should reduce the information to the key ideas and terms. Information reduction prevents memory overload. Trivial details can interfere with your ability to recall key ideas.

Where You Study

Even if you know how and what to study, you still may be unable to study because you do not know *where* to do it. Having the right place to study can make a lot of difference in your ability to concentrate. One student made out a schedule and was determined to study English literature from seven to ten o'clock, but he chose to study in the wrong place:

Determined to do his reading on schedule, he sat down at his desk promptly at seven. First, he discovered that his pencil was out of lead and needed a refill before he could make any notes. Walking across the hall to the room of a friend to see if he had some lead, he found an interesting discussion going on about the merits of Fords versus Chevrolets. Becoming absorbed in this, it was some time before he remembered that he was supposed to be studying English. Starting back to his room, he recalled that there was a good TV program on. With the aid of a little wishful thinking, he convinced himself that he could be studying while watching TV in the lounge. Next, with his attention divided between the TV and the book, he found himself daydreaming about the weekend coming up. And so it went. Ten o'clock came, time to go out for a bite to eat—and still no work done.[1]

A common problem of studying is concentration (or its opposite, distraction). Part of the problem of distraction is purely physical: noises, conversation, people walking by, etc. You solve this problem by finding a well-lighted, quiet study place. But finding a study place is not enough; you must also *make* your study place. You create your study place through studying. How does this work? Your behavior is, to some extent, controlled by your immediate environment. When you are in a place where you are accustomed to eating, you tend to feel like eating; when you are in a place where you are accustomed to sleeping, you tend to feel sleepy; and when you are in a place where you are accustomed to studying, you tend to feel more like studying. What you do is to some degree controlled by such "stimuli" as the people around you, the place you are at, and the situation you are in. Studying should not be done where other things are done; if you do study in such places, your mind will wander to those other things.[2] If you study at the kitchen table, you may be distracted by thoughts of eating; if you study in bed, you may be distracted by feelings of sleepiness. If you feel like smoking, eating, sleeping, or daydreaming, leave your study place and go elsewhere; otherwise, these competing activities will become more and more distracting in the future.

One college student went to a psychologist for help with her studying problems, and was advised to apply the concept of stimulus control:

Since she felt sleepy when she studied, she was told to replace a 40-w lamp with a good one and to turn her desk away from her bed. It was also decided that her desk was to control her study behavior. If she wished to write a letter, she should do so, but in the dining room; if she wished to read comic books, she should do so, but in the kitchen; if she wished to daydream, she should do so, but was to go to another room; at her desk she was to engage in her schoolwork and her schoolwork only.

This girl had previously had a course in behavioral analysis and said, "I know what you're up to. You want that desk to assume stimulus control over me. I'm not going to let any piece of wood run my life for me."

"On the contrary," I said, "you *want* that desk to run you. It is like having a sharpened knife in a drawer. You decide when to use it; but when you want it, it is ready."

After the first week of the regimen, she came to me and gleefully said, "I spent only ten minutes at my desk last week."

"Did you study there?" I asked.

"Yes, I did," she said.

"Good," I said, "let's try to double that next week."

For the next few weeks we did not meet, but she subsequently reported that during the last month of the semester she was able to spend three hours a day at her desk for four weeks in a row, something she had been unable to do previously. When she sat at her desk she studied, and when she did other things she left her desk.[3]

You can improve your ability to concentrate by creating your own special study place based on this simple rule: when you want to do something besides study, you have to do it elsewhere.

When You Study

Knowing how, what, and where to study are of little use unless you are able to find the time to do it. You must know when to study and be able to schedule your time accordingly. Many things compete for your study time. One student, Kenny, describes the problem as follows:

My problem is the controversy between girls and studies. In order to make good grades I should stay in and study at nights and on week ends. This conflicts with my social affairs. . . . Another of my problems is . . . applying my time to my best advantage in study. When I get home in the afternoon there is usually work that my mother wishes me to do and it takes most of the time before dinner to complete. . . . By the time I get through I either have no time left to study or the things I have studied are forgotten.[4]

Scheduling is essential to effective study. Most of us waste time. If you plan your studying with a schedule, you will be able to make the most effective use of the time you have available. You will, for example, be able to schedule your studying so that you study each subject close to its classtime; you will be able to distribute your studying, to avoid massed practice; and you will be able to make sure that you study enough before tests. You should plan to study only for short periods of about half an hour, then take a few minutes' break before continuing. The break consists of a kind of "reward" for the previous period of studying. According to *the law of effect* (see pages 106–107), responses followed by rewards tend to be strengthened; if you reward yourself for studying, your study habits should be strengthened and your ability to concentrate on what you are reading will improve. Stop studying for a while when you find your mind wandering or your eyes drooping; get up and do something else. Reward yourself.

An important consideration in scheduling is the possible interaction between different study sessions; under some circumstances, studying one subject actually interferes with your ability to learn another subject. Interference that results from previously studied material is called *proactive interference;* interference that results from material studied afterwards is called *retroactive interference*. If you study German, then French, and then Spanish, your ability to learn French may be interfered with proactively by your study of German, and retroactively by your study of Spanish. In general, the more similar two subjects are, and the less time that elapses between the two study periods, the more interference will result. This is stated in *the principle of proactive and retroactive interference: a memory can be interfered with by similar memories that are acquired before (proactive) or after (retroactive) the memory in question.* In other words, similarity breeds confusion.

The principle of proactive and retroactive interference: A memory can be interfered with by similar memories that are acquired before (proactive) or after (retroactive) the memory in question.

Sometimes people forget because one memory interferes with another. It is easy to remember one telephone number; but if you had to remember twenty of them, you would probably make mistakes. Melton and Von Lackum asked subjects to memorize lists of nonsense syllables (such as LUB, PEF). One group of subjects (group 1) memorized two lists and was asked to recall the second list. Another group (group 2) memorized two lists and was asked to recall the first one. Other subjects memorized only one list, resting either before or after, and then tried to recall the list. Group 1 (proactive interference) and group 2 (retroactive interference) did more poorly on the recall task than did subjects who memorized only one list. Those who memorized only one list suffered much less memory interference.

Melton, A. W., and Von Lackum, W. J. Retroactive and proactive inhibition in retention: evidence for a two factor theory of retroactive inhibition. *American Journal of Psychology,* 1941, **54,** 157–173.

Underwood, B. J. Interference and forgetting. *Psychological Review,* 1957, **64,** 49–60.

The remedy for interference is proper scheduling. Similar subjects should not be studied close together; two language classes or two math classes should be well spaced in your study schedule. You may also increase the distinctiveness (thereby reducing the interference) between two subjects by taking notes for these subjects using two different colors of paper.

Steps to Better Studying

A proven alternative to the method of studying you are now following is the "SQ3R" method.[5] This is a systematic approach to studying that emphasizes active practice of the material. The letters in "SQ3R" stand for the actual steps of the procedure: "Survey," "Question," then three "R" steps, "Read," "Recite," and "Review."

Step 1. Survey. Get an overview of the assignment by noting the title of the chapter, reading the introduction, checking the main headings, and reading the summary at the end. With the perspective gained from such a survey, you will read the material with more comprehension and remember it better. The survey provides a context of meaning within which the material to be learned can be embedded.

Step 2. Question. Ask yourself questions about the material you are about to study. Sometimes authors will place such questions at the beginnings of chapters, but more often you will have to make up the questions yourself. You can do this by transforming chapter titles and headings into meaningful questions. Asking questions provides a purpose to your reading and study; you become more actively involved in the process of studying, and you tend to remember what you read longer. Questioning also tends to focus your attention on the more important points to be covered in the assignment, so that you will be less distracted by the small details.

Step 3. Read. Read actively, noting important terms, italicized words, and main ideas, and try to answer the questions you began with. You should be working on one small unit of the assignment at a time, usually one headed section. If you find your mind wandering, if you begin daydreaming or get sleepy, you should study one more page and then quit. Do not continue to study when you cannot concentrate. When you read, you must be alert.

Step 4. Recite. Recitation is both the most neglected aspect of study and the single most important aspect of study. When you recite, you are actively restating what you have just read, either aloud, or silently to yourself, or by writing it down on paper. After you read each section of the material, you should try to use your own words to summarize, restate, and list the key ideas in the passage, trying to answer the questions you had when you began. Material that you read without restating in any way you tend to forget rapidly; when you restate it to yourself or on paper, you retain it longer. Therefore, stop at the end of each headed section and give yourself a verbal synopsis of what you have just read; then scan back over the section to make sure that you got the major points. You should spend at least as much time in this recitation process as you spend in reading itself.

Step 5. Review. Review what you have studied when you are through. Reviewing should be an active process, involving recitation, and not just a passive rereading or scanning of notes. You can actively review from your notes by examining main topics you have written down, then trying to restate the main points under each major topic. You can review from your text by scanning the headings, then trying to restate the main points under each heading. This kind of active rehearsal of the material you are learning should be done immediately after you have finished studying it, and also several times between then and the exam over it.

Taking Tests

Knowing how, what, where, and when to study is the prerequisite for doing well on examinations. However, many people still have problems in taking an exam. Jeff describes his problem as follows:

I have trouble with multiple choice and essay exams. It seems like I never have enough time to finish the exams before I start debating with myself about the answers to different questions. On essay exams I feel so discouraged and I always leave out important points.

Before taking any test you should take practice tests similar to what you expect to find on the actual test. Many workbooks and study guides that accompany textbooks contain practice exams and questions. Also, try to find old exams given by the same instructor and determine what types of questions the instructor prefers. Look for important questions in content areas that are stressed on the old test. Also, try to determine if the questions come from the lectures, the readings, or both. It may be helpful to ask the instructor what will be emphasized on the exam. You might also benefit from making up your own questions from the readings and lectures and exchanging them with other students in the class.

The strategy for taking multiple choice exams differs from the strategy for essay exams. In taking multiple choice exams, it is important to read the questions carefully and to answer them quickly. Determine how many questions there are on the test and approximately how much time you should spend on each item. If you have 30 minutes for a 60-item multiple choice exam, you should allow an average of 30 seconds per question. If you aren't sure of the answer to a question, place a mark next to it and finish the rest of the exam. In choosing an answer it will save time if you eliminate the obviously incorrect answers first. Studies have shown that it is okay to change your answer: If you feel that your first choice may be wrong, you are more likely to be correct if you change it. Finally, it is important that you don't read into the questions more than the instructor actually intended.

Answering essay questions usually requires some time for thinking and for organizing an answer. It is a good idea to prepare a brief outline of your answer after reading the question carefully. This will allow you to feel organized and to include all the important points. It is important to use examples to support your main points in the essay and to answer directly the essential points of the question. You should plan to leave some time to reread your answer to make sure you haven't made any careless mistakes or left out any important points. It is also important to make sure your writing is legible and readable.

Getting Work Done

The test is usually only one part of the grade in a course. Many courses require a major project or term paper that is due near the end of the course. Joan did well on her test but had a problem completing term projects on time. She described her political science project as follows:

The first day of class I knew I would have to turn in my project the week before finals. There always seemed to be other, more pressing things to do for my courses. When I would make some time to work on my project, I had a hard time getting started and never seemed to accomplish much. I finally had to stay up late every night the week before the project was due. I didn't finish typing the paper until the day after it was due. The professor took off half a grade because it was late.

Joan's experience is not unusual. Most of us have worked on major projects both inside and outside of school that end up being crammed into a small amount of time.

In order to overcome procrastination, it is necessary first to break down a project into smaller workable tasks that can be completed in a set amount of time. Since it is important that your tasks do not overwhelm you, each one should call for only as much work as feels comfortable. A schedule should be drawn up for each task, and a deadline date for each should be included. Completing the first few tasks on time will provide motivation for doing later tasks.

It may be necessary to provide external rewards for completion of each task. For example, going to a weekend movie or dinner could be made dependent on completing a task by Friday. For some people it may be necessary to break down and reward tasks on a daily basis. This type of reward for small segments of behavior demonstrates the principle of shaping, or successive approximations, and was introduced by B. F. Skinner in his work with laboratory animals.

Another method of motivating completion of tasks involves a fine, or "response cost," to be paid if the work is not completed. One type of response cost might involve agreeing to do some disliked work for someone else. For example, a student may arrange to clean the bathroom and all the windows in a friend's home, if he or she does not finish the first three chapters in the textbook by the deadline date.

Exercise—Getting Work Done

This exercise is designed to give you some practice in setting up a program to overcome procrastination.

Step 1. Choose at least one of the tasks listed below.

1. Cleaning and organizing your desk
2. Looking for a part-time job
3. Completing a term paper in one of your current classes
4. Sending out Christmas cards
5. Preparing for a final exam

Step 2. On a sheet of paper, list five to ten smaller tasks that are part of the goal of completing the larger task you have chosen.

Step 3. Determine a schedule and date for completion of each of the subtasks.

Step 4. List three possible rewards for completion of the subtasks.

Step 5. List three possible response costs for failure to complete a subtask.

Try to determine what problems might arise if you try to implement one of these programs. Do you feel that you could do it yourself, or do you need help from your friends or relatives? What would you do to change the program if you failed the first two weeks? How would you reward yourself for completing subtasks ahead of schedule?

Summary

Studying is an important skill if you know how, what, where, and when to study. To study effectively, it is important to repeat the material to be learned many times. The practice should be spaced out, not crammed into the last minute. It is important to narrow down what you study to key ideas and terms. Do your studying in a quiet, well-lit area reserved for studying only and try to schedule your studying time. One approach to systematic studying that has been found to be effective is the "SQ3R" method. The steps in this approach are Study, Question, Read, Recite, and Review. Mastering study skills is the first step toward doing well on examinations. It is also important to know what to expect on tests as well as how to take multiple choice and essay exams.

Completing major projects in school or at home is often delayed until the last minute. By breaking down a task into subtasks, scheduling deadlines for each subtask, and rewarding successes and fining failures, it is possible to overcome procrastination.

Notes

1. Morgan, C. T., and Deese, J. *How to study.* New York: McGraw-Hill, 1969.

2. Beneke, W. M., and Harris, M. B. Teaching self-control of study behavior. *Behavior Research and Therapy,* 1972, **10,** 35–41.

3. Goldiamond, I. Self-control procedures in personal behavioral problems. *Psychological Reports,* 1965, **17,** 851–868.

4. Henry, J. *Culture against man.* New York: Vintage Books, 1965.

5. Robinson, F. P. *Effective study.* New York: Harper and Bros., 1946.

Suggested Readings

Armstrong, W. *Study tips, how to study effectively and get better grades.* New York: Barron's Educational Services, 1975.

Gilbert, D. W. *Study in depth.* Englewood Cliffs, N.J.: Prentice-Hall, 1966.

Maddox, H. *How to study.* New York: Fawcett Premier Books, 1963.

Robinson, F. P. *Effective study.* New York: Harper & Row, 1970.

Simms, T. F. *Improving college study skills.* Beverly Hills, Calif.: Glencoe Press, 1970.

Smith, S. *Best methods of study.* New York: Barnes and Noble, 1970.

Walter, T., and Siebert, A. *Student success: How to be a better student and still have time for your friends.* New York: Holt, Rinehart and Winston, 1975.

Chapter Four

Written by Stephanie Crane/Drawn by Ben Black

Improving
Your Memory

A man came to my laboratory who asked me to test his memory. At the time the man (let us designate him S.) was a newspaper reporter who had come to my laboratory at the suggestion of the paper's editor. Each morning the editor would meet with the staff and hand out assignments for the day—lists of places he wanted covered, information to be obtained in each. The list of addresses and instructions was usually fairly long, and the editor noted with some surprise that S. never took any notes. He was about to reproach the reporter for being inattentive when, at his urging, S. repeated the entire assignment word for word.

I gave S. a series of words, then numbers, then letters, reading them to him slowly or presenting them in written form. He read or listened attentively and then repeated the material exactly as it had been presented. I increased the number of elements in each series, giving him as many as thirty, fifty, or even seventy words or numbers, but this, too, presented no problem for him.

The experiment indicated that he could reproduce a series in reverse order—from the end to the beginning—just as simply as from start to finish; that he could readily tell me which word followed another in a series, or reproduce the word which happened to precede one I'd name.

As the experimenter, I soon found myself in a state verging on utter confusion. An increase in the length of a series led to no noticeable increase in difficulty for S., and I simply had to admit that the capacity of his memory *had no distinct limits.*[1]

Language, thought, habit, even perception depend upon memory. The psychological present — this moment as we experience it — rests on, incorporates, and is built from a lifetime of accumulated experience. The past lives in the present through memory. Memory is so basic and so essential to thought and action that we sometimes take it for granted.

Identifying Memory Problems

Perhaps you have particular memory problems. Use the following check-list to identify your most difficult ones.

_____ I never seem to remember people's names until I have met them three or four times.

_____ I have to write down friends' phone numbers because I always forget them.

_____ I sometimes miss an appointment because I haven't written it down.

_____ In school I have a hard time memorizing important dates.

_____ Memorizing English or foreign vocabulary words always takes so much time for me.

_____ Sometimes I forget many of the key facts I have memorized the night before an exam.

_____ Memorizing math and science formulas takes me forever.

Amnesia

If you checked some of the items above, you may think that you have a bad memory problem. But imagine what it would be like to have no memory at all. You would not be able to speak, to read, to recognize places and objects, to care for yourself; you would be able to move, but not with purpose; you would show no human intelligence: you would in effect not be human. Less severe memory problems also have profound consequences. Amnesia, the partial or complete loss of memory, can result either from a blow to the head or from psychological trauma.

A nineteen-year-old college student suffered a head injury in an automobile accident while driving home for Christmas. When he came to, he was completely disoriented and could not remember even his own name. After a few hours he recovered some of his early memories, including his name and his life up to two years prior to the accident; for that two-year period, however, his mind was still a blank. When asked where he lived, he stated an address in another city—an apartment his family moved away from over a year previously. By ten days after the accident his memory was essentially completely restored; however, he could not remember what happened immediately before the accident. The events of those few seconds were forever lost to him.

Repression

Most of our losses of memory are not so devastating as that experienced by the victim of amnesia. The little things, the hundreds of mostly insignificant names and dates, the telephone numbers, the grocery lists — these seem just to fade away; while we are thinking of something else, they edge out of mind. Not all forgotten things are lost in this way: some are forgotten "on purpose"; they are forgotten because they are too painful to remember; they are *repressed*. Repression is the unconscious blocking of the recall of painful events or frightening feelings. Repression is a way of coping with an ugly reality, as the following case shows:

Irene was a girl of twenty years, who was greatly disturbed by the long illness and death of her mother. Her mother had reached the last stage of tuberculosis, and lived alone in abject poverty with her daughter, in an attic. The girl watched her mother during sixty days and nights, working at her sewing machine to earn a few pennies to sustain their lives. When finally her mother did die, Irene became very much disturbed emotionally. She tried to revive the corpse, to call the breath back again. In her attempts at placing the limbs in an upright position, the mother's body fell to the floor, whereupon she went through the strain of lifting her back into bed, alone. Certainly, such experiences could not be forgotten in the ordinary course of things. Yet in a little while Irene seemed to have grown forgetful of her mother's death. She would say, "I know very well my mother must be dead, since I have been told so several times, since I see her no more, and since I am in mourning; but I really feel astonished at it all. When did she die? What did she die from?"[2]

Irene had repressed the painful memory of her mother's death.

Two Kinds of Memory

There is not just one kind of memory. Being able to remember a license plate that you have glanced at is one thing; being able to remember the date of your birth is something else. One kind of memory — "short-term memory" — specializes in retaining information very briefly; it holds your sensory impressions in temporary storage. A second kind of memory — "long-term memory" — takes the temporarily stored information and makes a relatively permanent record of it. Different brain processes are apparently involved in these two kinds of memory. A brain injury may impair short-term memory, leaving the individual forgetful of recent events but fully able to recall events occurring some time ago; or the

injury may impair long-term memory, leaving the individual able to remember only very recent events. The latter problem is illustrated in the
following case history:

[In one case] memory disorder followed a brain operation performed in
an attempt to alleviate epilepsy. The extent of the man's deficit was
shown by the fact that after the operation and 10 weeks prior to the
report, he and his family had moved; but he had not yet learned his new
address, nor could he find his way home alone, and he was unable to
locate frequently used objects in the house. For example, he would have
to ask his mother where the lawn mower was, even though he had used it
the day before. He would do the same jigsaw puzzles day after day and
would reread the same magazines without giving any evidence that the
contents were familiar to him. Thus he seemed to have lost entirely his
ability to retain new information over long periods. However, the rational and apparently normal way in which he behaved indicated that
some short-term retention must have been occurring.[3]

Encoding, Storage, Retrieval

At the end of the movie, your friend asks you to name the director. You
don't know, and make one of three replies: "I didn't notice," "I forgot," or
"I can't remember." Each response suggests a different reason for failing
to know the answer. What are these different reasons?

When you say "I didn't notice," you indicate that the name did not
register, that the information somehow never reached you in a form to remember. This reflects the first of three essential memory processes
—*encoding,* taking the information in and registering it in a form that
can be retained. If the information is not encoded, you will not know
it later because you never got it in the first place. When you say "I
forgot," you indicate that you succeeded in registering or encoding the
information, but you were unable to *retain* it; this reflects the second of
the three essential memory processes—*storage,* maintaining the information over time. When you say "I can't remember," you indicate that
you succeeded in encoding and storing the information, but you cannot
now *recall* it; this reflects the third essential memory process—*retrieval,*
searching for and obtaining the information from memory. Using memory
successfully requires all three processes: registering (encoding), retaining (storage), and recalling (retrieval). Figure 4.1 summarizes how these
processes affect incoming information.

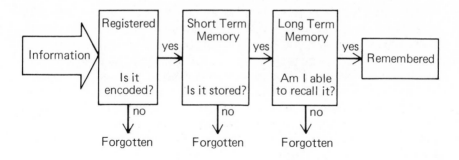

Figure 4.1 *The Memory Process*

Often you have memory problems resulting from encoding failures—you never succeeded in getting the information to memory in the first place. People don't notice a lot of things; it is generally known that witnesses of a crime typically give widely differing reports of what happened. Noticing is an active process; it is not something that just happens to you: looking, touching, sniffing, listening—all are activities, things that you do in order to obtain information. The failure to properly encode can at times have comical results:

A congressman once publicly criticized the Department of Agriculture for wasting the taxpayers' money in printing useless pamphlets. According to the congressman, they printed pamphlets about everything except the love life of the frog.

Following the congressman's speech, the Department of Agriculture began to receive orders for *The Love Life of the Frog.* Since the orders continued to arrive, the department eventually had to make a public announcement stating emphatically that there was no such pamphlet on the love life of the frog. After the public denial, letters requesting *The Love Life of the Frog* began to arrive by the hundreds. Finally, the secretary of agriculture, in a national address, stated that the department had never printed such a pamphlet and had no intention of doing so. Following the broadcast, thousands of orders for the pamphlet arrived in the mail.

For many people, the information never got across; they failed to encode it.

Sometimes you know *that* you know, but you don't know *what* you know. What was the name of your fifth-grade teacher? If you can't recall, perhaps you have her name "on the tip of your tongue" — you can almost remember it, but not quite. In such a case, the name has been encoded and stored, but you are unable to retrieve it. When a name is "on the tip of your tongue," you can sometimes remember it by trying out various possibilities, saying them aloud until one sounds familiar. When a name is "on the tip of your tongue," you can often identify the first letter in the word and perhaps even the number of syllables, though the word itself remains inaccessible.

The "tip-of-the-tongue" phenomenon suggests that words are stored in such a way that those with the same beginning letters are associated in memory. How otherwise could you know the right beginning letter of a missing name? When you have a name "on the tip of your tongue," it must be that you have found the right general location in memory, but not yet the right particular word. Further evidence for the claim that words with the same beginning letter are associated in memory comes from studies showing that if you are given the first letter of a name you are trying to remember, this hint makes it much easier to recall the name.[4] Because such hints are used to help retrieve information already stored in memory, they are called "retrieval cues."

Mnemonic Devices

A mnemonic device is a memory aid, a strategy for improving memory. Such strategies must be based on the principles by which memory functions. It is known that memory is organized; items in memory are not filed away independently, at random, but are highly associated — bound in a network of relationships. Most mnemonic devices take advantage of this fact and ensure that new items to be remembered are connected to or associated with old items already in memory. Association is a kind of "memory glue." This mnemonic strategy was used by S., the man with the fantastic memory described at the beginning of the chapter:

When S. read through a long series of words, each word would elicit a graphic image. And since the series was fairly long, he had to find some way of distributing these images of his in a mental row or sequence. Most often (and this habit persisted throughout his life), he would "distribute" them along some roadway or street he visualized in his mind . . . he would take a mental walk along that street . . . and slowly make his way down, "distributing" his images at houses, gates, and store windows.[1]

By pairing items to be remembered with familiar images along a street, S. was able to bind new items into a network of associations; when it came time to recall the items, he would simply take an imaginary "walk" along the street. The familiar images along the street would then serve as retrieval cues, facilitating recall.

On occasion you may feel that you have too much to remember. One way to cope with this problem is to reduce the number of items to be remembered, without reducing the total amount of information to be stored in memory. The trick in this strategy is called "chunking." Studies show that the number of different items that your short-term memory can handle at one time is limited to about five to seven items.[5,6] The letters O-N-T-H-E-N-A-I-L are more difficult to remember than the words ON THE NAIL, formed by clustering the letters into three groups. Chunking involves clustering associated items; a more economical repackaging of the material to be remembered. An important form of chunking is outlining: you organize the material to be remembered into meaningful units, or clusters of associated items; then you name or symbolize each cluster, and memorize the names of the clusters. Chunking simplifies the material to be remembered, and thus reduces memory load. Or, conversely, through chunking, memory load can be kept constant while the amount to be remembered is increased.

Improve Your Memory

You can improve your memory by improving any of the three functional processes that make up your memory: encoding, storage, or retrieval. Most systems for improving memory concentrate on making the storage process more efficient; however, by improving any of the three processes you will be better able to remember names, dates, shopping lists — even chemical equations, psychological principles, or Balkan geography.

Improving the Encoding Stage

Step 1. Concentrate on what you are trying to memorize. Shut out all other matters and focus on the subject at hand. Encoding must begin with attention. Remember that if the material is not encoded or is encoded improperly, you will not be able to use it, even with the best memory system.

Step 2. Observe as many different things about the material as possible. Notice the details. For example, if you are trying to learn a new person's face, observe the eyes, forehead, chin, ears, and so on. Look for similarities and differences between new and old.

Step 3. Talk to yourself about the material. If you encode verbal as well as sensory impressions, you will have a double file, two chances instead of one. When you are observing a new face, say to yourself, "Well, he has a high forehead, thin lips, a scar on the chin, etc."

Exercise—Improving the Encoding Stage

In order to get some practice improving the encoding stage, you may want to try this simple exercise. Try to remember what the people look like who sit next to you in all your classes. What characteristics of their faces can you pick out to help you distinguish them? Now encode these characteristics with both sensory and verbal impressions.

Improving the Storage Stage: Three Methods

Method One

The first method for improving memory storage is by reducing memory load through a chunking procedure using acronyms. An acronym is formed through the first letters of several other words; the word "NATO" is an acronym standing for the North Atlantic Treaty Organization. Since the first letter of a word serves as an effective retrieval cue, your memory of the first letters provides the gateway to the full memories.

Step 1. Put the material to be remembered into a number of isolated words to be remembered. For example, the names of the twelve cranial nerves, if you are studying neuroanatomy.

Step 2. Write down the first letters of each of the words.

Step 3. Try to juggle the letters to form some word. If you can form such a word, then memorize it; its letters will serve as cues for the words you want to remember.

Step 4. If you cannot do step three, or if the words must be remembered in a fixed order, use each letter as the first letter of a new word, and make the words spell out a rhyme or a sentence. The first letters of the new words are now your keys to the original words to be remembered. For example, the first seven presidents of the United States are cued by the first letters of this phrase: "Whales And Jellied Macaroons, Mar-malade And Jam" (Washington, Adams, Jefferson, Madison, Monroe, Adams, and Jackson).

Method Two

The second method for improving memory storage also works by reduc-ing memory load through chunking. The idea is to simplify the material, through chunking, so that the amount does not exceed your memory capacity; then to use "memory glue" (association) to retard forgetting. The method works particularly well for speeches and for written prose.

Step 1. Outline the material, using headings and subheadings consist-ing of no more than one or two key words each. If you have a speech or a chapter of a text you want to remember, these key words should be drawn from the material so that they remind you of ideas or facts you want to remember. In effect, you are breaking up the continuous prose into chunks and labeling each chunk with a key word. You should have no more than five major chunks; each major chunk can also be broken down into five or fewer smaller chunks.

Step 2. Take these key words, in order, and weave them into an in-teresting, bizarre, or funny story. This will be easiest when most of your key words are relatively concrete, as opposed to abstract, words. When done, you should be able to imagine your story and recognize each of your key words as it comes up; each key word will remind you of the chunk of material that it represents (it will be a retrieval cue).

Method Three

The third method for improving memory storage employs a mnemonic image system. In this method, you firmly fix an ordered set of vivid im-ages in your mind, then associate the material to be remembered with the set of images. The imaginary street map that the man S. used is an example of this method: he imagined himself walking down the street, and "placed" the items of the list along the way — next to a gate, by a lamppost, on a fence, etc. — then, when he wanted to recall the items, he took the walk again in his imagination, and was able to "see" the items as he passed by. You can try this system — you don't need S.'s phenomenal memory in order for it to work. A second variant of this method is to use a mnemonic rhyme, as in the following example:

Step 1. Memorize the following rhyme:

One is a gun

Two is a shoe

Three is a tree

Four is a door

Five is knives

Six is sticks

Seven is oven

Eight is plate

Nine is wine

Ten is hen

Eleven is "penny-one," hotdog bun

Twelve is "penny-two," airplane glue

Thirteen is "penny-three," bumblebee

Fourteen is "penny-four," grocery store

Fifteen is "penny-five," big beehive

Sixteen is "penny-six," magic tricks

Seventeen is "penny-seven," go to heaven

Eighteen is "penny-eight," golden gate

Nineteen is "penny-nine," ball of twine

Twenty is "penny-ten," ball-point pen[7]

Step 2. As you say each line to yourself, imagine as vividly as possible each item described. Do not, for example, imagine an abstract, general door; instead, imagine a particular door — perhaps a great iron door with a large metal knocker that clangs when rapped. Try to imagine what the item feels like, or smells like, or sounds like, as well as what the item looks like.

Step 3. You now have a mnemonic system that will help you memorize lists, in order, up to twenty items long. To memorize such a list, begin with item one and imagine it in some dramatic, bizarre, or amusing relation with the first item on your list. For example, if the first item to be remembered is "coffee," you might imagine yourself taking a water pistol *gun* (from the mnemonic rhyme) and squirting *coffee* on a charging grizzly bear. If the second item on your list is "soup," you might imagine yourself drinking chicken *soup* out of an old smelly pink *shoe* (from the mnemonic rhyme). In each case, the idea is to combine your mnemonic rhyme image with the item to be remembered in a vivid way.

Step 4. To reproduce the list, all you have to do is to say the rhyme to yourself. For example, with the grocery list above, you would say, "One is a gun" . . . water gun . . . squirting *coffee;* "Two is a shoe" . . . pink shoe . . . drinking *soup,* etc.

Improving the Retrieval Stage

You have many memories hidden away that are relatively inaccessible. The lack of accessibility, according to some scientists, is the single most important memory problem. If you could find the key to open the closed doors in your mind, you could relive many past experiences you thought were lost. Finding the right key — the right retrieval cue — is important. Memory is highly organized: memories are associated and interconnected. Following these associations and interconnections, tracking them down, often leads you to the memory you are trying to recall.

Step 1. Whenever possible, modify your surroundings in some way that will "cue" your memory. The old "string around the finger" serves this purpose; of course, it is important to make a strong association between what you want to remember and the string — otherwise you will only remember that you have forgotten something. Another example would be moving your phone to a different but noticeable place in order to remind yourself to make an important phone call.

Step 2. When you are trying to recall something, "free associate" to the first thing that comes to your mind — think about whatever words come to mind, without censorship. After a while, you may reach what you want to recall, thanks to the myriad of associations in memory.

Step 3. When trying to remember a particular event, retrace your steps to the point just before the event occurred. You can do this in fact or in imagination. For example, if you have forgotten where you put your glasses last night, walk through the rooms where you were, doing what you did last night, and you may find the memory cued by this reenactment.

Step 4. When trying to recall a name, say the alphabet to yourself. Free associate to each letter, saying words that come to mind starting with the letter. Your brain's alphabetic filing system may help you find what you want.

Exercise—Using the Retrieval Stage

Use the techniques you have just learned to try to remember the following information:

1. The name of your math teachers in junior high school.
2. Where you were and what you were doing exactly one year ago today.
3. The address of a friend who now lives in another city.

Which of the tasks was the hardest to remember? Why? Which of the four steps listed in improving the retrieval stage did you find most helpful?

Absentmindedness

How many times have you forgotton to mail an important letter? Do you ever spend time searching for lost keys or a misplaced notebook? Have you ever missed an important appointment or forgotten to pick up someone? All these situations are memory problems. They are all annoying and aggravating, and they cause you to waste much time and energy.

The key to overcoming absentmindedness is to picture what you are doing at the very instant you are doing it. The technique involves making a mental picture, an association, of the object to be remembered.

You are finished studying for the night and place your notebook down on top of your record turntable. To avoid spending time looking for it in the morning you make an imaginary mental picture of your notebook revolving around the turntable. This picture allows you instantly to think of both the notebook and where you put it.

The idea is to force yourself to make this type of association. Another common example involves locating keys.

Jack ran into his apartment because his phone was ringing. As he opened the door he left his keys in the lock. At that instant he imagined a gigantic key opening his front door. When he was through with his phone call it was easy for him to remember where he left his keys.

Forgetting to take a book that is needed for a class or a letter that has to be mailed can also be frustrating. In this type of situation it is best to associate the important object (letter or book) with an object you cannot avoid before leaving for school. For example, you could associate the letter with the doorknob of your front door, or the book with the lock on your car door. Every time you look at the lock it will make you think of the book.

This technique for overcoming absentmindedness requires you to use your imagination and to increase your concentration by closely observing your own behavior. You have to practice making associations, and concentrate on what you are doing at the very instant you are doing it.

Summary

Memory is important in almost everything we do. Loss of memory — amnesia — can cause serious problems in everyday living. At times, memories are forgotten; we repress thoughts that are too painful to remember. There are two types of memory: long term and short term. All information to be remembered must be encoded, then stored, and finally retrieved when you want it. To improve memory, mnemonic devices can be used. These devices work by associating new information with old memories. If there is too much information to remember, chunking or grouping information together can reduce the memory load. You can improve memory by improving any of the three systems that make up your memory — encoding, storage, or retrieval. Absentmindedness, a common memory problem, can be overcome by learning to make immediate mental associations.

Notes

1. Luria, A. R. *The mind of a mnemonist.* New York: Avon Books, 1968.

2. Morgan, J. J. B., and Lovell, G. D. *The psychology of abnormal people.* London: Longmans, 1928.

3. Howe, M. J. A. *Introduction to human memory.* New York: Harper & Row, 1970.

4. Earhard, M. The facilitation of memorization by alphabetic instructions. *Canadian Journal of Psychology,* 1967, **21,** 15–24.

5. Miller, G. A. The magical number seven, plus or minus two: some limits on our capacity for processing information. *Psychological Review,* 1956, **63,** 81–97.

6. Mandler, G. Organization and memory. In K. W. Spence and J. T. Spence (eds.), *The psychology of learning and motivation, Vol. II.* New York: Academic Press, 1968.

7. Bower, G. H., and Reitman, J. S. Mnemonic elaboration in multilist learning. *Journal of Verbal Learning and Verbal Behavior,* 1972, **11,** 478–485.

Suggested Readings

Howe, M. J. A. *Introduction to human memory.* New York: Harper & Row, 1970.

Loftus, E. F., and Loftus, G. R. *Human memory.* New York: Wiley, 1976.

Lorayne, H., and Lucus, J. *The memory book.* New York: Ballantine Books, 1974.

Luria, A. R. *The mind of a mnemonist.* New York: Avon Books, 1968.

Young, C. V. *The magic of a mighty memory.* New York: Parker, 1971.

Zielke, W. *Conditioning your memory.* New York: Sterling, 1970.

Chapter Five

THERE ARE NO
SHORT CUTS TO
EXPANDING
AWARENESS—
LIKE, IN MOST CASES
YOU GET
WHAT YOU PAY FOR.

THANKS
FOR TELLING ME
BECAUSE I WAS
JUST GOING TO BUY
A USED MANTRA
AT A
HALF PRICE SALE.

Written by Stephanie Crane/Drawn by Ben Black

Expanding Awareness

One day a man of the people said to Zen Master Ikkyu: "Master, will you please write for me some maxims of the highest wisdom?"

Ikkyu immediately took his brush and wrote the word "Attention."

"Is that all?" asked the man. "Will you not add something more?"

Ikkyu then wrote twice running: "Attention. Attention."

"Well," remarked the man rather irritably, "I really don't see much depth or subtlety in what you have just written."

Then Ikkyu wrote the same word three times running: "Attention. Attention. Attention."

Half-angered, the man demanded: "What does that word 'Attention' mean anyway?"

And Ikkyu answered gently: "Attention means attention."[1]

We are enclosed, out of contact with the world; we are only half awake; we grope in the dark. Yet the world invites awareness: it abounds in energy and we possess senses tuned to that energy; senses for exploring things close up — tasting and touching; and senses for exploring things at a distance — seeing and hearing and smelling. We could be intimately in contact with the flow of energies in the world and in our own bodies, but we often are not.

Attention determines what enters consciousness; we are aware only of the subjects of our attention. Awareness follows attention, but attention is limited; we cannot attend to everything. Our senses are bombarded with information about the state of the world or the condition of our bodies; we attend, however, only to a fraction of what is there. We are limited in how much information we can process at once; we therefore select from the whole, a part — that part that is illuminated by the spotlight of our attention. This perceptual limitation is expressed in *the principle of selective perception: only a small portion of the world accessible to our senses is attended to and perceived.*

The principle of selective perception: Only a small portion of the world accessible to our senses is attended to and perceived.

When several people are talking at once, you can typically follow only one of them, but whichever one you choose. Cherry presented subjects with two simultaneous messages, one to the right ear and one to the left. He asked subjects to attend to one of the messages and repeat it as it was delivered. Subjects could easily do this; but when they were asked about the content of the other message, subjects typically knew almost nothing. They could identify some gross characteristics of the source, but they knew little of what had been said. Subjects attended to and perceived only a part of their sensory world.

Cherry, E. C. Some experiments on the recognition of speech, with one and two ears. *Journal of the Acoustical Society of America,* 1953, **25,** 975–979.
Treisman, A. M. Selective attention in man. *British Medical Bulletin,* 1964, **20,** 12–16.

Imagine that you have a small flashlight to find your way in the dark. If the light is diffused broadly in a wide beam, you will see many dark shapes very dimly; much more than your path would be lit. If the light is focused in a narrow beam, you will see clearly what lies ahead in spite of the limitation of your small light.

Because of the limitations on attention and perception, attention must be focused in order for you to see; most often, however, our minds are dwelling on many things at once. Attention is scattered, diffused. We seem to live in the past (our past categories) and the future (our future images) instead of the present; and so we miss the immediate feelings of the present. The need to focus attention was best expressed in an early saying of the Buddha:

In what is seen there must be just the seen; in what is heard there must be just the heard; in what is sensed (as smell, taste, or touch) there must be just what is sensed; in what is thought there must be just the thought.[1]

Too often attention is scattered, so that memories, expectations, and conceptualization are all mixed with what is sensed. Perhaps our largest deficit in awareness lies in sensing our own bodies. The cultivation of the senses, particularly the proprioceptive, or body-senses, has been neglected in our education. Language and logic are taught diligently, but the inner sensory world, our contact with our own bodies, has been virtually ignored.

Except for sensations of pain and very general feelings of comfort or discomfort, the sensations from within are like stars, which only appear when the artificial lights are turned off. When there is quiet enough, they can be very precise. . . .

As long as the head is still busy, full sensory receptivity is impossible; while with increasing stillness in the head, all perception, traveling unimpeded through the organism, automatically becomes sharper and more in context. In this new stage of more awareness and permissiveness the self-directive powers of the organism reveal themselves ever clearer, and we experience on a deeper level the unexpected transformations we can undergo.[2]

One way to increase your awareness of your inner body sensations is to focus your attention on them, to let your attention wander throughout your body and to notice — perhaps for the first time — how each part feels. A person who did this in a Gestalt therapy session was astonished at the results:

Normally—that is, before I let my "attention wander through my body"—I was aware of my body sensations merely as a general hum, a kind of poorly defined sense of general vitality and warmth. However, the attempt to subdivide this into component sensations was a source of genuine amazement. I became aware of a series of tensions in various parts of my body: knees and lower thighs as I sit in a chair; the region of the diaphragm; the eyes, shoulders and dorsal neck region. This discovery was quite astonishing to me. It was almost as if my feeling had entered a foreign body with tensions, rigidities, and pressures entirely different from mine. Almost immediately upon discovery I was able to relax these tensions. This, in turn, caused me to be aware of a sense of looseness and even elation; a very sudden freedom, pleasure and readiness for anything to come. Aside from these pleasurable sensations I was not aware of any emotions, anxieties, fears, connected with these tensions and their relaxation. In addition, despite the fact that I had bared the existence of these tensions and succeeded in relaxing them, they invariably returned, and later sessions repeated this discovery-relaxation-satisfaction cycle.[3]

An ancient method of focusing attention, turning off symbolization, and thus expanding awareness is meditation. There are a number of different ways to meditate; only one of these will be presented here.

Meditation

A firsthand account of a Zen meditation experience in a training session with a Zen master:

I made up my mind to follow obediently the direction of the Master for five days without doubting, relying completely on the Master. . . .

In the morning of the fifth day, I got up at five and began to sit. I returned to the state of the previous night. And unexpectedly soon a conversion came. In less than ten minutes I reached a wonderful state of mind. It was quite different from any which I had experienced in *seiza* (sitting quietly) or other practices. It was a state of mind incomparably quiet, clear, and serene, without any obstruction. I gazed at it. Entering this state of mind, I was filled with a feeling of appreciation, beyond usual joy, on my reaching such state of mind, and tears began to flow from my closed eyes.[4]

The joy accompanied a state of consciousness brought about through meditation, a mental exercise available to everyone. A second account of an experience in a Zen meditation training session:

It was the fifth day. I took no particular cognizance of the fact. Looking back on it, I was eating more slowly; my movements were slower. What I did not choose to give my attention to . . . I was unaware of. What I chose to attend to . . . I was acutely aware of.

After the usual morning nap, we went upstairs. Seated again, we were given the fifth exercise, a variation of the previous one. . . . Gradually I must have become completely focused on the exercise. I do not think that anything else went through my mind.

And then—it was late in the morning—a white, clear screen came before my eyes. In front of the screen passed or, rather, floated simple images—faces, objects. I have no clear recollection of the images. A rush of feeling came over me.

I burst into tears; the tears became quiet sobbing.

I do not remember at what point I had stopped the exercise.

I can state my feeling but I am not sure I can communicate it with any real meaning. I would not like to be mysterious; I would like to communicate it clearly, at the same time knowing that it may be impossible.

My feeling was that I was seeing something of great importance, as if everything fitted together for the first time. What had all my life struggles been about? Things were very clear and very simple.[5]

What is the experience that led these two men to the profound feelings of clarity and joy? Meditation requires bodily relaxation — usually in a sitting or lotus posture — and a passive awareness that can be induced in a variety of ways. Attention is shifted from outward activity to inner process and experience. By sitting in a quiet place with your eyes closed, breathing regularly, the sources of external stimulation and distraction are greatly reduced; you can tune in more easily to your inner processes. Different techniques of meditation involve different ways of helping you to tune in to your inner processes; with one form you concentrate on your breaths; with another form you concentrate on a word—a mantra—such as OM.[6]

Physiological studies of meditation have shown that oxygen consumption, carbon dioxide elimination, heart rate, and respiration all decrease significantly during the meditative state.[7] The pattern of electrical activity of the brain also undergoes systematic changes in meditation.[8] Practitioners report that meditation helps you to pay attention, makes you more sensitive to small cues, induces great calm and relaxation of tensions, and improves sleep. Following an extensive experience with meditation, one author reported:

The heightening of the awareness of my sense impressions . . . appeared in retrospect to be most important. I had discovered a value in things that I knew could always be recalled, and there was a deeper sense of the uniqueness of each sound, sight, and touch, that was permanently satisfying. . . . The development of a sensitivity of this sort results in living with nature and not just as an observer of it. . . . It was an unexpected gift . . . this enrichment of reception that so increased one's joy of perception. . . .

We are all unconscious artists, we weave the stuff of beauty from the properties and ingredients of matter. A rose is only a rose because man sees it as such; without him it would only be a pattern of energy vortices. Because of this new realization, I took pride in all sorts of beauty that before I had ignored. Sound and sight are purely personal interpretations; we should therefore enjoy as sensually as possible this artistry of our own creation.[9]

How to Meditate

Step 1. Go to a quiet room where you will be undisturbed and sit in a relaxed manner. Keep your back relatively straight and allow your head to tilt slightly forward. Place your hands in your lap.

Step 2. Become passive and unresponsive in your thoughts. Let your thoughts move through you without reacting. The ideal is for your mind to become a room with open windows, through which your thoughts can move without becoming trapped.

Step 3. Focus your attention on your breathing. You breathe in and out all day and night, but you are never mindful of it, you never for a second concentrate your mind on it. Now you are going to do just this. Breathe in and out as usual, without any effort or strain. Now, bring your mind to concentrate on your breathing in and out. When you breathe, you sometimes take deep breaths, sometimes not. This does not matter at all. Breathe normally and naturally. The only thing is that when you take deep breaths you should be aware that they are deep breaths, and so on. In other words, your mind should be so fully concentrated on your breathing that you are aware of its movements and changes. Forget all other things, your surroundings, your environment; do not raise your eyes and look at anything. Try to do this for five or ten minutes.[10]

Step 4. Note your daily progress. At the beginning you will find it extremely difficult to bring your mind to concentrate on your breathing. You will be astonished how your mind runs away. It does not stay. You begin to think of various things. You hear sounds outside. Your mind is disturbed and distracted. You may be dismayed and disappointed. But if you continue to practice this exercise twice a day, morning and evening, for about five or ten minutes at a time, you will gradually, by and by, begin to concentrate your mind on your breathing. After a certain period you will experience just that split second when your mind is fully concentrated on your breathing, when you will not hear even sound nearby, when no external world exists for you. This slight moment is such a tremendous experience for you, full of joy, happiness and tranquility, that you would like to continue it. But still you cannot. Yet, if you go on practicing this regularly, you may repeat the experience again and again for longer and longer periods. That is the moment, when you lose yourself completely in your mindfulness of breathing. As long as you are conscious of yourself you cannot concentrate on anything.[10]

Using Biofeedback

On Friday, March 20, 1970, a thirty-two-year-old woman suffering from an excruciating headache was taken to the emergency room of New York Hospital–Cornell Medical Center, on East Seventieth Street, by ambulance. The young woman, Robin Bielski, had awakened the previous Saturday with a dull ache in the back of her head and neck. . . . Over the next few days, the pain got progressively worse. She went to her regular doctor, and he referred her to a neurologist. The neurologist performed a spinal tap—a standard diagnostic test for damage to the central nervous system. The results were negative.[11]

Further tests showed that Robin had suffered a cerebellar hemorrhage, a bursting of blood vessels in a brain structure near the back of the skull. The hemorrhage resulted from chronic hypertension, dangerously high blood pressure; the reduction of that pressure was now a matter of life or death for Robin Bielski. On the recommendation of her physician, she joined an experimental program aimed at teaching people how to lower their own blood pressure through a procedure called biofeedback.

Body Communication

When you try to do something, how do you know that you've done it? You know you've kicked the wall with your foot because your toe hurts — your sense of touch provides information that the act was completed. You reach out to press a light switch; you can feel the switch with your finger when you contact it and you can see the light come on when the switch is depressed. The sensations from your fingers and eyes are *feedback,* providing information about the success or failure of your actions. *Biofeedback* is biological feedback: information about the state of your body. Just as a thermostat requires information feedback from a room thermometer in order to regulate temperature, you must have information feedback from your senses to regulate your bodily processes, to learn new skills, and to control your motor behavior. This relationship is expressed in *the feedback principle: feedback facilitates the learning and voluntary control of responses.*

Some feedback you are consciously aware of — such as the pain in your toe after you kick the wall; other feedback you are unaware of. Many bodily processes are regulated by subconscious feedback mechanisms that continue to work whether you are awake or asleep. Normally, body

The feedback principle: Feedback facilitates the learning and voluntary control of responses.

A blind man could learn to bowl if someone told him how he was doing; that is, if he had feedback. With knowledge of results, or feedback, you can learn to produce and control many different responses. Hardwyck and Petrinovich used feedback to help subjects stop sub-vocalizing (silently "saying" words while reading). The experimenters recorded muscular movements of subjects' necks and throats. A machine converted these movements into a tone that subjects could hear; when subjects sub-vocalized less, the tone became softer. With this feedback, the subjects gained control over the response and stopped sub-vocalizing. Without feedback, subjects continued to sub-vocalize.

Green, E., Walters, E., Green, A., and Murphy, G. Feedback technique for deep relaxation. *Psychophysiology,* 1969, **6,** 371–377.

Hardwyck, C., and Petrinovich, L. Treatment of subvocal speech during reading. *Journal of Reading,* 1969, **12,** 361–368.

Kamiya, J. Operant control of the EEG alpha rhythm and some of its reported effects on consciousness. In C. Tart (ed.), *Altered States of Consciousness.* New York: Wiley, 1969.

temperature and blood pressure are two such processes. Robin Bielski's brain was given continual feedback about her blood pressure, but she was totally unaware of the message. She could not sense that her arterial muscles were dangerously tensed, constricting her vessels and raising her blood pressure. Without this feedback, voluntary control was impossible.

At some level, however, Robin was in communication with her arteries. Specialized cells called neurons carry messages from the brain to the arterial muscles directing them to contract; other neurons carry sensory information back from the arteries to the brain, providing information feedback about blood pressure; but the information in this case is not normally available to consciousness.

Like all of us, Robin could tense or relax the muscle in her arm whenever she chose to do so. Other responses, however, are not so easily controlled. The regulation of blood pressure is directed by an evolutionarily ancient part of the brain located just above the top of the spinal cord. This ancient part of the brain operates, for the most part, below the level of consciousness. (Consciousness, or awareness, seems to be a function of a different part of the brain, the wrinkled surface called the cortex.) For Robin Bielski, the problem was to try to gain some conscious control over that part of her brain responsible for blood-pressure regulation—a so-called "involuntary" reaction.

Recent studies show the effect of providing electronically amplified biofeedback for certain "involuntary" reactions. Rats can be taught to blush with one ear at a time if they are provided feedback about the blood flow in their ears.[12] Rats can also speed up or slow down their heart rate when they are rewarded for it; some rats have even been induced to commit a bizarre kind of suicide by slowing their hearts to the point that they stopped. People can also learn to control their heart rate if feedback is provided. This feedback may be given in the form of an audible tone or a colored light that goes on when heart rate is right:

Washington, Jan. 9—The patient sits in a hospital bed in Baltimore, watching three little lights arranged like a traffic signal—red on top, yellow in the middle, green on the bottom.

The idea is to keep the yellow light on simply by thinking about it. The stakes are high. The patient suffers from a dangerous disturbance in heart rhythm. He is being trained to maintain normal heart beat by an effort of the mind.[13]

Biofeedback, such as the colored lights for the heart patient above, provides knowledge of the success or failure of your actions, and makes voluntary control possible—even for many involuntary reactions.

Exercise—Becoming Aware of Biofeedback

In order to experience variations in body feedback, try to determine your pulse rate for a one-minute period in each of the following situations:

1. Just waking up in the morning
2. During a meal
3. Watching an exciting TV show or movie
4. During a test
5. Waiting to be picked up for a date or before picking up a date
6. During a lecture
7. Right after completing an exercise session
8. Talking to a friend
9. Before going to sleep at night

Do you think your pulse rate would vary much in the same situations if you measured it the next day? Can you think of other biological processes you could measure without equipment?

Learning to Keep Control

Robin Bielski's life was threatened by her excessively high blood pressure. A way had to be found to bring the pressure down. She was invited to participate in an experimental biofeedback program, under the direction of Dr. Neal Miller, designed to teach her how to control her own blood pressure. The first problem was to provide her with biofeedback about her blood pressure; if she could know when it went up or down, then she could possibly learn to gain voluntary control over its changes. In each of many daily training sessions, a special machine measured her blood pressure and provided immediate feedback by emitting a "beep" when she succeeded in lowering it. After a couple of weeks of training, her blood pressure began to go down; after about six weeks of training it reached the normal range. How did she do it? She reports:

At first, it seemed that lowering my pressure was only a simple muscular trick. I thought it was a matter of relaxing my stomach, my chest, my breathing, but none of these worked all the time. I found I could drop my pressure quickly by fooling with my muscles, but I could only sustain the drop if I "relaxed" my mind. It all seemed to depend on clearing my mind of all stressful thoughts.[11]

Unfortunately, there have been few reports of clear, medically significant, permanent improvements in cardiac or blood pressure control through biofeedback. It works sometimes for some people, but its usefulness as a general medical tool has yet to be shown.

Brain Waves

The young woman sits cross-legged on the wooden floor of her Los Angeles apartment and places a small electronic machine in front of her. She squeezes paste from a tube onto two electrode disks at the end of wires running from the machine, then attaches the electrodes to her head. Her eyes close and her head slumps forward. In a few moments a quiet tone comes from the electronic machine. She opens her eyes and the tone stops; she closes her eyes and, a short time later, the tone continues. Her brain waves are turning the tone on and off.

Brain waves are patterns of electrical activity recorded from the scalp that reflect the underlying electrical activity of the neural cells in the brain. The young woman in the example above is using a small biofeedback machine to help her learn to produce a particular kind of brain wave called *alpha*. Alpha, a brain wave of about 10 cycles per second, is detected by the machine when it occurs and a tone is turned on to provide feedback.

The subjective state associated with the production of alpha waves has been described as "relaxed awareness," "tranquility," and "inner peace." Others have described it as a "blank mind" with no visual images or strong emotion.[14] People who have experienced both alpha production with biofeedback and transcendental meditation report that the subjective states are somewhat similar.[15] During an alpha training session with biofeedback, one person reported:

It sounds funny, but . . . well, okay . . . it seems like there was some kind of force on the inside, flowing through my forehead out . . . not a hard pressure but you can feel it, like when you move your hand through flowing water.[16]

Those who regularly practice alpha production often describe the alpha state as a mystical, transcendent state of consciousness. Others merely report that it relieves their anxieties and makes them feel good.

The biofeedback machine tells you when you are producing alpha by emitting a steady tone. With this feedback you have the opportunity to discover how to produce alpha; that is, to find out exactly what you have to do to produce this state. Once you make this discovery, you may no longer need the feedback machine. You may, in effect, internalize the feedback system so that you are able to discriminate when you are and are not in the alpha state on the basis of internal cues.[17]

How to Produce Alpha

Learning to control your brain waves is learning to produce certain subjective states that are associated with different brain waves. These states can be learned with biofeedback, and sometimes they can be learned without biofeedback, by using a simple verbal description. For many people, alpha can be produced with a verbal description of the associated subjective state.[18] Here is one procedure to try:

Step 1. Sit down in a comfortable chair in a dark room.

Step 2. Close your eyes and relax for a minute (keep your eyes closed for the duration).

Step 3. Begin breathing slowly, deeply, and regularly.

Step 4. Empty your mind of all visual images, problems, and tensions. Make your mind as "blank" as possible.

Step 5. Focus your attention inward; imagine your mind as a dark, still lake.

Muscle Activity

A young man sits in a large, comfortable reclining chair and places two electrodes over his eyebrows on the frontalis muscles. A third electrode is placed over a bone in his arm. As the machine is turned on, he sees a rapid blinking of lights on the machine. He begins to relax his muscles and the lights start to blink slower. His muscle activity is making the lights blink faster and slower.

Biofeedback of muscle activity is called electromyogram (EMG) feedback. An EMG records the pattern of this electrical activity of the muscles. The man in the example above is using EMG biofeedback to help him reduce tension headaches. Using EMG biofeedback enables him to develop control over very low levels of muscle activity simply by receiving biofeedback signals similar to the ones described earlier for brain waves.

EMG biofeedback is often supplemented by other therapy techniques, such as the progressive muscle relaxation technique (discussed in Chapter Six).

EMG biofeedback may be the most useful feedback technique. Almost everyone has experienced some type of headache. Simple tension headaches can occur when the scalp muscles contract. Often there is accompanying tension in the shoulders or other muscles. EMG biofeedback combined with relaxation techniques has been shown to be very effective in reducing this type of headache. Some other treatment applications of EMG biofeedback include insomnia, alcoholism, anxiety, hypertension, asthma, and muscle spasms. EMG biofeedback can also be used to reduce body tension or to increase the muscle activity of nerves supplying injured or damaged muscles.

Inner Freedom

Outer freedom implies personal control over movements and expression; inner freedom implies personal control over such inner processes as thoughts, emotions, and states of consciousness. Outer freedom is limited by social and political controls, such as custom and law. Inner freedom can be limited only by constricted consciousness: we fail to exercise our inner freedom, to probe the limits of it, because we are unaware of the possibilities and have inadequate feedback. The inner changes that occur are accompanied by cues too subtle to sense under normal conditions; thus we often do not know what our inner state is. Some forms of meditation have the aim of quieting input and focusing attention on these subtle cues; biofeedback has the aim of amplifying these subtle cues so that they can be perceived and discriminated. In both cases the idea is to complete the feedback loop so that we can begin to develop self-control over these inner processes.

Expanding inner freedom means more voluntary, conscious control over states of consciousness — tranquility on demand — and over anxieties and emotional reactions. Expanding inner freedom means weakening external environmental controls over our behavior. Perhaps the inner peace associated with alpha comes from increased personal power and expanded freedom. As one participant in an alpha training session commented:

"It's a kind of personal ecology trip—you don't despoil your internal environment with artificial ingredients; you use only what you already have."[19]

Another participant said simply:

"It gave me a sense of dignity."[19]

To Sleep

Sleep is a state of consciousness that is distinctly different from the waking state. When you sleep you are less aware of the world around you.

There are five different stages of sleep. As you begin to fall asleep, you enter stage one. As your sleep becomes deeper, you progress through stages two, three, and four. At each succeeding stage, you become less reactive to external noise. Blood pressure, heart rate and respiration all decrease. It is more difficult for someone to wake you up as your sleep becomes deeper.

After you have been asleep for about an hour, you usually return to stage one sleep. But, instead of awakening, your closed eyes begin to move very quickly, mental activity increases, and bodily functions become aroused. Even with all this activity your muscles become extremely re-laxed. This fifth stage of sleep is called rapid eye movement (REM) sleep. This is the stage where dreams generally occur. Following a period of REM sleep, you cycle through the sleep stages once again. Four or five such cycles occur each night. As an adult, you spend as much as 25 percent of your sleep time in REM sleep. If you sleep seven or eight hours per night, you probably spend as much as two hours every night in REM sleep. Dreaming could occur approximately every 90 minutes.

It is clear that sleep and REM sleep are necessary for normal human functioning. Peter Tripp, a New York disc jockey, stayed awake for 200 hours to raise money for a charity. The following is a description of some of his behavior at 110 hours of sleep deprivation.[20]

Loss of concentration and mental agility were not the worst, however . . . at 110 hours there were signs of delirium. As one of the doctors recalled, "We didn't know much about it at the time because he couldn't tell us." From his latter statements, his curious utterances and behavior at the time, it became clear Tripp's visual world had grown grotesque. A doctor walked into the recruiting booth in a tweed suit that Tripp saw as a suit of furry worms. A nurse appeared to drip saliva. A scientist's tie kept jumping. This was frightening, hard to explain, and sometimes Tripp grew angry and wondering if this were a bona-fide experiment or a masquerade. Around 120 hours, he opened a bureau drawer in the hotel and rushed out calling for help. It seemed to be spurting flames. Tripp thought the blaze had been set deliberately to test him. In order to explain to himself these hallucinations—which appeared quite real—he concocted rationalizations resembling the delusions of psychotic patients.[20]

Sleep deprivation can lead to depression, disorganized activity, and hal-lucinations. Keeping a person awake is surely an effective torture. Loss of REM sleep can also lead to nervousness and irritability. However, the body has an amazing ability to catch up on REM sleep if it has been deprived of it.

To Dream

I drew with my finger, moistened by saliva, a wet cross on the palm of my left hand, with the intention of seeing whether it would still be there on waking up. Then I dreamed that I woke up and felt the wet cross on my left hand by applying the palm to my cheek. And then a long time afterwards I woke up, really, and knew at once that the hand of my physical body had been lying in a closed position undisturbed on my chest all the while.[21]

What do you dream about? The content of dreams varies. In recent years dreams have been studied by psychologists, in laboratories, by waking people up during REM sleep. One study found that the most frequent themes of college students' dreams were: falling, being attacked or chased, trying repeatedly to do something, schools, teachers, studying, and sexual experiences.[22] Dreams usually concern two or three people and familiar objects (e.g., your house or car).[23]

Where do these dream images actually come from? A great many can be traced to your recent daily activities. Images can also come from early memories that have been revived by an image in your dream. Imagery of what is actually happening to you while you are sleeping, such as a change in room temperature, may be incorporated into your dream. Finally, dream images are often derived from your physiological state. Pregnant women often have dreams concerning their babies.

People are generally puzzled by their dreams, and many theories have tried to explain the functions of dreams. Early theorists felt that dreams helped to eliminate mental tensions that had built up during the day. Freud stated that the purpose of dreaming is to satisfy a wish.[24] He felt that the dream guards your sleep: It enables you to carry out impulses, unfulfilled during the day, that might have disturbed your sleep.

Carl Jung is believed to have analyzed over 100,000 dreams. He felt that you dream about things that you are lacking in your waking life.[25] His theory of dreams incorporates aspects of mysticism and religion.

A common theory of dreams states that their function is simply that of problem solving. Dreaming may be a continuation of thinking about your daily problems. A dream may show you how to deal with your needs and wishes.

These various theories of dreams have led to methods of interpretation and analysis. But first you must be able to recall your dreams.

Dream researchers generally have concluded that everyone does dream. The difference is that some people can recall their dreams better than others. A number of suggestions have been made by psychologists to help you recall your dreams.

A Step-by-Step Procedure to Help Recall Dreams

Step 1. Have a pencil and paper or a tape recorder at your bedside so that you will be ready to record your dream. Make sure there is a light available in case you awake from a dream in the middle of the night.

Step 2. Use an alarm clock rather than a clock-radio. A clock-radio allows you to wake up gradually and your dream may fade from memory.

Step 3. Before you go to sleep tell yourself that you are going to remember your dream. Think about ideas that interest you that you would like to dream about. You are more likely to remember a dream that can be used constructively.

Step 4. You should try to be somewhat tired, but not exhausted, when you go to bed. Drinking, taking drugs, or overeating may interfere with dreaming.

Step 5. When you awake, the first thing you should ask yourself is "Have I been dreaming?" Lie quietly without much movement, and let your mind concentrate on whatever comes up. Do not think of what you have to do during the coming day.

Step 6. When you have remembered a dream, write it down or record it immediately. Even if it is vague, you will probably be able to slowly fill in the details.

Step 7. Have recording materials with you during the day in case people or events touch off dreams from the previous night.

Step 8. Keep a dated journal of your dreams. There may be an interesting sequence to them.

Summary

We are bombarded by information but can only attend to a limited amount. Attention determines what is allowed into our conscious mind, and our attention is very often scattered. Very few of us are even aware of the information coming from our own bodies.

Meditation is one technique used to focus attention and to expand awareness. During meditation, attention is shifted to an inner relaxed experience. Biofeedback, the process of receiving information about body functions, is another method that can be used to expand awareness. Feedback from blood pressure, brain waves, and muscle activity has been used to deal with a variety of medical and psychological problems.

Sleep is another level of awareness that has been studied extensively. There are five different stages of sleep that you pass through each night. REM sleep is the stage where your dreaming usually occurs. Dream content varies widely. A number of theories have been developed to account for dream images and their functions. Before trying to understand your dreams, however, you must be able to recall them. A number of techniques have been used to help people recall their dreams.

Notes

1. Kapleau, D. *The three pillars of Zen.* New York: Harper & Row, 1966.

2. Selver, C. Report on work in sensory awareness and total functioning. In H. A. Otto (ed.), *Explorations in human potentialities.* Springfield, Ill.: Charles C Thomas, 1966.

3. Perls, F., Hefferline, R. E., and Goodman, P. *Gestalt therapy.* New York: Delta Books, 1951.

4. Kitahara, S. A Zen training session. *Psychologia,* 1963, **6,** 188–189.

5. Huber, J. *Through an eastern window.* Boston: Houghton Mifflin, 1967.

6. Naranjo, C., and Ornstein, R. E. *On the psychology of meditation.* New York: Viking Press, 1971.

7. Wallace, R. K. Physiological effects of transcendental meditation. *Science,* 1970, **167,** 1751–1754.

8. Anand, B. K., Chhina, G. S., and Singh, B. Some aspects of EEG studies in yogis. *Electroencephalography and Clinical Neurophysiology,* 1961, **13,** 452–456.

9. Shattock, E. H. *An experiment in mindfulness.* London: Rider, 1958.

10. Rahula, W. *What the Buddha taught.* New York: Grove Press, 1959.

11. Jonas, G. Visceral learning — I. *New Yorker,* 1972, **48,** Aug. 19, 34–57.

12. Miller, N. E. Learning of visceral and glandular responses. *Science,* 1969, **163,** 434–445.

13. Schmeck, H. M., Jr. Control by brain studied as way to curb body ills. *New York Times,* Jan. 10, 1971.

14. Stoyva, J. M. The public (scientific) study of private events. In E. H. Hartmann (ed.), *Sleep and dreaming.* Boston: Little, Brown, 1970.

15. Kiefer, D. Meditation and biofeedback. In J. White (ed.), *The highest state of consciousness.* Garden City, N.Y.: Anchor Books, 1972.

16. Green, E. E., Green, A. M., and Walters, E. D. Voluntary control of internal states: Psychological and physiological. *Journal of Transpersonal Psychology,* 1970, **2,** 1–26.

17. Brown, B. B. Recognition of aspects of consciousness through association with EEG alpha activity represented by a light signal. *Psychophysiology,* 1970, **6,** 442–452.

18. Beatty, J. Similar effects of feedback signals and instructional information on EEG activity. *Physiology and Behavior,* 1972, **9,** 151–154.

19. Karlins, M., and Andrews, L. M. *Psychology: What's in it for us?* New York: Random House, 1973.

20. Luce, G. G., and Segal, J. *Sleep.* New York: Coward, McCann, 1966.

21. Van Eeden, F. V. A study of dreams. *Proceedings of the Society for Physical Research,* 1913, **26,** 431–461.

22. Griffith, R. M., Miyagi, O. and Tago, A. Universality of typical dreams: Japanese versus Americans. *American Anthropology,* 1958, **60,** 1173–1179.

23. Hall, C. S., and Van De Castle, R. L. *The content analysis of dreams.* New York: Appleton-Century-Crofts, 1966.

24. Freud, S. *The interpretations of dreams.* London: Hogarth Press, 1953.

25. Jung, C. *Man and his symbols.* New York: Dell, 1968.

Suggested Readings

Brown, B. *Stress and the art of biofeedback.* New York: Bantam, 1977.

Cartwright, R. D. *A primer on sleep and dreaming.* New York: Addison-Wesley, 1978.

Dement, W. C. *Some must watch while some must sleep.* Stanford, Calif.: Stanford Alumni Association, 1972.

DeRopp, R. S. *The master game: Pathways to higher consciousness beyond the drug experience.* New York: Delta Books, 1968.

Faraday, A. *The dream game.* New York: Harper & Row, 1974.

Fixx, J. F. *The complete book of running.* New York: Random House, 1977.

Glasser, W. *Positive addiction.* New York: Harper & Row, 1976.

LeShan, L. *How to meditate.* Boston: Little, Brown, 1974.

Naranjo, C., and Ornstein, R. E. *On the psychology of meditation.* New York: Viking Press, 1971.

Tart, C. T. *Altered states of consciousness.* New York: Wiley, 1969.

Teyler, T. J. *Altered states of awareness.* San Francisco: Freeman, 1971.

Chapter Six

Written by Stephanie Crane/Drawn by Ben Black

Learning to Relax

Jennifer felt terrible. Her dark hair looked disheveled and her eyes had acquired a look of worry. She had always been a rather easygoing person, but now with problems at home she was becoming increasingly nervous and tense. She had recently been surprised and greatly upset by her parents' unfriendly separation. They were both making demands on her time that she couldn't fulfill and also keep up with her work at school. Jennifer's friends described her as "jumpy" and "on edge." She lacked her usual energy and felt constantly tired. Just before final exams, she became extremely nervous and found it difficult to concentrate on her studies.

You can relieve tension through relaxation, but most people don't know how to relax. Extreme tension not only is a very unpleasant feeling, it can interfere with many things you have to do. Think about the last time you got very nervous. What happened? Check your symptoms of tension:

_____ Sweating, particularly on forehead, neck, and underarms

_____ Fast, shallow, and irregular breathing; shortness of breath

_____ Increased heart rate and blood pressure; a pounding heart

_____ Muscular tension, especially in the back of your neck

_____ Overreaction, jumpiness; bothered by small noises

_____ Irritability

_____ Muscular tremor

_____ Stomach upsets; stomachache, knot in your stomach, "butterflies"

_____ Diarrhea or constipation

_____ Icy hands and feet

_____ Chronic fatigue

_____ Headache

Mind over Body

The tension Jennifer experienced comes from tensed muscles that have received messages from the brain to contract. When you are very nervous, many muscles are activated and tightened unnecessarily; for example, the muscles in your shoulders and the back of your neck may be tensed for a long time, and afterwards will ache. Besides these transitory aftereffects of nervous tension, there are many other longer lasting and much more serious consequences of prolonged states of tension. The mind and the body are not separate, independent entities: any change in the body is accompanied by a change in mental or emotional state, and any change in the mind is accompanied by a corresponding change in the body.[1] The changes in the body that accompany chronic feelings of worry and anxiety are often serious. This relationship is called *the psychosomatic principle: prolonged psychological distress can produce physical symptoms.*

Ulcers, asthma, high blood pressure, and several skin disorders have been shown in some cases to be psychosomatic, being influenced by prolonged states of tension. Ulcers have been induced in laboratory monkeys through psychological stress. Tension often precipitates asthmatic attacks in persons with that disorder.

Flora F. was the second of three daughters. . . . From her first year of life she suffered from attacks of bronchial asthma. . . . Her customary mood was one of sadness, dominated by longings for her mother. She was extremely sensitive to loss, or the threat of it, which often precipitated her asthmatic attacks. One severe attack occurred when she learned that her doctor, social worker, and nurse on the asthma project were all about to leave. Another major attack followed a visit to an aunt who had shown her a picture of her dead mother.[2]

Your skin may be sensitive to your level of anxiety and tension. Extended states of tension may disturb your body's production of antibodies, resulting in different kinds of allergic reactions. The skin and the mucous lining of the nose are particularly vulnerable to these reactions. One study demonstrated the effect of psychological tension on the nose:

The psychosomatic principle: Prolonged psychological distress can produce physical symptoms.

The term "psychosomatic" refers to the effect of the mind on the body. Many physical problems have been related to psychological distress. Since "mind" is a function of the brain, it is actually the brain that produces the physical symptoms. Sawrey and Weisz placed rats in a psychologically distressing situation: their cage was constructed so that they had to cross an electrified grid to reach food and water. For an hour every two days, the grid was turned off. Another group of rats was placed in a nonelectrified cage and allowed access to food and water only one hour every two days. After thirty days, rats in both groups were examined. The rats that were simply deprived of food and water were fine, but many of the rats in the electric shock condition had developed ulcers.

Block, J. Further consideration of psychosomatic predisposition factors in allergy. *Psychosomatic Medicine,* 1968, **30,** 202–208.

Friedman, S. B., Ader, R., and Glasgow, L. A. Effects of psychological stress in adult mice inoculated with Coxsackie *B* viruses. *Psychosomatic Medicine,* 1965, **27,** 361–368.

Sawrey, W. L., and Weisz, J. D. An experimental method of producing gastric ulcers. *Journal of Comparative and Physiological Psychology,* 1956, **49,** 269–270.

We did a study of patients who had colds and nasal infections, asking them, when they came in for medical care, to come back when they had recovered. As each returned to us, recovered, we measured the blood flow, the freedom of breathing, the swelling, and the amount of secretion in his nose. Then we began to talk with him about the event or events that had occurred before he became ill. After this conversation—about his mother-in-law, for example, or his new job—we repeated the measurements, and discovered that our talk had renewed the cold symptoms.

Biopsies of nasal tissue confirmed that we caused tissue damage by talking about psychologically charged events. The mother-in-law example is not merely facetious, by the way. A person often catches a cold when his or her mother-in-law comes to visit. So many patients mentioned mothers-in-law so often that we came to consider them a common cause of disease in the U.S.[3]

Apparently, mothers-in-law can affect your nose. Another case shows the effect of nervous tension on the skin:

Anna A., a twenty-seven-year-old nurse, was engaged to be married and was somewhat anxious and uncertain about this adventure. A week before her wedding day she developed a severe attack of urticaria (hives): most of her body was covered with raised white, intensely itchy wheals. However, she continued with the preparations for the wedding. Two weeks after her marriage, she reappeared at the hospital, radiantly happy and with quite clear skin.[2]

Exercise—Discovering Muscle Tensions

Before learning about the different techniques you can use to ease tension, it may be helpful to identify the muscle groups that become tense in your daily activities. It is possible to divide the muscles into the following seven groups:

1. Muscles of the dominant arm
2. Muscles of the nondominant arm
3. Facial muscles (eyes, eyebrows, nose, mouth)
4. Neck and throat muscles
5. Muscles of the chest, shoulders, upper back, and abdomen
6. Muscles of the dominant thigh, calf, and foot
7. Muscles of the nondominant thigh, calf, and foot

Try to keep a record for two or three days of tenseness that occurs in each of these muscle groups. Record the situation, the time of day, and who was present each time tension occurred. By analyzing this data it may be possible to determine what situations lead to tension and which muscle groups are the key to your own relaxation.

Easing Tension

You can ease your tension by relaxing your body. Relaxing is not an activity that you do; instead, it is the result of not doing something else (tensing). But to stop tensing is not easy; you often do not know when you are tensing and when you are not. One problem in combating tension is to become more sensitive to the feedback from your muscles, which tells you when you are tense. Another problem is to discover what relaxation procedure works best for you personally.

Exercising, paradoxically, is a method of relaxation many people use. You might think that the deliberate tensing of your muscles in walking or calisthenics would have just the opposite effect, but apparently this is not so. Due, perhaps, to a negative practice effect (see Chapter Eight), increasing your physical exercise actually helps to reduce your physical tension. Soaking in a hot tub is another commonly used and effective method for relaxing. Two more complex methods of inducing relaxation are (1) autohypnosis, and (2) progressive relaxation. The first, autohypnosis, involves focusing attention, self-suggestion, and breathing exercises; the second, progressive relaxation, is a procedure for teaching deep muscular relaxation throughout the body.

Autohypnosis

Jennifer found it very difficult to get to sleep the night before a big test at school. After reviewing for the test, she would stay awake for hours worrying; facts would intrude unwanted into her mind; she just couldn't calm down. The next day she would be tired from lack of sleep and would make careless mistakes on the exam. After learning about autohypnosis, a simple relaxation technique, she was able to ease her tension and get more rest.

Hypnotizing yourself is not something magical or esoteric. You do not become a robot, lose your consciousness, or feel weird. In fact, you may have hypnotized yourself before and not have been aware of it. You recover from the hypnotic effect naturally, in the course of a few minutes, feeling refreshed. You do not have to worry about how you will "come out of it" — this is automatic. If you put yourself "under," you will wake in a few moments without help. Try these simple steps:

Step 1. Find a soft, comfortable chair in a very quiet room. Arrange the chair so that it is facing a relatively blank wall at a distance of five to ten feet. Place a thumbtack in the wall about a foot above your eye level when you are seated in the chair.

Step 2. Sit in the chair, staring fixedly at the tack while keeping your head relatively level. Breathe regularly, slowly, and deeply, counting backwards with each breath from ten to one. Do not permit your eyes to move from the tack.

Step 3. When you reach *one,* continue staring at the tack. As you do so, imagine that your arms and legs are becoming increasingly heavy; do not move your arms and legs — imagine what it would feel like if they were too heavy to move.

Step 4. Continue staring fixedly at the tack. Now imagine that your eyelids are becoming increasingly heavy. Imagine that they are heavier and heavier. Imagine that they have lead weights attached to them. Think to yourself that it is hard to keep your eyes open, that they want desperately to close. At this point, let your eyes close (you may find that they will "close by themselves").

Step 5. Begin counting backwards from ten as you breathe deeply and slowly with your eyes closed. Focus your attention on your breath — imagine that your breath is visible, that it is purple clouds of mist or smoke, and that you are watching it slowly go in and out. Try to ignore all sensations except those associated with breathing. Do not move or attend to any part of your body.

Step 6. As you reach *one* in your counting, imagine yourself lying back in a tub of hot water; your head is relaxing comfortably and your body is floating gently in the warm water. Try to feel the warmth from the water on your skin. Try to float as a limp rag. Tell yourself to go limp, to float, to relax completely. Continue to breathe deeply and slowly. Continue this stage for as long as you can focus on floating; if your mind begins to wander, to worry, to plan, or remember — stop, open your eyes, and get up.

Progressive Relaxation

Often you don't realize you are tense; only later when you feel the ache in the back of your neck, the tightness around your eyes, or an unexplained tiredness, do you realize that you have been tense for some time. Tension dissipates with relaxation; but before you can learn deep muscular relaxation, you have to learn to recognize your muscular tension at the time it occurs, not afterwards. If you can recognize when you are tense and where you are tense, you can relax more completely. In accordance with *the feedback principle,* you have to know what you are doing before you can stop doing it. The method of progressive relaxation teaches you to become more aware of the tensions in your body.

There are two important concepts in progressive relaxation training.[4,5] The first is the "tension sensation," the bodily experience of a contracting muscle. Each muscle or set of muscles controls a body movement. One goal of progressive relaxation training is to gain awareness of the muscles involved in particular body movements. The second important concept is "relaxation." Relaxation is the opposite of tension or contraction. Relaxing a muscle does not involve further work; it is simply the cessation of contracting or tensing. Progressive relaxation training teaches awareness of tension and the ability to relax that tension. Try the following step-by-step procedure:

Relaxation Training

Allow yourself at least one-half hour for the session. Select a quiet room with a couch or bed in which you will not be disturbed. Loosen any tight-fitting clothing. Until you learn the procedure, you will want to sit up with the book in your lap so that you can read each step as you proceed; after you become familiar with the method you may wish to go through the entire session lying down on the bed or couch with your eyes closed. The method is called "progressive" relaxation because it progressively relaxes the body in a step-by-step procedure, beginning with the hands, then moving up the arms to the head, then moving down the body to the feet.

Step 1. Clench your right fist and feel the tension sensations in your arm. Clench your fist even tighter, noticing the tightness and the tension in your arm muscles. Now, completely relax your arm, letting your fingers partially straighten out. Observe the difference in the way your arm muscle feels.

Step 2. Repeat Step 1, only clench your fist slowly and release it slowly until it is completely relaxed. Pay attention to the difference in the way your arm muscles feel when tensed or relaxed.

Step 3. Clench your left fist while keeping the rest of your body as relaxed as possible. Feel the tension sensations in your left arm. Clench your fist tighter, and then completely relax. Notice the difference in the way your arm muscle feels.

Step 4. Repeat Step 3 more slowly; then completely relax.

Step 5. Bend both arms at the elbows and tense your biceps — the muscles in the front part of your upper arms. Imagine that you are lifting a heavy weight toward your chin. Notice the tension in your biceps. Tense them tighter, and then relax them completely, letting your arms straighten out. Feel the difference between being tense and relaxed.

Step 6. Repeat Step 5 more slowly.

Step 7. Straighten both of your arms, pressing the backs of your hands down against your legs until you feel the tension in the backs of your arms. Now relax and notice the difference.

Step 8. Let your arms completely relax. Lay them at your sides. Search for any tension sensations in your arms and relax them for about a minute. Just let your arms go completely limp. Imagine that the tension is flowing down your arms and out your fingers, leaving your arms completely inactive, limp, and heavy.

Step 9. Wrinkle your forehead by raising up your eyebrows as high as you can. Feel the tension throughout your forehead. Then relax your forehead; notice how it smoothes out.

Step 10. Frown hard, feeling the tension between your eyes. Now, relax and feel the difference.

Step 11. Close your eyelids tightly. Notice the tension all over your eyelids and around your eyes. Relax, but keep your eyes closed.

Step 12. Firmly clench your teeth, closing your jaws tightly. Feel the tension sensations in your lower jaw and temples. Now, relax and let your lips part; let your jaw hang loose.

Step 13. Press your head back, feeling the tension in your neck. Turn your head left, then right, noticing the different tensions in the sides of your neck. Bend your chin toward your chest. Now let your neck completely relax.

Step 14. Shrug your shoulders. Feel the tension in the tops of your shoulders and the sides of your neck. Relax and notice the difference in the way the muscles feel.

Step 15. Let your shoulders go completely relaxed, and then your arms, neck, jaws, eyelids, and forehead. Imagine the tensions from these areas flowing out, down your arms and out your fingers. Be limp and loose. Notice the absence of tension sensations in these areas.

Step 16. Inhale deeply, and notice the tension in your chest. Hold your breath and observe the sensations of tightness in your muscles. Now relax completely by exhaling.

Step 17. Breathe slowly and regularly, letting the air go out of your lungs when you relax. Do this while relaxing the rest of your body.

Step 18. Tighten your stomach muscles and keep them tight. Notice the tension in your abdomen. Relax and notice the difference.

Step 19. Arch your back, feeling the tension sensations on both sides of your spine. Relax everywhere except in this part of your spine. Now relax your back as well.

Step 20. Breathe regularly while relaxing your arms, head, neck, upper and lower torso. Relax any area in which you feel tension sensations. Let these areas be loose and inactive.

Step 21. Straighten your legs and press your heels down hard against the floor or bed. Feel the tension in your thighs and buttocks. Now relax and feel the difference.

Step 22. Keep your legs straight and point your toes by moving your feet away from your face. Notice the tension in the calves of your legs. Relax, letting your feet move back to a normal position.

Step 23. Move your feet in the opposite direction, back toward your face. Notice the tension in your shins at the front of your lower legs. Relax the muscles in your shins and calves, letting your feet be limp and loose.

Step 24. Relax your feet, legs, lower torso, upper torso, arms and hands, neck, jaws, and face. Relax everywhere, feeling no tension. Breathe slowly and deeply, imagining all tensions to flow down your body and out your toes, leaving your body inactive, limp, and heavy. Remain totally inactive for a few minutes.

Any of the steps in this sequence can be isolated and more fully explored and repeated in further sessions. Doing this will enable you to detect very small tensions in your muscles. The more aware you become of your muscle sensations, the easier it will be for you to relax. Your training might be helped by putting the steps of the procedure on tape so that you can follow them without interruption. You can also extend the training by following the steps while sitting or standing. This will help you gain further control over your ability to relax while in public.

Deep muscle relaxation is something you learn how to do by practicing. The progressive relaxation procedure outlined here, with practice, will increase your awareness of and your ability to control nervous tension. But even the first time you try it, you will feel more relaxed.

Summary

Tension is the result of tightened, tense muscles. Extended states of tension may lead to serious physical problems, such as ulcers and high blood pressure. It is possible to identify seven major muscle groups where tension may be located. Exercise and soaking in a hot tub are two simple methods of reducing tension. Two more complex methods of inducing relaxation are autohypnosis and progressive relaxation. Progressive relaxation consists of learning to discriminate between the sensations of tension and relaxation.

Notes

1. Green, E. E., Green, A. M., and Walters, E. D. Voluntary control of internal states: Psychological and physiological. *Journal of Transpersonal Psychology,* 1970, **2,** 1–26.

2. Treisman, M. Mind, body, and behavior: Control symptoms and their disturbances. In P. London and D. Rosenhan (eds.), *Foundations of abnormal psychology.* New York: Holt, Rinehart and Winston, 1968.

3. Holmes, T. H., and Masuda, M. Psychosomatic syndrome. *Psychology Today,* April 1972, 71–72, ff.

4. Jacobson, E. *Anxiety and tension control: A physiological approach.* Philadelphia: J. B. Lippincott, 1964.

5. Wolpe, J., and Lazarus, A. A. *Behavior therapy techniques: A guide to the treatment of neuroses.* New York: Pergamon, 1968.

Suggested Readings

Benson, Hubert. *The relaxation response.* New York: William Morrow, 1975.

Bernstein, D. A., and Borkovec, T. *Progressive relaxation training: A manual for the helping professions.* Champaign, Ill.: Research Press, 1973.

Jacobson, E. *Anxiety and tension control: A physiological approach.* Philadelphia: J. B. Lippincott, 1964.

Walker, C. E. *Learn to relax: Thirteen ways to reduce tension.* Englewood Cliffs, N.J.: Prentice-Hall, 1975.

Chapter Seven

Written by Stephanie Crane/Drawn by Ben Black

Reducing Anxieties and Fears

Hugh O'Brian, actor:

As a kid, I worked as a window-washer to earn a few bucks. One morning I was doing the windows on the eighth floor of a 15-story building when the safety belt—that's the lifeline that connects you to the building—gave way. I managed to catch on to a ledge, but had to dangle over one of Chicago's busier intersections until I was hauled to safety. Ever since, unenclosed heights are not for me. A plane is fine, but I can't take a terrace on top of a skyscraper with nothing but a railing between me and the ground. I refuse to give in to a phobia. I try to fight it. That's why I took up parachute jumping. I both won and lost the battle. I have jumped repeatedly—but never without nausea . . . panic . . . fear.[1]

Jacqueline Susann, writer:

A moth, a grasshopper, any creepy-crawly thing can reduce me to a quivering lump. Once when I was in summer stock, a piece of "hay" tickled my leg. I brushed at it and it flew off on its own power! Somebody said, "How sweet—a praying mantis." Sweet indeed! As it prayed, I died.[1]

Henry Fonda, actor:

Several years ago, after completing a film with my buddy, Jimmy Stewart, I was feeling down—way down. Jimmy asked me why, and I leveled with him. "I'm afraid I'll never work again," said I. "Not you, too!" he answered. "I thought I was the only person who ever felt that." But that's still my ever-present fear—failure; never being asked to work again; no one wanting me.[1]

We often live with worry and anxiety. Although these are unpleasant, even painful experiences, we seem unable to avoid them. Sometimes fear intrudes into our lives, distorting our thoughts and decisions. Anxiety drives us—forward to impossible achievement, or backward, fleeing from imagined harm. We sometimes sweat, tremble, and lie awake with fear. Our hearts pound, our mouths are dry, our heads ache with fear. The intensity of the feelings and the magnitude of the disruption in our lives often are quite incompatible with the extent of true danger. Among our fears may be social rejection, failure, elevators, thunder, small insects.

What Are Your Fears?

_____ Looking foolish

_____ Making mistakes

_____ Not being a success

_____ Speaking before a group

_____ Auto accidents

_____ Thunder

_____ Receiving injections

_____ Crowds

_____ Fire

_____ Human blood

_____ Airplanes

_____ Doctors

_____ Suffocating

_____ Being criticized

_____ Spiders

_____ Falling

_____ Dogs

_____ Enclosed places

_____ Cancer

_____ Failing a test

_____ Loved ones being injured

_____ Snakes

_____ Untimely death

_____ Being alone

_____ High, open places

_____ Insects

_____ Large open spaces

_____ Elevators

_____ Feeling rejected by others

_____ Darkness

_____ Mental disturbance

_____ Loss of temper

_____ Dirt

_____ Being stared at

_____ War

_____ Going blind

_____ Being crippled

_____ Drowning

Hidden Causes

Wendy woke with a scream. Her heart was pounding and her breath came in gasps. For a moment, she was certain that she was in terrible danger. The sheet was damp from her perspiration. What had happened? She could not make it out. All she remembered was a dark, swirling image in a dream. And even that was being forgotten as she settled back into sleep.

Why do we feel what we feel? Why do we do what we do? Sometimes we understand what is going on with us, and sometimes we don't; the reasons are unclear. We may feel compelled to strive for success without knowing why. We may instinctively dislike someone, but not be able to justify it. We may feel vaguely uneasy and anxious but be unaware of what is bothering us. Our motives are sometimes unconscious; they are below the level of awareness.

Just as the body may be invaded by microorganisms and may take defensive action against them without our awareness, so psychological needs may be frustrated and defensive behavior undertaken with no awareness or conscious choice on our part. For example, show-off behavior and negativism are usually defensive reactions to the frustration of needs for adequacy, social approval, and acceptance, but in some cases, not only the defensive tactics but even the feelings of inadequacy that prompt them are below the level of consciousness.[2]

The role of unconscious motivation has been investigated through hypnosis. In one study, an individual was hypnotized and put into a deep trance; the hypnotist then induced a conflict between an "irresistible impulse" and a "moral prohibition." A strong desire to do something was frustrated by the feeling that it was wrong. The individual was given the following posthypnotic suggestion:

When you awaken you will find next to you a bar of chocolate. You will have a desire to eat the chocolate that will be so intense that it will be impossible to resist the craving. At the same time you will feel that the chocolate does not belong to you and that to eat it would be very wrong and very bad. You will have no memory of these suggestions when you awaken, but you will, nevertheless, react to them.[3]

When the individual came out of the trance, he began to act very strangely; he was obviously in great distress, but he did not know why. The reasons had been made unconscious. The hypnotist reported:

When the subject was aroused, he looked casually about the room, yet avoided the table near him on which I had placed a bar of chocolate. He complained of a feeling of dizziness and of faintness. He asked for a glass of water and then decided to get it himself. He stood up from the chair, took two or three steps, then fell backward remarking that he felt so faint that he could hardly walk. His face was blanched and when his pulse was taken it was found to be rapid and thready. His forehead was covered with cold perspiration. He complained of feeling chilly. He then began to shiver and shortly after exhibited generalized muscle tremors. Almost compulsively his head moved sideways as he glanced furtively at the table. The moment he caught sight of the bar of chocolate his tremors became much more violent. He breathed deeply and seemed to go into a faint, leaning backward in the chair with his eyes closed. He remarked that he had no idea why he felt so bad and when questioned whether he would like a piece of candy, he shook his head emphatically and stated that he disliked chocolate bars. When I attempted to hand him the candy he became agitated and complained of such great physical distress that I found it necessary to rehypnotize him and remove the conflict.[3]

Just as the hypnotized subject was influenced by unconscious impulses and conflicts, your behavior may be influenced at times by conflicts of which you are unaware. The mind is only partly conscious. There are memories and desires below the level of your awareness. *The principle of unconscious determination* asserts that *behavior is influenced at times by emotions, impulses, and memories of which we are not currently aware.*

Defense Mechanisms

A normal way of coping with anxiety and frustration is to mobilize psychological defenses against the threat. These defensive tactics, though unconscious, are so common that they have been classified and named. You will recognize some of these defense mechanisms as ways you use to cope.

Repression is the forgetting of painful memories or frightening impulses. Material that is repressed is pushed out of consciousness so that the anxiety associated with it is lessened. If you have repressed the mem-

The principle of unconscious determination: Behavior is influenced at times by emotions, impulses, and memories of which we are not currently aware.

Orne, Sheehan, and Evans examined the effects of a hypnotic suggestion on a person's behavior. Subjects in one group were excellent hypnotic subjects and subjects in another were not but were instructed to pretend to be hypnotized. All were given a hypnotic suggestion to touch their foreheads when they heard the word, "experiment"; they were told they would not remember this instruction. Outside of the experimental setting, none of the pretending subjects consistently responded to the word "experiment." Hypnotized subjects who were unaware of the suggestions, however, always responded to the word "experiment" when away from the experimental setting. They could not say why they touched their foreheads; the reasons were unconscious. Of course, what is conscious at one time may be unconscious at another. Incidents are "forgotten," yet they may continue to influence our lives.

Freud, S. The unconscious. In S. Freud, *The Standard Edition of the Complete Psychological Works of Sigmund Freud, Vol XLV*. London: Hogarth Press, 1957.

Orne, M. T., Sheehan, P. W., and Evans, F. J. Occurrence of posthypnotic behavior outside the experimental setting. *Journal of Personality and Social Psychology,* 1968, **9**, 189–196.

Sheehan, P. W., and Orne, M. T. Some comments on the nature of post-hypnotic behavior. *Journal of Nervous and Mental Disease,* 1968, **146,** 209–220.

ory of your father's death, you cannot recall the details of the incident, although you may be aware that he is dead; you can thus avoid the pain and trauma you would experience in reliving the tragedy.

Displacement is the redirection of hostile feelings from an unsafe to a safe target. Anger that is displaced is anger that is directed not toward the person who caused it, but toward a second party. A child who is spanked by a parent may displace the anger and kick, not the parent, but the cat — an innocent second party. If your day at school has been upsetting, you may come home and yell at your younger brother (displaced aggression).

Rationalization is a way of explaining away all your difficulties in a fashion that protects your ego and self-esteem. You rationalize your failures by inventing logical excuses for them. Suppose you tried to win a contest but failed; what could you do to feel better? You could say, "I didn't want to win anyway"; "the contest was rigged"; "I didn't really try"; or, "the contest actually wasn't worth the effort." Each of these rationalizations serves to defend your ego and self-esteem against the embarrassment of failure.

Projection is a way of denying your own feelings and attitudes and attributing them to others ("projecting" them onto other people). To admit that you feel angry may make you anxious; to defend yourself against this anxiety, you may insist that others are angry at you, rather than the other way around.

Emotional insulation is a way of defending yourself against hurt by withdrawing your emotional investment from your work and relationships. Rather than risk great disappointments, you are cautious and more reserved, and you are careful not to let your hopes get too high. If you take no risks, if you are careful not to put your ego on the line, no one can hurt you. You withdraw into a protective shell to ward off frustration and disappointment.

Letting Off Steam

In the late 1800s, Joseph Breuer, a Viennese physician and colleague of Sigmund Freud, began treating a young woman in her early twenties for a very peculiar condition. One arm and both legs were paralyzed; her neck muscles were permanently contracted; she had periods of nausea and coughing; and she experienced difficulties with her vision and hearing. In terms of physical disease, the particular pattern of symptoms did not make sense. Under hypnosis she was able to talk about her suppressed feelings and memories of her father's long illness and death. In the course of this treatment, she came to understand the unconscious psychological origins of her physical symptoms, and the symptoms disappeared. The patient was completely cured.

Today, most psychotherapy is a kind of "talking cure" — the client talks to the therapist, revealing conflicts, frustrations, and painful memories and feelings, and subsequently feels better. The therapist participates in the interaction by clarifying, interpreting, probing, reflecting, and advising.

Catharsis means to discharge emotional tensions through expressing them; for example, by "letting off steam" or "talking it out." By "getting things off your chest" — getting your hurt out into the open — your bad feelings will often diminish. As Cicero said, "Friendship improves happiness and abates misery, by the doubling of our joy and the dividing of our grief."

Grief shared is grief reduced; disclosure relieves tension. When you feel upset or angry and talk to someone, or otherwise actively express your feelings, you feel better. Releasing strong emotions through crying also has healing effects.[4] When some depressed persons express their feelings, they feel less depressed.[5] And experiments have shown that anger can be reduced by talking it out.[6] Furthermore, when you get things out in the open, you yourself can often see them more clearly and objectively. Additionally, those you talk with may be able to help you by contributing information or pointing out possibilities you have overlooked.

When you get it off your chest, not only do you experience relief, but you may bring unconscious material to consciousness. Feelings, impulses, and memories of which you are unaware may emerge from your unconscious mind; thus if you tune in to what you say and feel when you disclose your feelings to friends, you can learn about yourself. Of course, if you tell the wrong person, you may wind up feeling worse: you don't want to suffer punishment from a hostile listener; you want to experience acceptance from a caring friend. With an accepting listener, catharsis is a practical strategy for relieving tension.

Learning Fear

Early in this century the Russian physiologist Ivan Pavlov showed that involuntary reactions can be controlled by harmless objects or events with which they become associated through a learning process that is called *classical* or *respondent conditioning.* An alcoholic is made to drink whiskey with a special drug, Antabuse, added to produce extreme nausea. After several experiences with this potent mixture, the subject associates the taste of alcohol with the reaction of nausea; eventually any alcoholic drink — without the drug — elicits nausea. The effect is produced by classical conditioning and follows from *the law of contiguity: a stimulus that repeatedly occurs at about the same time as a response may acquire the power to elicit that response.* A stimulus (liquor) repeatedly occurring about the same time as a response (nausea) eventually acquires the power to elicit the response (nausea).

John Watson, an early behaviorist, taught an infant boy to be afraid of a white rat by associating the harmless rat with the occurrence of an unexpected loud noise; whenever the infant saw the rat, he would also hear a sudden loud noise behind his head. The rat was always accompanied by a frightening gong. Over several repetitions of the pairing of rat with loud noise, an association was established through *the law of contiguity,* and the rat alone thereafter elicited fear: whenever the infant saw the rat, he would scream with terror.

Specific fears of objects and situations may result from conditioning.

The law of contiguity: A stimulus that repeatedly occurs at about the same time as a response may acquire the power to elicit that response.

Pavlov allowed a dog to see but not to eat some powdered meat, and then measured the salivary response of the dog; there was almost none. Pavlov then allowed the dog to both see and eat the meat powder a number of times. Eating the meat powder produced a reflexive salivary response. Thus, seeing the meat powder (stimulus) was repeatedly paired with salivation (response). Following this, when the dog simply saw the meat powder, it began to salivate. The sight of meat powder had become associated in the dog's mind with the response of salivating. In a similar manner, people learn to fear fire: the sight of fire has become associated with the response of pain.

Pavlov, I. P. *Conditioned Reflexes.* London: Oxford University Press, 1927.
Watson, J. B., and Rayner, R. Conditioned emotional reactions. *Journal of Experimental Psychology,* 1920, **3,** 1–14.
Wolpe, J., and Lazarus, A. A. *Behavior Therapy Techniques: A Guide to the Treatment of Neuroses.* New York: Pergamon, 1966.

You were not born afraid of spiders, blood, or heights: these are learned fears, acquired through a history of interaction with the environment and with other people. Like the infant who is terrified of a rat, you have learned many of your fears.

Sometimes a single dramatic and unpleasant experience can condition fear reactions. A child was struck by a car one day while walking alongside a road. She was knocked down and bruised, but not severely injured. The experience, however, was very frightening. For about a year thereafter, she was unable to cross the street without considerable anxiety; this single incident had conditioned her to fear automobiles. As described at the beginning of this chapter, Hugh O'Brian's fear of unenclosed heights was learned from one traumatic experience.

The little girl's conditioned association of fear with automobiles eventually subsided and disappeared. If fear is learned, then it can be unlearned.

Unlearning Fear

How can you unlearn fear? Since fear is learned through a conditioning process, the same process can be applied to unlearn fear. Many fears gradually subside with time, as the initially frightening experience fails to recur. In the little girl's case just described, the fear diminished as new experiences with cars occurred without pain; these new experiences constituted new conditionings, so that the fear reaction was eventually replaced with other, more pleasant, conditioned responses. This re-conditioning process can be done more systematically. The idea is to pair the feared object or situation with some pleasant emotion or reaction so that the fear reaction will be replaced by enjoyment.

The re-conditioning process has to be gradual. You don't take a child who is afraid of the water and throw him or her in the pool. You would first encourage the child to play in a very shallow puddle, then in the shallow end of the pool, and only later in the deep water. The technique for gradually re-conditioning fears is called *desensitization.* Desensitization reduces the fear reaction and replaces it with relaxation; through this process, you can actually learn to relax in the presence of spiders, snakes, blood, heights, or other feared objects and situations.

Remarkably enough, you can re-condition your fears through your own imagination. You can imagine your fears away. The process depends upon your ability to relax while imagining whatever frightens you. It has been shown that if you do this over and over, you can probably face in real life whatever has frightened you, and remain relaxed. The less fearful response transfers from your imagination to real life.

But how can you relax while imagining snakes? The secret is simple: you have to learn gradually. You first try to imagine a garden hose on the ground, while relaxing. Then you imagine a dead snake in a jar across the room. At each stage you gradually increase the fearfulness of your image while remaining relaxed. The images you begin with should be ones that are remote in distance, time, or likeness to the object or situation you fear; the images you end with should be the ones that initially aroused your intense fear.

The different images that you imagine should be arranged in a hierarchy, ranging from a completely neutral image at the top (the first stage) to an intensely feared image at the bottom (the final stage). Desensitization occurs as you successfully imagine each image in the list while remaining relaxed, starting with the top (least feared) and progressing to the bottom (most feared). As soon as you detect the least intrusion of fear while imagining a particular image, go back up your hierarchy to an image that invokes no fear at all. After much practice, you will find that you will be able to imagine items at the very bottom of the hierarchy while remaining at ease; when you are able to do this, your fear is desensitized. An example of a fear hierarchy appears below, constructed for a person with an intense fear of speaking in front of a group of people:

1. Reading about speeches alone in a room, one or two weeks before you have to give the speech.
2. Discussing the coming speech a week before, in class or after.
3. In the audience when another person gives a speech (one week before your own speech).
4. Writing the speech in the study area.
5. Practicing the speech alone in your room.
6. Getting dressed the morning of the speech.
7. Activities just before leaving for the speech.
8. Walking to class on the day of the speech.
9. Entering the room.
10. Waiting while another person gives a speech.
11. Walking up before the audience.
12. Presenting the speech (seeing the faces, and so on).

The desensitization hierarchy structures a gradual approach to the feared object, person, or event. You begin by imagining yourself in the situation at the top of the list while you are in a relaxed state; only after you are able to imagine this situation with comfort do you proceed to the next, more frightening situation on the list. Small steps are essential at this point; if you try to progress too rapidly, if you try to take steps which are too large, then you may become anxious and find it impossible to relax while imagining the items on the hierarchy.

The story at the beginning of the chapter describes how Hugh O'Brian has been unsuccessful in reducing his fear of heights by parachute jumping; he may have had better luck if he had started more gradually. The gradualness of the list can be constructed through time, distance, or intensity. The public speaking hierarchy just presented gradually moves through *time,* from two weeks before the speech until the moment of the speech itself. A hierarchy based on *distance* might be constructed for a fear of snakes; at the top of the hierarchy you might have a situation in which you are viewing a snake that is 50 feet away; at each successive step of the hierarchy, you would get closer, until the bottom item of the list might involve your picking up the snake.

Desensitize Your Fears

Step 1. Make a list of the things you are frightened of; the list at the beginning of this chapter will provide a start.

Step 2. Pick one of the fears (e.g., fear of public speaking) and make a list of about 15 different situations that elicit the fear; make sure that you include some situations that elicit the fear intensely and others that elicit the fear only slightly, so that the full range of the fear is represented. Write these on cards.

Step 3. Arrange the cards in order, ranging from the least feared situation (on top of the pile) to the most feared situation (on the bottom).

Step 4. Take the cards to a quiet room where you can sit or lie down in comfort. Take a few minutes to become as relaxed as possible. Deep and regular breathing will help you relax. For more details on how to relax, see Chapter Six.

Step 5. Imagine as vividly as possible the situation on the top of your hierarchy (on the first card). It is important that you visualize this in as much detail as possible and that you maintain complete relaxation while doing so.

Step 6. If you feel the slightest anxiety or fear, stop visualizing the scene and make your mind blank while you relax and breathe deeply. When you are completely relaxed, return to your hierarchy and visualize the item on your list.

Step 7. Go on to the next most feared item on the list (the next card) only when you are able to visualize the first item while maintaining complete relaxation. You should not go on to another card until you can imagine the scene described on the one you're on with complete ease and have visualized it several times while completely relaxed.

Step 8. Spend 15 to 30 minutes per day working on your hierarchy, relaxing and visualizing the scenes listed. It will probably take you some time to work your way through the hierarchy so that you are able to visualize the items at the bottom of the list with ease; do not hurry the process. When you have finished a hierarchy, construct another list for another one of your fears and begin working through that one.

Watching Others

A little girl seemed to enjoy petting large dogs, ever since she was very young. Her father remembered the first time they were walking in the park and a large, friendly dog approached them. She seemed to be afraid because the dog was so big, but after he went over and started petting the dog, and the dog started to lick him, she approached the dog and soon made friends with it.

This illustrates *modeling,* another method of reducing fear. In the 1960s Albert Bandura, a psychologist at Stanford University, demonstrated that learning could occur by observing other people's behavior and the consequences of their behavior. The people whose behavior is imitated are called models. As children, we often learn the appropriate way of behaving by watching adult models. We learn that an animal is friendly because we observe other people approaching the animal and having a good experience.

Using modeling to reduce fears involves gradual exposure to, and practice in approaching, the fear. Modeling could be done using a film, but is more effective if it is live. For example, let's say you were afraid of a harmless sheep dog. In the beginning modeling session you might simply observe a model interacting with the dog in his cage for a few minutes. Over the course of the next few sessions, the model might gradually increase his contact and interaction with the dog. You might then be encouraged to approach the dog while holding the model's hand. Gradually, the model's assistance is removed as you become more and more independent.

Rewarding Your Thoughts

Another method of reducing anxiety and fears involves your imagination. In real life, anything that increases the chances of a behavior occurring in the future is called a reinforcement. For example, receiving praise from your instructor for a good question will probably increase the likelihood of your asking questions in class in the future. Using reinforcement is part of the operant conditioning method of changing behavior by manipulating consequences. It is based on *the law of effect,* which states that actions followed by favorable consequences tend to recur.

Joseph Cautela was the first psychologist systematically to apply behavioral principles to imagined themes. Cautela felt that stimuli presented in imagination could affect real-life behavior.

Covert reinforcement is different from desensitization. Desensitization is based on the principles of classical conditioning, which involves involuntary biological responses that are elicited by presentation of a stimulus. Covert reinforcement is based on the principles of operant conditioning, which involves voluntary responses emitted by the organism that are followed by reinforcement.

Applying the Covert Reinforcement Method

Step 1. Visualize a scene that is very reinforcing. For example, if you like to listen to rock and roll music, you might imagine yourself listening to a

> *The principle of covert reinforcement: A reinforcement presented in imagination can increase the likelihood of a behavior occurring in the future.*
>
> Covert reinforcement means that the stimulus and the reinforcement are presented in imagination. Cautela has demonstrated that reinforcing appropriate responses to a feared situation in imagination can help overcome the fear in real life. He reports the case of a student with test anxiety who imagined himself in the feared testing situation and was reinforced throughout the scene by imagining himself skiing. The student was then able to take, and pass, an important exam.
>
> Cautela, J. R. Covert reinforcement. *Behavior Therapy,* 1970, **3,** 33–50.
> Marshall, W. L., Boutelier, J., and Minnes, P. The modification of phobic behavior by covert reinforcement. *Behavior Therapy,* 1974, **5,** 469–480.

song you really enjoy. It may be helpful to be able to imagine two or three different rewards.

Step 2. Imagine the situation that makes you anxious. Try to break the scene down into 10 or 15 small steps as was done in the desensitization procedure.

Step 3. After confronting each small step in your imagination, try to imagine your reinforcement. Keep imagining it for about 10 seconds. Repeat the entire scene a second time.

Step 4. Practice each scene at least four times a day.

Step 5. Try and actually confront the feared situation. Just before you try, you should reinforce yourself with your imagined scene.

Summary

Anxiety and fear are often a disturbing part of our lives. Anxieties may arise from unconscious conflicts, but they are usually held in check by defense mechanisms such as repression or rationalization. One way of relieving anxiety is through a catharsis or release of emotional tension. Another theory states that anxiety might arise from conditioning, and be relieved through the re-conditioning technique of desensitization. This technique combines the use of progressive relaxation with images of the feared situation. Another technique for reducing fear is called modeling. By watching and participating with the model, previously feared behaviors can be overcome. Covert reinforcement is a technique that uses rewarding images to successfully overcome fear. You should choose the technique that you feel will work best for your fear. Don't be afraid to try different techniques. If one technique is not helpful, another one may be successful.

Notes

1. Fears of the famous. *Good Housekeeping,* 1973, **176,** 106–107.

2. Coleman, J. C. *Psychology and effective behavior.* Glenview, Ill.: Scott, Foresman, 1969.

3. Wolberg, L. R. Hypnotic experiments in psychosomatic medicine. *Psychosomatic Medicine,* 1947, **9,** 337–342.

4. Sadoff, R. L. On the nature of crying and weeping. *Psychiatric Quarterly,* 1966, **40,** 490–503.

5. Beck, A. T. *Depression: Causes and treatment.* Philadelphia: University of Pennsylvania Press, 1967.

6. Feshbach, S. The drive reducing function of fantasy behavior. *Journal of Abnormal and Social Psychology,* 1955, **50,** 3–11.

Suggested Readings

Marks, I. M. *Fears and phobias.* New York: Academic Press, 1969.

Melville, J. *Phobias and obsessions.* New York: Coward, McCann and Geoghegan, 1977.

Rachmen, S. *Phobias: Their nature and control.* Springfield, Ill.: Charles C Thomas, 1968.

Rathus, S. A., and Nevid, J. S. *Behavior therapy strategies for solving problems in living.* New York: Signet, 1978, pp. 36–64.

Smith, M. J. *Kicking the fear habit.* New York: Dial Crest, 1977.

Chapter Eight

Written by Stephanie Crane/Drawn by Ben Black

Breaking Bad Habits

Peter had quit smoking twice before, but had returned to the habit the first time after a two-month period, and the second time after a one-week layoff. His first return involved taking one cigarette when offered at a social get-together—"for the hell of it." He knew that smoking the one cigarette did not lead to the physical need to smoke more. So he began to smoke a few a day. Within two weeks, he was back at his pre-quitting level of two packs a day. He quit smoking the second time one week before final examinations in college. As the stresses of the examination period increased he found himself more strongly drawn to smoking, especially as he watched other students lighting up "to relax." The third attempt to quit smoking arrived unexpectedly—he awoke one morning hacking. He reported that "two hours must have passed before I could catch my breath right." Once he caught his breath, he resolved "with every fiber of my being that I was never going to touch another damn cigarette again!"[1]

You can break some of your bad habits. Habits have been learned, and many of them can be unlearned. Most often we feel that we can't do anything about our bad habits — that they are beyond our control. Often we have tried to do something about them and have failed, have felt weak and guilty, and have resigned ourselves to our "fate."

Before continuing, check those habits you would like to change.

_____ Drinking   _____ Joint cracking

_____ Smoking cigarettes   _____ Taking pills

_____ Overeating   _____ Smoking marijuana

_____ Biting fingernails   _____ Gambling

_____ Shoplifting   _____ Always arriving late

_____ Swearing   _____ Free spending

_____ Procrastination   _____ Grinding teeth

_____ Being untidy   _____ Pulling hair

_____ Arguing   _____ Not studying

_____ Lack of exercise

De-automatize Yourself

The prerequisite for self-control is self-awareness. You will not be able to exercise voluntary control over your actions if you do not know what you are doing. Like willpower, self-awareness is not a character trait or aspect of your moral fibre; it depends specifically upon what you do. You can learn to behave in ways that maintain self-awareness.

Many of your actions are relatively automatic; you are not aware of doing them deliberately. Of course, sometimes it is adaptive to behave automatically; for example, driving a car involves many different muscular actions that must be coordinated. It would be unsafe to drive completely deliberately, so that each action is voluntary. Your driving skills need some automatization in order to be smooth and coordinated; if you have to think about each muscle action, you will not be able to think about the road and the traffic ahead.

But sometimes you are automated when you don't want to be. You may not want to bite your fingernails "automatically" or smoke without even being aware that you are doing it. You may not want to eat "unconsciously." If you feel like a passenger in your own body, you may want to put yourself back in the driver's seat. The novelist Colin Wilson describes his automatic behavior as an "inner robot." He says:

I am writing this on an electric typewriter. When I learned to type, I had to do it painfully and with much nervous wear and tear. But at a certain stage a miracle occurred, and this complicated operation was "learned" by a useful robot whom I conceal in my subconscious mind. Now I only have to think about what I want to say; my robot secretary does the typing. He is really very useful. He also drives the car for me, speaks French (not very well), and occasionally gives lectures at American universities. [My robot] is most annoying when I am tired, because then he tends to take over most of my functions without even asking me. I have even caught him making love to my wife.[2]

Can your robot be dismissed? You would not want to do so completely, even if you could. But you can regain voluntary control over many individual habits that are now relatively automatic. The technique for de-automatizing yourself is called *massed* or *negative practice*. It consists of the simple act of doing on purpose what you are now doing unconsciously and automatically. Negative practice helps you to achieve awareness of your habitual actions, and awareness increases your capacity for voluntary control. Freedom — in the sense of self-control — increases when it is exercised. Actions become more voluntary when they are practiced voluntarily. This effect is demonstrated in the case below of a young woman with the bad habit of grinding her teeth, a habit called *bruxism.*

The patient, a 26-year-old female, was treated for a severe and chronic case of bruxism by the technique of massed practice. She was instructed to grind her teeth nonstop for one minute, then to rest for one minute, and to repeat this procedure five times per trial. She was required to undergo six trials daily for approximately two and one-half weeks.

At the end of this period her husband reported that involuntary gnashing of her teeth, which had occurred mainly while she was asleep, was no longer present.

At a follow-up after almost a year, the woman's improvement had been maintained.[3]

You can de-automatize yourself through negative practice. Negative or massed practice helps you to achieve awareness of your actions. Sometimes, as in the case just cited of the woman who gnashed her teeth, awareness alone is sufficient to bring about self-control. Even when it is not sufficient, awareness is a necessary first step toward control.

Break the Links

Awareness may not be enough: Peter is perfectly aware that he is smoking at the moment he does it, but he still is unable to stop. In this case, his environment may be controlling him. Behavior is influenced by the environmental context in which it occurs — what comes before it and what comes after it.

Some things you do only under certain conditions or in certain places; the antecedent circumstances — all that happens before the action — affect your behavior. You may be more likely to smoke after eating, or more likely to bite your nails when you are bored. Your behavior is to a certain extent controlled by these antecedent stimuli. In order to break your habit, you may have to break its link to antecedent stimuli.

Your habits are also influenced by what follows them. The consequent stimuli—all that happens after the action—affect your behavior. Both animals and humans are relatively rational: they tend to act to minimize pain and maximize pleasure—that is, to bring about favorable consequences. The consequence of an act can be thought of as "the payoff." In order to break your habit, you may have to change its payoff.

The Payoff

Operant conditioning is a type of simple learning based upon results, or consequences. People learn what acts have good results. The principle underlying operant conditioning is *the law of effect: acts with favorable consequences tend to be repeated; acts with unfavorable consequences tend to be abandoned.*

The law of effect: Acts with favorable consequences tend to be repeated; acts with unfavorable consequences tend to be abandoned.

Thorndike placed cats in small, closed boxes. When the cat pressed a lever in the box, the box would open and the cat could escape (a favorable consequence). Thorndike found that a cat would repeat the exact behavior that preceded the opening of the box. For example, a cat that pressed the lever by lying on its side and rolling into the lever would repeat this exact behavior when placed in the box again. It would not press the lever in some other way. The most important type of favorable consequence is a reward, such as food if you are hungry, attention and affection if you are lonely, or money to buy what you want. A second type of favorable consequence is the end of something unpleasant.

Krasner, L. The operant approach in behavior therapy. In A. E. Bergin and S. L. Garfield (eds.), *Handbook of Psychotherapy and Behavior Change: An Empirical Analysis.* New York: Wiley, 1971.

Skinner, B. F. Superstition in the pigeon. *Journal of Experimental Psychology,* 1948, **38,** 168–172.

Thorndike, E. L. *Animal Intelligence.* New York: Macmillan, 1911.

A "favorable consequence" is technically called "reinforcement"; giving your hungry dog a food reward after it fetches the paper has the effect of reinforcing, or strengthening, the fetching trick. An "unfavorable consequence" is technically called "punishment"; swatting your dog after it jumps on your chair has the effect of suppressing or weakening that habit.

What constitutes an unfavorable consequence? Pain, frustration, embarrassment, deprivation, and fear are a few of the unpleasant consequences we seek to avoid. What constitutes a favorable consequence? Food when you're hungry and water when you're thirsty are two primary reinforcers; but anything that satisfies a need or brings you happiness or pleasure can serve to reinforce an act. A movie when you're bored, a pair of new shoes, the smile of a special friend, a warm bath, your favorite record — all of us have our own personal rewards. Acts with favorable consequences, ones favorable to you, are acts you tend to repeat.

According to *the law of effect,* many of your bad habits are maintained because they work, they pay off for you, they have favorable consequences. For example, in Peter's case, one of the favorable consequences of smoking was relaxation. If you can control the consequences of behavior, you can control the behavior itself. It follows that if you remove the favorable consequences of an act, the act should occur less often. The idea that you can break a bad habit by removing the favorable consequences that maintain it follows from *the extinction principle: an act that repeatedly occurs without reinforcement will cease.*

When a child throws a tantrum, there are consequences. Some of these consequences may be favorable to the child. If these consequences are removed, the tantrum behavior may diminish.

A psychologist was called in to help parents control the tantrums of their two-year-old son. The child would scream and rage every time the parent would attempt to leave the room after putting him down to sleep in the evening; as a result, the mother or father was forced to stay with the child for up to two hours each night until the child fell to sleep. According to the psychologist's analysis of the situation, the attention given by the parents to the child was a favorable consequence for the child; every time he threw a tantrum, he got attention from his parents. In accordance with *the extinction principle,* the psychologist instructed the parents to remove the reinforcer—that is, to discontinue giving the child attention every time he threw a tantrum. The result was that the child gradually stopped throwing tantrums and went quietly to sleep when put to bed.[4]

What are the favorable consequences of *your* bad habits? What is pleasant that your habit helps you achieve? What is unpleasant that your habit helps you avoid? The answers may not be obvious. One college

The extinction principle: An act that repeatedly occurs without rein-forcement will cease.

Skinner placed rats in a box where they were reinforced with food for pressing a lever. After a number of trials, reinforcement was discontinued; no food followed the pressing of the lever. Following this, the rats pressed the lever less and less until they almost stopped completely. The act ceased because it was no longer reinforced.

Sherman reports the case of a seven and one-half year old boy, Glen, who disrupted his class at school by frequently calling out answers without raising his hand. The consequent attention from the teacher, even though it was criticism, was apparently reinforcement that maintained Glen's shouting. The problem was solved when the teacher began to ignore Glen when he shouted out and to give him attention when he raised his hand with the right answer. The shouting response stopped because it was no longer reinforced.

Sherman, A. R. *Behavior Modification: Theory and Practice.* Monterey, Calif.: Brooks/Cole, 1973.

Skinner, B. F. *The Behavior of Organisms.* New York: Appleton-Century-Crofts, 1938.

student's poor study habits resulted in the following favorable consequences: (1) the increased attention of her parents, who had become involved in their own problems to the extent of ignoring her; (2) the avoidance of hard work; (3) the avoidance, for long periods, of anxious thoughts about schoolwork (by not thinking about school at all); and (4) the friendship of a young man who also had poor study habits.

Punishment

Self-punishment is an attempt at self-control that is used more often than self-reinforcement. We talk about "kicking ourselves" for some actual or imagined transgression or mistake. We curse ourselves for our "weakness." We heap guilt and abuse upon ourselves when we fail to keep our resolutions. We are proficient at punishing ourselves.

One bizarre variety of self-punishment is the "pocket shocker" — an electrical device small enough to carry in your pocket, that can be used to shock yourself as punishment for failing in your self-control program. A similar device is an electrified cigarette case; the only way you can get a cigarette is to endure a painful electric shock.

Self-punishment involves certain problems. According to *the law of effect,* acts followed by punishment should decrease or be weakened; but the act of delivering punishment to yourself is itself a punished act— and it should become more and more difficult to apply. The act of shocking yourself with a "pocket shocker" is followed by punishment (a painful shock). In fact, self-punishment is often abandoned quickly by those who attempt it — perhaps because of *the law of effect.* When acts of self-control are followed by punishment, they tend not to be repeated.

A second problem with punishment is that it leads to anxiety and bad feelings associated with the whole situation in which the punished act occurs; when you repeatedly feel pain, fear, or guilt in a particular situation, eventually the situation itself develops the power to elicit bad feelings. If you repeatedly punish yourself for failing to study sufficiently, you will eventually develop bad feelings about studying — feelings you may choose to avoid by avoiding school.

Antecedents

Self-control requires that you act on and control your environment because circumstances in your environment influence your behavior. Controlling circumstances following actions — consequences — is only half of the job; the remaining half involves controlling circumstances preceding actions — antecedents. These antecedent circumstances influence your habit; for example, your smoking behavior may be partially controlled by a prior cup of coffee or the sight of someone else smoking.

You can disrupt the control that antecedent situations have over your behavior; their power to control your bad habits can be weakened. There are three strategies for weakening this control: (1) Antecedent control can be weakened by avoiding the antecedents for a period of time. Don't go on coffee breaks for a while if you are sorely tempted to smoke during them. Avoiding the antecedent is the first control strategy. (2) If you cannot avoid the antecedent situation, you can nevertheless weaken its controlling influence by using the second strategy — pausing. On his coffee break, Peter feels he must have a cigarette, so he smokes one, but first he pauses and waits for a couple of minutes before he lights up. If this is done consistently, it will weaken the power of the situation to control the behavior. (3) The third strategy for weakening antecedent control is to learn to do something else in the tempting situation, something that is incompatible with the bad habit. Keeping your hands in your pockets is incompatible with biting your fingernails. Chewing gum is incompatible with smoking. Praising is incompatible with fighting, etc. In order for the incompatible behavior to replace your bad habits, however, it must have favorable consequences; you must reinforce yourself for the incompatible activity. One way to reinforce yourself is to give yourself a special treat for every day that you succeed in replacing the bad habit with the new and incompatible response.

A man who had unsuccessfully tried to quit smoking several times did an analysis of the situations in which he had returned to smoking after having "quit" for a few days. He found that he was likely to go back to smoking at work if he took a coffee break or ate lunch with his friends, several of whom smoked. Their cigarettes looked so inviting that he would bum one and then be "hooked" again. In stage one of his plan, he avoided these antecedents for two weeks, carefully explaining to his friends what he was doing, and reinforcing himself for successful avoidance. He was not tempted so much on the weekends because he spent them with his wife, who did not smoke. . . . Now his task was to remain vigilant for tempting antecedents and to reinforce himself for not smoking when the antecedent occurred. He was able to tell when such an antecedent was occurring, because he would suddenly remember how much he wanted a cigarette. The morning cup of coffee, a meal, a relaxed period, another smoker, a party—these were often the kinds of tempting antecedents that he had to learn to deal with.[5]

If the smoker could disrupt situational control over the habit, he would feel less temptation to smoke. He tried to avoid "tempting antecedents" — those situations in which he would feel an irresistible urge to smoke — and he also rewarded himself when he was able to resist his urge to smoke.

Six Steps toward Self-Control

Step 1. Select a problem behavior and state it in terms of what you do or don't do. You must actually list the specific actions involved. Examples: "I bite my fingernails," or "I don't study enough."

Step 2. Observe your behavior for about a week and keep a record of it, writing down the number of times a day that it occurs or the length of time spent on it. If you don't always know when you do it, gain awareness through a program of negative practice. Also observe the antecedents and consequences of the behavior, noting the situations in which it occurs or fails to occur, and the favorable or unfavorable consequences.

Step 3. Disrupt antecedent control, by avoiding the antecedent situations, pausing when tempted, and deliberately doing something that is incompatible with the bad habit.

Step 4. Identify your reinforcers — those things that you like best, seek out, or do most often. Don't forget the simple things — hot showers, ice cream, reading the paper, watching TV, drinking coffee. Include only those reinforcers that you have direct control over; you can't give yourself a million dollars or the smile of a special friend.

Step 5. Use your reinforcers to change your behavior. Program your consequences by reinforcing yourself for making small changes in the desired direction. Save your reinforcers to use in your self-control program; you get a hot shower in the morning, for example, *only* if you do not smoke for half an hour after supper. You get to watch your favorite TV show this evening *only* if you reduce your smoking today by twenty percent. You get to make that rewarding telephone call *only* after you have successfully studied one chapter in your text. In devising your program, it is important to make sure that your overall frequency of reinforcement does not drop drastically; if anything, it should increase. This should not be hard to do, since normally most people are relatively stingy with their self-reinforcement.

Step 6. Continue to observe and record your behavior so that you will know how you are doing. Monitoring your behavior, in itself, is an aid to self-control. If your records show that you are not successful, you should regard it — not as a failure of willpower — but as a failure of your particular reinforcement program; accordingly, your response to failure should be a revised program or alternative plan, not guilt and not self-punishment. A common failure in self-control programs is to require too much improvement before reinforcement is given.

Weight Control

It has been estimated that there are between 40 to 80 million overweight people in the United States. Overeating is a learned habit, which can be changed through changing the behaviors associated with overeating. Changing eating habits involves more than a knowledge of what you eat. It involves how you eat (rate of eating, how you chew your food); when you eat (e.g., while watching TV or between breakfast and lunch); and where you eat (e.g., in bed or in certain restaurants). These are the antecedents to overeating. These are the variables that must be controlled, weakened, or eliminated to successfully control overeating.

There also must be a payoff for changing eating patterns. For many people the payoff is a healthy feeling and the energy they have from being thinner. For others, it relates to their physical appearance and self-image. Some people must lose weight or risk the chance of serious illness.

Managing Eating Behavior

Managing eating habits is a gradual way to lose weight, but generally leads to more permanent weight control than "fad" diets. Research on overeating has shown that overweight people respond to external cues such as the time of day or how food looks and smells rather than internal cues of hunger.[6] To manage eating habits, then, you must first become aware of the food cues in your environment.

Overweight is not simply the result of overeating. Most overweight people do not get enough exercise. Increased mechanization in our society is one reason for inadequate exercise.[7] Research has shown that programs which combine changing eating habits with exercise are the most successful weight reduction programs.[8] You can start today to increase your energy expenditure by doing simple exercises, such as parking your car a few extra blocks away from your destination and walking or taking the stairs instead of the elevator. More strenuous exercise, such as swimming, racquetball, skiing, or jogging, would undoubtedly be helpful to a complete weight management program.

One pound is approximately 3500 calories. If you want to lose one pound per week, you would have to reduce your normal intake by 500 calories a day. This would be accomplished simply by increasing your energy expediture by 500 calories, decreasing your food intake by 500 calories, or ideally, a combination of both.

Exercise — Learning about Your Daily Energy Expenditure

Most people know how to count calories. There are many guides available that list the calories of almost every food. However, many people are not aware of how many calories they burn off during the day. To learn about your own daily energy expenditure, add up the number of calories consumed per day for a three- or four-day period using the following list.[7]

	Calories per minute
1. Personal necessities	
Sitting, eating	1.5
Sleeping	1.2
Washing and dressing	2.6
2. Locomotion	
Cycling, 5.5 mph	4.5
Cycling, 9.4 mph	7.0
Cycling, 13.1 mph	11.1
Driving a car	2.8
Walking, 2 mph	3.2
Walking, 3 mph	4.4
Walking, 4 mph	5.8
Walking downstairs	7.1
Walking upstairs	18.6
3. Sedentary occupations	
Classwork, lecture	1.7
Sitting, reading	1.3
Standing, light activity	2.6
Typing, 40 words/min., mechanical typewriter	1.7
Typing, 40 words/min., electric typewriter	1.5
4. Domestic work	
Bed making	3.5
Dusting	2.5
Ironing	1.7
Preparing a meal	2.5
Scrubbing floors	4.0
Shopping with heavy load	4.0
Window cleaning	3.5
5. Light industry	
Assembly work in car factory	2.3
Carpentry	3.8
Farming chores	3.8
Farming, haying, plowing with horse	6.7
House painting	3.5
Metal working	3.5
Mixing cement	4.7

	Calories per minute
Stone masonry	6.3
Truck and automobile repair	4.2
6. Heavy work	
Dragging logs	12.1
Drilling coal or rock	6.1
Felling trees	8.6
Gardening, digging	8.6
Pick and shovel work	8.6
7. Recreation	
Canoeing, 2.5 mph	3.0
Canoeing, 4 mph	7.0
Cross country running	10.6
Dancing, waltz	5.2
Dancing, rumba	5.7
Golfing	5.0
Gymnastics exercises:	
Balancing exercises	2.5
Trunk bending	3.5
Mountain climbing	10.0
Playing baseball (except pitcher)	4.7
Playing basketball	8.6
Playing football (American)	10.2
Playing pingpong	4.9
Playing tennis	7.1
Playing squash	10.2
Playing volleyball	3.5
Skiing, level hard snow, moderate speed	10.8
Skiing, up hill hard snow, maximum speed	18.6
Sprinting	23.3
Snowshoeing 2.27 mph	6.2

Is your energy expenditure similar each day? What are the antecedents for increased calorie expenditure for you?

A Step-by-Step Approach to Manage Overeating

In addition to the general procedures to use for self-control (see pages 110–111), specific procedures have been developed to deal with the problem of overeating.

To Weaken or Eliminate the Antecedents of Overeating

Step 1. Eat in one room, preferably in one place in that room, and don't engage in other activities (e.g., reading or watching television) while eating.

Step 2. Plan meals for a specified time and eat every planned meal. Don't prepare more than you need. Clear plates directly into the garbage. Leave the table after finishing your meal.

Step 3. When eating, use smaller plates, take small bites, and chew and swallow your food before taking more.

Step 4. Take breaks during meals; put your utensils down for a few minutes during the meal.

Step 5. Let other people bring their own sweets. Try not to serve high-calorie foods at meals.

Step 6. Avoid the purchase of problem foods. Shop from a list and only after a full meal.

Step 7. Make a list of activities that you enjoy that are incompatible with eating. Try to engage in one of these activities instead of snacking.

To Manage the Consequences of Eating

Step 1. Write out a contract indicating how many pounds you have to lose and the amount of time you have to lose it. You should not try to lose more than one pound weekly.

Step 2. Provide yourself with feedback on controlling the antecedents by recording the number, or frequency of their occurrence, each day.

Step 3. Provide yourself with feedback on the amount of food eaten by keeping track of the number of calories consumed per day.

Step 4. Provide yourself with feedback on energy expenditure by recording the number of calories expended through exercise per day.

Step 5. Arrange to have other people (husband, wife, boyfriend, girl friend, mother or father) provide a reward for a gradual weekly reduction of calories and/or increase in exercise. Food should not be used as a reward.

Step 6. Reward yourself for calorie reduction and/or exercise by buying yourself small gifts each week you are successful.

Step 7. Arrange for negative consequences to follow a failure to reduce calories or increase energy expenditure every week. The following are examples of possible negative consequences:

1. Arrange to do a disliked chore that seems never to get done (e.g., clean the toilet, wash windows).
2. Do not allow yourself some well-established rewards (e.g., no television for the next week).

Step 8. Pay attention to social rewards (e.g., compliments) from other people for continued success in the program.

Step 9. If greater social support is needed, join one of your local weight groups (e.g., Overeaters Anonymous or Weight Watchers).

When you have reached your goal, many of these steps should remain as part of your everyday eating habits. If you find yourself gaining a few pounds, reinstate the program until you return to your goal weight.

Summary

Bad habits have generally been learned and therefore can be changed or unlearned. Self-control is the key to breaking bad habits. Negative or massed practice is one way to become aware of these habits and possibly to gain control over them. However, it also may be necessary to change the antecedents and consequences of the behavior in order to establish control. Changing antecedents can be accomplished through avoidance, pausing, or participating in incompatible behaviors. Consequences can be manipulated by applying *the law of effect* and *the extinction principle.* Consequences also can be changed through punishment.

Overeating is one of the most common bad habits. Psychologists have developed specific techniques for managing overeating antecedents and consequences. Combining these strategies with an effective exercise program will enable an individual to gain control over this habit.

Notes

1. Rathus, S. A., and Nevid, J. S. *Behavior therapy strategies for solving problems in living.* New York: Signet, 1977.

2. Wilson, C. Existential psychology: A novelist's approach. In J. F. T. Bugental (ed.), *Challenges of humanistic psychology.* New York: McGraw-Hill, 1967.

3. Wolpe, J., and Lazarus, A. A. *Behavior therapy techniques: A guide to the treatment of neuroses.* New York: Pergamon, 1966.

4. Williams, C. D. The elimination of tantrum behavior by extinction procedures. *Journal of Abnormal and Social Psychology,* 1959, **59,** 269.

5. Watson, D., and Tharp, R. *Self-directed behavior: Self-modification for personal adjustment.* Monterey, Calif.: Brooks/Cole, 1972.

6. Schachter, A., and Gross, L. P. Manipulated time and eating behavior. *Journal of Personality and Social Psychology,* 1968, **10,** 98–106.

7. Stuart, R. B., and Davis, B. *Slim chance in a fat world: Behavioral control of obesity.* Champaign, Ill.: Research Press, 1972.

8. Harris, M. B., and Hallbauer, E. S. Self-directed weight control through eating and exercise. *Behavior Research and Therapy,* 1973, **11,** 523–529.

Suggested Readings

Kanfer, F. H., and Goldstein, A. P. *Helping people change: A textbook of methods.* New York: Pergamon, 1975.

Mahoney, M. J., and Thoresen, C. E. *Self-control: Power to the person.* Monterey, Calif.: Brooks/Cole, 1974.

Stuart, R. B., and Davis, B. *Slim chance in a fat world: Behavioral control of obesity* (rev. ed.). Champaign, Ill.: Research Press, 1978.

Thoresen, C. E., and Mahoney, M. J. *Behavioral self-control.* New York: Holt, Rinehart and Winston, 1974.

Watson, D., and Tharp, R. *Self-directed behavior: Self-modification for personal adjustment.* Monterey, Calif.: Brooks/Cole, 1972.

Chapter Nine

Written by Stephanie Crane/Drawn by Ben Black

Relating to Children

"In my experience," Roger would say when delivering an opinion.

He was six. He had opinions about chemistry, astronomy, governmental affairs, human behavior and life in the Ice Age. Some of his views were right and some were wrong. He liked to preface them all with a thoughtful and considered, "In my experience."

"Does a mouse know it's a mouse?" Roger asked me when he was five. "What do you mean?" I asked. "Well, like I know I'm me. Does a mouse know he's a mouse." I was cagey. "Tell me what you think," I said. "Well, I think a mouse doesn't know it's a mouse, but I don't know why I know that." Roger thought some more. "Well, a dog is smarter than a mouse. Does a dog know it's a dog?" He looked doubtful.[1]

In your first four years of life, you gain about half of your adult level of general intelligence; by the age of six, you have almost two-thirds of your adult intelligence.[2] Learning begins with the first breath of life and advances most rapidly during the early years. In later childhood, intelligence expands more slowly, and in late adolescence it reaches a maximum, showing little further advance with age. Because of the tremendous intellectual growth in early childhood, your help at that time can be particularly significant.

To relate effectively to children you must understand their perceptions and their reality. Two popular but uninformed views of children are the "vegetable" theory and the "miniature adult" theory. According to the former, infants are little more than vegetables during the first few months of life, doing nothing but sleeping, eating, and eliminating; unlike adults, they lack consciousness, experience, and memories — they are mindless blobs. According to the miniature adult theory, children are exactly like adults, except smaller. Almost fifty years ago John Watson, the founder of behaviorism, wrote:

119

There is a sensible way of treating children. Treat them as though they were young adults. Dress them, bathe them with care and circumspection. Let your behavior always be objective and kindly firm. Never hug and kiss them, never let them sit in your lap. If you must, kiss them once on the forehead when they say good night. Shake hands with them in the morning. Give them a pat on the head if they have made an extraordinarily good job of a difficult task. Try it out. In a week's time you will find how easy it is to be perfectly objective with your child and at the same time kindly. You will be utterly ashamed of the mawkish, sentimental way you have been handling it.[3]

Few — if any — psychologists would offer that advice today. We now know that children are neither vegetables nor tiny adults: they have a distinctly different way of thinking; they are intelligent, but use their intelligence in ways often lost to adults. Understanding their intelligence and their distinctiveness has revolutionized our attitudes toward children. As Harvard psychologist Jerome Kagan observed, "In the past decade we have learned more about the first five years of life than had been learned in 300 years before."[4]

Alien Minds?

The world you see and the way you think are not altogether shared by children. For example, newborn babies cannot focus on objects located at different distances away from them; their eyes are like "fixed-focus" cameras, set at about eight inches. This means that things closer and farther than that distance are blurred. Their focusing gradually improves with age, so that by four most children can focus their eyes automatically for things nearer and farther than eight inches. The acuity of children's eyes—their ability to see fine lines and points as distinct—does not approximate the adult level until ages eight to ten. Compared to adults, children are more susceptible to certain perceptual illusions and less susceptible to others.[5]

Children not only see things differently, they think less abstractly: they are more dependent on tangible, concrete, particular things and are less able to understand or use classification, principles, and logical categories. Jean Piaget, a Swiss psychologist and pholosopher, has for many years studied the abstract-concrete difference between thinking in adults and children. According to Piaget, there are four qualitatively different periods of intellectual development in children, and all children pass through these periods in precisely the same order. Just as people experience physical growth in a fixed order (baby first, child second, adult last), Piaget argues, people experience the stages of intellectual growth in a fixed order. A fixed order does not imply a fixed rate, however; for both physical and intellectual growth, different people progress at different rates. There is considerable individual variation in the ages at which intellectual stages are reached. However, the vast amount of research stimulated by Piaget's theory has, in general, confirmed *the principle of invariant succession of stages: children pass through a fixed sequence of stages of cognitive development.*

The principle of invariant succession of stages: Children pass through a fixed sequence of stages of cognitive development.

The mental development of a child occurs in a series of qualitatively different steps, steps that all children move through in the same order. Piaget performed many "naturalistic experiments," observing children doing simple things in natural settings. He presented them with certain problems to be solved. Piaget observed that children had to be able to solve certain kinds of problems before they could solve others; the ways in which children attempted to solve problems also followed a certain sequence. Although the sequence of cognitive stages follows a fixed order, different children move through these stages at different rates.

Inhelder, B., and Piaget, J. *The Early Growth of Logic in the Child.* New York: Harper & Row, 1964.
Piaget, J. *The Origins of Intelligence in Children.* New York: International University Press, 1952.

Stage One: Sensorimotor Stage (0–2 years, on the average): During the early part of this period, as far as the infant is concerned, objects are "out of sight, out of mind." The infant behaves as though the only things that exist are those that are present and perceptible. If an infant of 6 months witnesses a ball rolling behind a chair, the ball, for the infant, ceases to exist. Gradually, during the sensorimotor period, a sense of object permanency develops so that things that are out of sight temporarily can still remain in mind. Piaget describes this period as a world of motor movement and sensation, in which the child comprehends its world through touching, tasting, sniffing, and manipulating. This period ends as the child develops the use of language and imagery.

Stage Two: Preoperational Stage (2–7 years, on the average): With the acquisition of language, the child begins to be able to think and solve problems, but only about fairly tangible items. A central feature of the preoperational stage is the child's egocentric point of view. The child cannot see other points of view, cannot shift perspective, cannot put self in the place of others. The child thinks that everyone else sees exactly the same view, even though others may be observing the world from other positions. This is not a matter of selfishness, but rather a limitation on perspective. This egocentrism extends to the child's conception of the natural world; the world and its principles and laws do not appear to be distinct from the child's wishes and desires. An example of preoperational egocentric thinking comes from Edward Bear—otherwise known as Winnie-the-Pooh:

That buzzing-noise means something. You don't get a buzzing-noise like that, just buzzing and buzzing, without its meaning something. If there is a buzzing-noise, somebody's making a buzzing-noise, and the only reason for making a buzzing-noise that *I* know of is because you're a bee . . . and the only reason for being a bee that I know of is for making honey . . . and the only reason for making honey is so as *I* can eat it.[6]

A second feature of the preoperational stage is the apparent irreversibility of thought patterns. The child can follow a line of reasoning, but cannot go back and reconstruct it to examine it for errors. The child can think, but cannot think about its own thinking process. Relations, too, are irreversible; thus, the child does not easily grasp the transitivity of the additive relation, "One plus two equals three"—the child must learn separately, "Two plus one equals three." This irreversibility of thought is shown in the following conversation with a four-year-old child:

"Do you have a brother?"

"Yes."

"What's his name?"

"Jim."

"Does Jim have a brother?"

"No."[7]

Stage Three: Concrete Operations Stage (7–11 years, on the average): The average child can now use logic when thinking about concrete things, and reason from the properties of classes (for example, come to a conclusion about a particular cow from what is known about cows in general). Generalizations and principles can be used, but must be closely linked to specific concrete examples. At the beginning of this stage, the child masters the crucial concept of *conservation*. Children have learned conservation when they recognize the invariance of objects under changes in position and shape; i.e., that certain properties of objects remain constant despite differences in appearance. Before the conservation concept is mastered, when a ball of clay is kneaded into the shape of a snake, the child will report that there is now more clay; when liquid is poured from a tall narrow container into a broad shallow container, the child will report that there is now less liquid; and when a bunch of marbles is spread out on the floor, the child will report that there are now more marbles. These three examples illustrate the non-conservation of substance, volume, and number, respectively.

Stage Four: Formal Operations Stage (11 and up): During this period the child becomes less dependent on concrete objects and specific examples, and more capable of thinking abstractly and hypothetically. For the first time, abstract formal systems can be understood — algebra and geometry can be systematically learned and comprehended. The enumeration and examination of hypothetical possibilities becomes possible, and the adult powers of complex logical reasoning develop. Children now are able to imagine what would happen if something were the case — even when it is not the case; this hypothetical and deductive reasoning approximates the level of complexity of adult reasoning power. During this stage, the adolescent becomes capable of performing scientific experiments; the various possible hypothetical outcomes can be imagined and then examined and tested. Freed from a dependence on concrete particulars, the child can now consider such abstract ideas as probability, calculus, and even proportions of proportions. It is during this stage, near the age of 15, when the adolescent achieves the adult level of cognitive maturity.

Exercise — Testing Piaget's Concepts

Piaget and other researchers have developed a number of tasks to test the principles of conservation. There are different aspects of conservation that take longer to develop than other aspects. A child should master conservation of length before he or she masters conservation of weight or volume.

Since conservation usually begins to develop at around age 7, it would

Figure 9.1 *Test for Conservation of Length*

be interesting if you could try these simple experiments on children from ages 5 through 12.

1. To test conservation of length, place 2 pencils of equal length parallel (separated by about 3 inches) to each other on a table (Figure 9.1, Step 1). Ask the child: "Are the pencils the same length?" After the child responds "Yes," move the top pencil about 2 inches to the left and repeat the question (Figure 9.1, Step 2).
2. To test conservation of volume, fill 2 tall, thin glasses with equal amounts of water (Figure 9.2, Step 1). Place them next to each other and ask the child: "Do the glasses contain the same amount of water?" After the child answers "Yes," pour one of the glasses of

Figure 9.2 *Test for Conservation of Volume*

water into a shorter, wider glass and then repeat the question (Figure 9.2, Step 2).

Why do you think conservation of length is easier to master? Would it be possible to teach children about conservation at an earlier age?

Responsive Environments

Intellectual development in children does not appear to be an automatic unfolding: it occurs through an intensive interaction with the environment. The physical environment of toys and books and snails and the social environment of people both contribute significantly to mental growth. Studies of the differential effects of different early environments have led scientists to speculate that intellectual development might be universally facilitated through developing more ideal environments for children. In his book *Intelligence and Experience,* Dr. Joseph McVicker Hunt predicts:

With a sound scientific educational psychology of early experience, it might become feasible to raise the average level of intelligence by a substantial degree . . . this "substantial degree' might be of the order of 30 points of IQ.[8]

A 30-point increase in IQ would constitute a huge leap in average intelligence — from retarded to normal, from normal to borderline genius.

Intelligence can be dimmed through inadequate environmental stimulation. Studies of children with inadequate early opportunities for learning show they suffer an intellectual deficit that often is never completely overcome. One author put it this way:

Millions of children are being irreparably damaged by our failure to stimulate them intellectually during their crucial years—from birth to six. Millions of others are being held back from their true potential.[9]

The human mind, however, is very resilient. Jerome Kagan, a prominent developmental psychologist, has recently shown that the profound intellectual retardation resulting from an impoverished early environment can be partially overcome.[10]

The child's early environment can be enriched by increasing stimulation and responsiveness. Opportunities for varied experiences — sensory experiences through nature and toys, language experiences through conversation and books, social experiences through interactions with adults and with peers — can be provided. The freedom to explore the environment can be encouraged; in this way, children learn to enjoy discovery.

Perceptual development is stimulated by environments which are rich in the range of experiences available; which make use of games, toys, and many objects for manipulation; and in which there is frequent interaction between the child and adults at meals, playtimes, and throughout the day.[11]

Scientists have recently been studying ways of giving infants an intellectual head start. Many questions are incompletely answered — we know that enriched, stimulating environments are superior, but what is the best kind of stimulation, at what age should it be provided, and how can lasting gains be made? These details have not yet been clarified.

For many years, Professor O. K. Moore has been perfecting an unusual responsive environment — a talking typewriter. The typewriter is linked to a small computer which is programmed to respond to typed input. The idea is to provide children with the opportunity to learn how to read and write by themselves. Children as young as three or four have learned to read fluently and to write their own stories. At first, whenever a key is struck, the typewriter repeats the letter out loud as well as typing it on a piece of paper. The child's fingernails are painted with different colors, coded to matching colors on the typewriter keys, in order to teach proper hand placement. Later, the typewriter system will display a word, such as c-o-w; the system spells the word, then pronounces the word, then selectively locks all typewriter keys except the one needed to type the first letter (then, when it is typed, the second, and so on). Thus, the child is guided through reading and writing by a gradual process of interacting with a responsive typewriter. Of course, unlike human teachers, the typewriter has infinite patience. It never gets angry or frustrated and it never has personality conflicts. As Maya Pines described her observation of the talking typewriter at work:

One spring morning, at Hamden Hall, I watched some of the youngest children, the nursery group, as they walked, skipped, or ran into the lab. First they went to a long table where a teacher painted their fingernails, dipping little brushes into open jars of bright-colored paints. Then they scattered to the six booths, to which they had been assigned at random.

An attractive little girl of four, who had been in the program nearly a year, sat next to a monitor and wrote her own sentences. She spelled the words out loud as she wrote: "After my nap I am going to the circus with my daddy . . ." "Do you want to read it?" asked the monitor when the story was finished. The little girl shook her head. "I want to read a book!" she said.[9]

Moore reports that using the talking typewriter system allows children to learn language skills on their own, because the skills are made intrinsically interesting — no external rewards are used. The system works. A number of six-year-olds who have gone through the program for a couple of years are able to read material at the level of the sixth or seventh grade.

One conclusion which follows from studies of child development is that children naturally, without being forced, strive for mastery over their environment and struggle to develop skills to manipulate their worlds. Children have more capacity for and more interest in learning than most people have realized. It does not follow, however, that they should be pushed into learning. Pushy parents can disrupt and interfere with the learning process. This does not mean that parents should stand back and do nothing; on the contrary, parents can and should arrange an optimum learning environment for their children. According to Piaget, Hunt, and other experts on intellectual development, the parental task is to provide experiences and circumstances that are slightly novel or incongruous, but not so strange that the child will withdraw from them or ignore them. The development of mastery and competence comes from the gradual expansion beyond the familiar. The child is internally motivated to solve problems at the leading edge of his or her familiarity; forcing the child may destroy this internal motivation. As Hunt says:

If a child is struggling to reach an object, and he is really working at it, the outstanding mother doesn't necessarily just kick the thing over to him. She kicks it closer, so that he has a pretty good chance of getting it, but she doesn't put it in his hands. We should follow the child's lead, but you don't have to force him. When parents begin to feel that someone else's child is getting ahead of theirs and they try to force him, then they have trouble.[4]

Sexism

We may block mastery and competence by rigidly expecting our boy-children and girl-children to grow up to be "masculine" and "feminine," to fit the molds that these terms imply. Boys traditionally are discouraged from learning about clothes, nursing, art, cooking, poetry, and other "feminine" domains; girls are discouraged from learning about mechanics, farming, math, carpentry, engineering, and other "masculine" domains.

Sexism is a form of prejudice, a prejudgment of people on the basis of their sex. Sexist statements such as "Men are insensitive" or "Women are illogical" are false because they are overgeneralizations; many men are very sensitive and many women quite logical. Individual people are always different from our stereotypes. When we pressure our children to conform to sexist stereotypes, we limit their possibilities for actualizing their own unique potentialities.

Girls are particularly limited by our sexist attitudes. Girls learn at an early age that it is OK to be sensitive, but not sensible; it is OK to be conniving, but never clever. Girls are stereotyped as "dumb blondes." Female children are taught to be passive and dependent; young women who are intellectually aggressive are punished; and the doors to graduate schools, professions, and executive suites are closed to competent female candidates.[12,13] Through this oppression there is a tremendous loss of human potential.

H. L. Mencken disagreed with the "dumb blonde" theory of female intelligence. He wrote:

Women decide the larger questions of life correctly and quickly, not because of intuition, but simply and solely because they have sense. They see at a glance what most men could not see with search-lights and telescopes; they are at grips with the essentials of a problem before men have finished debating its mere externals. . . . It is a rare, rare man who is as steadily intelligent, as constantly sound in judgment, as little put off by appearance, as the average woman.[14]

Are girls smarter than boys? It's not easy to find a way of measuring smartness to make such a comparison. We know that girls on the average begin speaking, reading, and counting sooner than boys. They begin speaking in sentences sooner than boys. There are fewer girls who must take remedial reading programs than boys. During the preschool years, girls score somewhat higher than boys on tests of general intelligence — the so-called IQ tests.[15]

But something happens on the way to high school. During high school, girls' grades begin to drop. They begin to score slightly lower than boys on IQ tests. Boys are markedly superior in arithmetical tests during high school. On the Scholastic Aptitude Test Scores (SATS), girls equal or slightly exceed boys on verbal skills; but boys markedly exceed girls on quantitative skills, averaging 50–60 points higher. Fewer girls than boys go to college.[15]

From the early school years on, boys do better than girls on tasks requiring spatial reasoning; boys are also more analytic in their thinking and girls more holistic and contextual. Girls tend to develop a different way of thinking than boys, and this difference increases with age and education.[16]

Because of differences in socialization — and perhaps in biology — girls and boys are cognitively different. Many scientists have proposed a dual system of cognition: one rational, abstract, and analytic; the other intuitive, concrete, and holistic. The former is typically associated with men and the latter with women, although it is clear that all persons use both systems to some extent. Women who have superior abilities at logical and abstract thinking are accused of "thinking like a man"; men who are intuitive are said to have "feminine intuition." Because of rigid sex-role expectations, boys are discouraged from being intuitive and girls from being analytic. A particular difficulty for girls is that only "masculine" thinking seems to be highly valued. In this society, the measure of intellectual promise — and often the gate to opportunity — are results of tests (IQ and SATS) that reflect only one kind of intelligence: abstract, logical, and analytic. There is no corresponding measurement and encouragement for intuitive and holistic thinking. In spite of the fact that some of the greatest minds of the century — such as Einstein — attributed their creativity to their intuitive intelligence, many people continue to think of intelligence as equivalent to logical analysis, and nothing more. Maslow argues against this narrow view:

We have learned to think of knowledge as verbal, explicit, articulated, rational, logical, structured, Aristotelian, realistic, sensible. Confronted with the depths of human nature, we psychologists learn to respect also the inarticulate, the preverbal and subverbal, the tacit, the ineffable, the mythic, the archaic, the symbolic, the poetic, the esthetic.[17]

If girls start off intellectually superior to boys, how do they end up scoring below them on IQ tests? An important clue lies in the timing of that change. The girls' IQ drops below that of boys at about the age when girls begin to strive vigorously for social acceptance. They begin to be sensitive to what it means in this culture to be "feminine" and "masculine," and they begin to adopt feminine ways.

Girls start off better than boys and end up worse. This change in their performance occurs at a very significant point in time. It occurs when their status changes, or to be more precise, when girls become aware of what their adult status is supposed to be. It is during adolescence that peer-group pressure to be "feminine" and "masculine" narrows.[18]

Women are supposed to act stupid: it is part of the female role. As adolescent girls begin to understand the expectations that others have for them, they begin to conform to those expectations. One author wrote:

In light of social expectations about women, what is surprising is not that women end up where society expects they will; what is surprising is that little girls don't get the message that they are supposed to be stupid until high school; and what is even more remarkable is that some women resist this message even after high school, college, and graduate school.[19]

How are so many women able to resist the pressures from peers, parents, teachers, and the images in the media? How do they resolve the conflicts they must feel between being feminine and fulfilling their intellectual potential? We know only that many women somehow find the courage to use their intelligence, to display their competence, to strive for success and fulfillment, and to live with the resultant conflicts.

Children naturally strive for mastery and competence. You can help or hinder them in this effort. You can help children grow by abandoning your stereotypes and by recognizing and fostering their individual interests, talents, and ways of thinking about themselves and the world.

Promoting Intellectual Growth

Step 1. Relate at the right level. Children at different stages of intellectual development require different kinds of explanations, stimulation, and interaction.

(a) When children are in the sensorimotor stage (up to age one or two), actively play with them, stimulating their senses and encouraging explorations in touching, smelling, and manipulating the world. Remember that sometime during this period, children will discover that objects continue to exist even when removed from their sight.

(b) When children are in the preoperational stage (from 2 to 7), they will solve problems by talking to themselves and acting out the circumstances involved. Touching and manipulating remain important beginning points for explanations; concrete instances of things have more meaning than generalizations. Remember that during most of this period, children will not understand the concept of conservation; their judgments of "more" or "less" may not agree with yours. You can set the stage for the mastery of the concepts of conservation by encouraging children to manipulate objects which demonstrate the principles (beads, clay, etc.); you can also encourage the mastery of conservation concepts by encouraging children to classify objects and events around them into groups or classes. There is no single right way to group things; encourage children to classify things in different ways.

(c) When children are in the concrete operations stage (from 7 to 11), they will still basically be thinking inductively — from the specific to the general; they still require concrete, specific examples. Remember that during this period, children will grasp the principles of conservation; but during the transition between comprehending and not comprehending these important concepts, they will not always be consistent nor will they always be able to generalize conservation concepts from one context to another.

(d) When children are in the formal operations stage (11 and up), less reliance needs to be placed on concrete objects or examples; they will become better able to conceptualize things verbally or symbolically, and better able to think abstractly. Reasoning from principles or rules now becomes more possible. Remember that the ability to hypothesize and imagine how things "could be" develops during the formal operations period.

Step 2. Provide a stimulating and responsive environment for children. Distinctive stimulation is especially important for younger children, below the age of six. Touching children, talking to them, showing them different sights and sounds, and providing them with objects to manipulate — all are important ways to enrich early environment. You can hang a mobile in the crib, play records for them to hear, or take them for walks. Remember not to overpower them with too many unusual sensations; stay on the edge of the familiar. Sights, sounds, and touches that are distinctive — that stand out and have differential consequences — are much more important than a general din of indistinguishable sensations. Become more responsive to children. An infant learns rapidly when its action or babble elicits some consequences from you or the world. This means that your children need your attention; interact with them, talk to them, play with them. When children are older, you can continue to provide different kinds of stimulation for them. For example, number concepts can be illustrated with a variety of different objects or even with sounds or touches. Letters of the alphabet can be seen, heard, and even touched. Make the children's world change; don't let it become static. Learning occurs best when children are in situations that are slightly novel or incongruous for them — not quite what they are used to. Introduce new toys or play objects into the children's life that are similar but not identical to those they are already used to. Modify the rules slightly for family games. Gradually enlarge their world — but do not push them into totally strange and novel situations.

Step 3. Use steps 1 and 2 only as rough guides. Relate to children as individuals, not as members of a group who should be in a particular stage of intellectual development or who should think and act as you believe other boys and girls think and act. Celebrate each child's unique potential.

What Were Your Problems as a Child?

Many children develop behavioral problems or have trouble in their relationships with parents, siblings, or friends. Some children will not listen to their parents, may get in fights with their siblings, or have trouble in school. Try to remember what problems you have had growing up.

_____ Crying or screaming frequently

_____ Afraid to go to school the first time

_____ Temper tantrums

_____ Going to bed promptly

_____ Sulking

_____ Not doing homework

_____ Not picking up your toys

_____ Arguing with your parents

_____ Arguing with your brothers or sisters

_____ Being disruptive in the classroom

_____ Not doing your chores around the house

_____ Not eating certain foods

_____ Disobeying rules

_____ Lying

_____ Petty thievery

_____ Washing and cleaning up

There are many other problems that could be listed. Try to think of the five problems that troubled you the most when you were a child. How did your parents handle these problems? How were the problems resolved?

Discipline

Here we are in the car, the whole family. We drove four hundred miles from Pittsburgh to New York. In the back of the car, Ivan behaved like an angel, quiet and deep in thought. I said to myself, "He deserves some praise." We were just entering the Lincoln Tunnel when I turned to him and said, "You are such a good boy, Ivan. You behaved so well. I am proud of you."

A minute later the sky fell on us. Ivan pulled out an ashtray and spilled its contents all over us. The ashes, the cigarette butts, and the smoke kept coming, like atomic fallout. We were in the tunnel, in heavy traffic, and we were choking. I could have killed him. If it were not for the other cars around us, I would have murdered him on the spot.[20]

If you were in this frustrating situation, what would your reaction be? Which of the following comes closest to what you might do?

Ignore the child.

Yell at him, shake him or slap him, and make him clean it up.

Say, "You brat, you did that for pure spite. Why are you so bad?"

Say, "You frightened the life out of me! I was afraid we were going to have a terrible accident! I'm just furious with you!"

Pull over to the side of the road as soon as possible and spank him.

Have a good laugh.

Your reaction in such circumstances influences the child's future behavior; discipline is a way of shaping or socializing the child to become an adult member of your community. Children usually behave, but sometimes they misbehave. What is and what is not "misbehavior" depends upon what you find unacceptable. What should you do with a child's unacceptable behavior? You have two main alternatives: (1) change your reactions, or (2) change the child's behavior.

The Right to Be Different

By changing yourself to become more accepting, you can sometimes solve the problem of a child's "misbehavior." Here, in effect, you liberalize your criteria for determining what is unacceptable. If a child does something that you cannot accept, this does not necessarily mean that the child is wrong and should change; a child has the right to be different from you. Certain things that children do are not properly "your problem." If children's behavior does not interfere with your life and your needs, then their behavior is their own business.

Only a child's *actions* can possibly affect you; only actions can interfere with your rights and needs. The child's thoughts, feelings, and wishes are beyond your power and your right to regulate. The child's actions should be socially acceptable, but in the realm of thought, wish, and fantasy — anything goes, nothing is wrong, and nothing should be regulated. The distinction between action and feeling is crucial: feeling angry at a sister is OK, but hitting her is not. It is reasonable to regulate hitting through discipline; however, the attempt to regulate angry feelings through discipline is very difficult and may lead to emotional difficulties in later life.

At times, a child's actions endanger lives or property, or interfere with your rights and needs. Discipline is used at such times to change the child's behavior and make it more acceptable to you. However, sometimes a child's behavior seems unacceptable because you have different values. The child wears the latest hair or dress style — one you find inappropriate; the child does not want to go to church, while you attend regularly; the child chooses friends you do not like — these conflicts are the result of differences in beliefs and values. Attempting to enforce your beliefs and values through discipline is a mistake; children are even more likely to reject values they are pressured to accept. Children and adults share certain rights, and among these is the right to believe what they want. In this country, this is a basic civil right, accorded to all citizens. Dr. Thomas Gordon, author of the book *Parent Effectiveness Training,* wrote:

Why don't parents comprehend that civil rights must begin at home? One reason why parents seldom think of their children as having civil rights is the widespread attitude that parents "own" their children. Holding this attitude, parents justify their efforts to mold their children, shape them, indoctrinate them, modify them, control them, brainwash them. Granting children civil rights or certain inalienable freedoms presupposes viewing children as separate human beings or independent persons having *a life of their own.*[21]

Like Father, Like Son

If discipline is ineffective in teaching values and beliefs, how then do children acquire them? The answer is surprisingly simple: children tend to imitate their parents; they identify with their parents and assimilate parental values and beliefs. Children emulate successful adults. Adults serve as models and children watch them closely and copy them. Studies show that children's religious, moral, and political beliefs generally resemble those of their parents. These beliefs are acquired through *the principle of imitation and identification: children tend to imitate adults whom they regard as successful and competent; under certain circumstances, children identify with adult models, by internalizing their values, beliefs, mannerisms, and personality dispositions.*

The principle of imitation and identification: Children tend to imitate adults whom they regard as successful and competent; under certain circumstances, children identify with adult models, by internalizing their values, beliefs, mannerisms, and personality dispositions.

Imitation refers to the performance of specific behaviors that other people have performed; identification refers to the internalization of certain beliefs, values, mannerisms, and personality dispositions that other people possess. Bandura and Huston asked children to solve a number of problems. While crossing the room to demonstrate the task, the experimenter repeated, "March, march, march," a behavior irrelevant to the task itself. When the children set out to do the task, they said, "March, march, march," in imitation of their adult model. Mussen and Rutherford found that children identified more with adult models who were warm and nurturing than with ones who were not. "Like father, like son" is more likely to be true when the father is warm and nurturing.

Bandura, A. Social learning theory of identificatory processes. In D. A. Goslin (ed.), *Handbook of Socialization Theory and Research.* Chicago: Rand-McNally, 1969.

Bandura, A., and Huston, A. C. Identification as a process of incidental learning. *Journal of Abnormal and Social Psychology,* 1961, **63,** 311–318.

Mussen, P. H., and Rutherford, E. Parent-child relations and parent personality in relation to young children's sex-role preference. *Child Development,* 1963, **34,** 589–607.

By living your values, by being a successful adult model, you can strongly influence the beliefs of children; but attempting to enforce thought-conformity through discipline does not work. Discipline works for actions, not ideas. The misuse of discipline can have profound effects. Parents have great power over the lives of their children, and this power is occasionally abused.

The Die Is Cast

Being human is not a birthright. Our humanness develops through our interactions with the world and with caring people. The growth of humanness can be blocked when these early interactions are dehumanizing: pain, starvation, terror, rejection — these harsh experiences distort normal personality development and may leave their ugly mark on the adult personality decades later.

What happens early in infancy can affect the whole course of your life. Sigmund Freud believed that the first few years of life determined the adult personality. He considered weaning and toilet training as critical early experiences. He proposed that harsh toilet training in infancy produced an adult personality disorder called the "anal character" — a person who is extremely stingy, stubborn, orderly, and compulsively clean. Freud also proposed that harsh and early weaning produced an adult type called the "oral character" — a person marked by excessive passivity, pessimism, and dependency. While Freud's hypotheses have not in general been confirmed by research evidence,[22] it has been found that harsh weaning and toilet training in infancy are associated with a variety of adult personality problems.[23,24] Furthermore, many other aspects of the infant-parent relationship have been found to precede adult problems. Such problems are prejudice,[25] juvenile delinquency,[26] and schizophrenia[27] may have roots in early childhood. According to the *principle of early determination, early childhood experiences affect adult personality.*

It is difficult to distinguish the effect on the adult personality of specific childhood experiences. Parents treating their children harshly in one area of behavior — such as toilet training — typically treat their children harshly in other areas. The independent effects of harsh toilet training may then be impossible to discover, as the following case shows:

In 1954 a British boy scout, sixteen years of age, stabbed and killed a woman of seventy-two. He had been afraid she would discover his forgery of some scout certificates; but this hardly explained why he stabbed her twenty-nine times. His mother's description of his childhood suggested some answers. Apparently, he was toilet trained by the age of nine months: his father, an ex-army officer, made him sit on the pot if necessary for hours. By nine months, too, he had been taught to put every toy away. His father apparently "kept on at the boy," who nonetheless seemed to worship him. As a child he was shy and timid. The sight of a broken toy made him cry with fright, and when he was older he disliked horror films. The mother also said she sometimes beat him. When angry, he would "just go white, clench his hands and say nothing, and in a moment it was all over." The boy himself said that he had a temper, but that he had always controlled it and could put anything unpleasant "completely out of his mind."[28]

Early experiences in infancy are not the whole story; the human personality is a vastly complex, fluid process. Your identity is influenced by all of your encounters, not just your early ones. You are changed by your experiences even now; but you carry with you the influence of your early history.

Physical Abuse

Parents have used an amazing variety of weapons to punish children — hands, belts, boards, chains, whips, to name a few. Punishment works — both for parents and, to a point, for children. It provides an outlet for parents to express their anger and aggression against children; and children are usually less likely to repeat actions for which they have been punished (in accordance with *the law of effect*). But punishment has certain unfortunate side effects. Aggressive parents who use harsh physical punishment often have children who copy them and display violence themselves (*the principle of imitation and identification*). Punishment also teaches fear and anxiety, and may, if severe, provide the basis for later emotional disturbance. Children tend to resist and avoid punishment. Resistance may take the form of defiance, rebellion, retaliation, lying, blaming others, and cheating. Alternately, the child may avoid the situation by withdrawing into fantasy, daydreams, apathy, depression, or drugs.

Though we live in a relatively prosperous and enlightened age, it is a time of anxiety and confusion for many parents; a few are unable to cope with their problems and explode into violence.

An eighteen-month-old baby in the Bronx . . . was hanged by her wrists and savagely whipped with a belt, then cut down and left to lie on the bathroom floor for almost two days suffering from a broken arm.[29]

Each year vicious beatings by parents leave children physically and psychologically injured. Child abuse cases increase year by year. Parents, frustrated by the difficulties and complexities of the modern world, increasingly turn against their children with displaced feelings of anger and violence. They are inventive in the sickening variety of their tortures:

Children have been brought into hospitals with skulls fractured and bodies covered with lacerations. One parent disciplined a child for presumptive misbehavior with the buckle end of a belt, perforating an intestine and killing the child. Children have been whipped, beaten, starved, drowned, smashed against walls and floors, held in ice water baths, exposed to extremes of outdoor temperatures, burned with hot irons and steam pipes. . . .

Are these events of great rarity? How prevalent can such occurrences be? Clearly data are hard to come by because in only the most extreme cases do such things come to public notice. Yet available information strongly suggests that the frequency is far greater than one may naively, or hopefully, imagine.[30]

What happens to children who are viciously whipped, burned, and beaten by their parents? Unfortunately, the abused children tend to grow up to be abusive parents.[11] The way adults treat their children appears to be heavily influenced by the way their parents treated them. We tend to adopt the child-rearing practices of our parents. Child abuse is part of an ugly circle: beaten children grow up to become brutal parents, who beat their own children, who in turn become brutal parents. The most violent adults — those convicted of first-degree murder — tend to have experienced as children "remorseless physical brutality" at the hands of their parents, according to one researcher.[31] Children tend to imitate their parents, according to *the principle of imitation and identification;* to some extent, "like father, like son" is true.

Verbal Abuse

Verbal abuse is a common mistake in child discipline. Insults and cutting comments destroy a child's sense of worth; if parents do not respect their children, children develop little self-respect. Parents often communicate their lack of respect to their children in various forms of verbal abuse:[20,21]

Insults and name calling: Calling the child "stupid," "bum," "jerk," or "spoiled brat." Makes the child feel unworthy, unloved, and just plain bad.

Threats and warnings: "You do that and you'll be sorry." "If you pester me any more you'll get a spanking." Makes the child feel afraid of the parent; also invites testing by the child to see whether or not the parent will follow through with the threat.

Interrogating: "Exactly how long did you study before the exam?" "Why do you hate your teacher?" "Why don't you get up on time?" Makes the child feel threatened; controls the conversation and forces disclosure. The answers to such questions are often used against the child.

Bossing and ordering: "Shut up and just do it." "Stop loafing and get to work." "Eat your spinach and don't argue." Communicates lack of trust of the child and parental indifference toward the child's wants and needs. Fosters either dependency or rebellion, not independence.

Interpreting and diagnosing: "You're saying that because you're jealous." "You're just doing that because you're tired." "You just want attention." Communicates parental attitude of superiority; makes children feel that parents can see through them; makes children stop revealing problems to parents.

Accusing: "You always lie." "You never mind." "People just can't depend on you to do what you say you'll do." "You always throw your clothes on the floor." Communicates parental attitude of disrespect for the child. Because such accusations are rarely completely true, the child feels a victim of injustice, and feels resentful.

Prophesying: "You'll end up in jail." "You'll wind up in the gutter." "Girls like you can never get a husband." "If you do that, nobody will like you." Communicates negative image of the child, and the child adopts the parental image as a self-image; motivates the child to act so as to fulfill the parental expectation.

Praising the personality: "You're a good boy, a perfect angel." "You're so sweet and kind." "You're very smart and pretty." Nobody can be sweet, smart, and pretty all the time. Praising makes the child feel guilty when he or she has unkind or "bad" impulses; makes the child feel manipulated. Later, the child will feel bad when *not* praised.

Through these different forms of interaction, parents often inadvertently communicate powerful negative expectations to their children. Children tend to conform to the expectations of their parents. When these expectations are negative, they affect the behavior of the children negatively. To some extent, what you expect is what you get.

Phil's parents were college professors who were strongly committed to the intellectual life. Before Phil was born they had long talks about how their child would be encouraged to think about world problems, to question assumptions, and to enjoy good books and music. Their hope, however, turned into frustration and anger when Phil showed little interest in such subjects in his first six years of life.

His parents began referring to him as "dense," "insensitive," and "hopelessly middle-class"; when his parents were angered, they would call him "stupid." Soon Phil, too, began to think of himself as slow and incapable of intellectual pursuits. As a consequence, he would not put himself into the position of having to engage difficult problems; he was certain he would fail. He took trade courses in high school and dropped out in the middle of his senior year. It was a clear case of self-fulfilling prophecy.

Parent-child relationships are usually characterized by relative love, acceptance, and respect. Sometimes, however, parents fail to communicate love and acceptance to their children. Some psychologists claim that the pattern of communication in certain families is disturbed, twisted, and paradoxical, and that the children of such families tend to suffer an abnormally high incidence of emotional disturbances such as schizophrenia.[32] The "double bind" is a particular type of communication between parents and children in disturbed families. A classic double-bind message is the injunction, "Be spontaneous!" If you obey this command, you have disobeyed it — you cannot deliberately be spontaneous. With a double bind, you are "damned if you do and damned if you don't"; the meaning of the message is ambiguous and confusing. Other double-bind message are, "Don't be so obedient!", "You should love me!", and "Have you stopped lying to me?" There is no reasonable response to these messages; if you obey the first message, you must disobey it. The second message suggests that loving and not loving are willful actions rather than feelings. The third message cannot be answered affirmatively or negatively unless the child confesses to lying. What is the meaning communicated with messages such as these? The child cannot decide. One variety of double-bind messages consists of one message that is verbal (e.g., "I love you"), and a second contradictory message that is nonverbal (e.g., facial expression showing resentment or contempt).

A mother visits her son, who has just been recovering from a mental breakdown. As he goes toward her (a) she opens her arms for him to embrace her, and/or (b) to embrace him. (c) As he gets nearer she freezes and stiffens. (d) He stops irresolutely. (e) She says, "Don't you want to kiss your mummy?"—and as he still stands irresolutely (f) she says, "But dear, you mustn't be afraid of your feelings."

He responds to her invitation to kiss her, but her posture, freezing, tension, simultaneously tell him not to. That she is frightened of a close relationship with him, or for some other reason does not want him actually to do what she invites him to do, cannot be openly admitted by the mother, and remains unsaid by her and the son. . . . She conveys, in effect, "Do not embrace me, or I will punish you," *and* "If you do not do so, I will punish you."[33]

You can experience children's behavior, but you cannot experience their experience. Experience is private, interior, hidden. Through our interactions with children we help them to develop a view of the world that is more or less shared by their family and their society: we teach them that that is a "cow," that germs cause disease, and that nature is wonderful. But experience cannot be so legislated. There is a fundamental difference between these two exchanges:

Child: That's a horse.

Parent: No, it's a cow.

Child: I'm cold.

Parent: No you're not. It's warm in here.

The latter constitutes an invalidation of the child's immediate experience. The parent denies the child's feelings, negates the child's experience. Children whose experience is consistently invalidated by their parents become confused and begin to mistrust their own perceptions, memories, and feelings. In extreme cases, invalidation may precipitate a profound emotional disturbance.

Maya's "illness" was diagnosed as paranoid schizophrenia. It appeared to come out of the blue. . . . She experienced herself as a machine, rather than a person. . . . She sometimes felt that her thoughts were controlled by others, and she said that not she but her "voices" often did her thinking. . . . Her difficulty was that she could not know when to trust or mistrust her own perceptions and memory or her mother and father.

Not only did both her parents contradict Maya's memory, feelings, perceptions, motives, intentions, but they made attributions that were themselves curiously self-contradictory, and . . . they spoke and acted as though they knew better than Maya what she remembered, what she did, what she imagined, what she wanted, what she felt, whether she was enjoying herself or whether she was tired.

We were not able to find one area of Maya's personality that was not subject to negations of different kinds.

For instance, she thinks she started to imagine "sexual things" . . . at the age of fourteen. She would lie in bed wondering whether her parents had sexual intercourse. She began to get sexually excited, and to masturbate. She was very shy, however, and kept away from boys. She felt increasingly irritated at the physical presence of her father. She objected to his shaving in the same room while she had breakfast. She was frightened that her parents knew that she had sexual thoughts about them. She tried to tell them about this, but they told her *she did not have any thoughts of that kind.* She told them she masturbated *and they told her that she did not.* What happened then is of course inferred, but *when she told her parents in the presence of the interviewer that she still masturbated, her parents simply told her that she did not!*[34]

What to Do Instead

There are two main approaches to child discipline: the power approach and the nonpower approach. The power approach depends upon the superior strength and resources of the parent to enforce parental expectations through rewards and punishments. The parent controls the child's behavior by controlling the good or bad consequences of that behavior. The nonpower approach informs, but does not coerce children. The parent communicates the effect of the child's actions on others, then the child decides what to do about it.

These two approaches to child discipline — power and nonpower — both have good and bad points. The power approach can be abused when severe punishment is used; the nonpower approach can be abused through various forms of miscommunication. There are many different approaches to child discipline; no single method is the best for everybody. Two methods will be described here. The reinforcement method, the best of the power approach, is a method based on tested principles of experimental psychology. The communication method, the best of the nonpower approach, is a method based on the principles of a form of psychotherapy.

Reinforcement Method

The reinforcement method is founded on the principles of operant conditioning: behavior is changed by manipulating consequences. According to operant conditioning and its *law of effect,* actions followed by favorable consequences tend to recur. From this point of view, misbehavior occurs because it is reinforced (it has favorable consequences).

With four children under six, Jody had her hands full. She had so little time after work to finish her chores around the house that she often could not give as much attention to the youngsters as she wanted to. One particularly bothersome habit the children had picked up was shouting at her, even in public. She would tell them over and over to speak quietly, that she wasn't deaf; but it did no good.

One evening while she was preparing supper, all four children were talking at once, trying to get her attention without success. Finally, four-year-old Lonnie shouted, "Mommie, Mommie, Mommie!!" She turned sharply and said, "Well, what is it?"

At that moment she realized why her children shouted at her: she responded only to the loudest voice when she was busy. Shouting worked.

Shouting had a favorable consequence: it got mother's attention, and attention is a powerful reinforcer of behavior.

If bad behavior is maintained with reinforcement, it might be eliminated if the reinforcement were omitted. If shouting were not followed by attention, shouting might be eliminated. According to *the principle of extinction,* actions will cease to occur if their reinforcement is omitted. The following case study shows what happens when a reinforcer is omitted:

Whenever he did not get his own way or did not receive the attention he wanted, Benjy would throw himself down, yell, scream, and hit his head on the floor.

Benjy was the first child in the family, and the arrival of his baby sister seemed to upset him terribly. The only way he could get his parents' attention now seemed to be to make a terrible racket and cause them to fear for his safety. When Benjy knocked his head on the floor for the first time, possibly accidentally, his mother quickly turned from the baby sister and picked him up and held him. Frequently when Benjy threw a temper tantrum his mother would yield to his desires, sometimes taking him out in the yard to play with him.

Benjy's parents felt his temper tantrums were growing worse and wondered if perhaps their actions were creating the tantrums. Therefore they decided to institute a new policy.

Whenever Benjy went into his temper tantrum act, his parents agreed that neither one would pay the slightest bit of attention to him. During the next several head-banging sessions he would ask his parents for a favor and if they denied it, he would bump his head some more. It was difficult for his parents to watch these episodes, so they simply walked out of the room. No longer did they grant favors after a tantrum.

Within a remarkably short time Benjy stopped the worst of his head-banging tactics. The action no longer paid off and, besides, it was painful to him.[35]

Just as reinforcement maintains bad behavior, it also maintains good behavior. Good behavior increases when it is rewarded. If you reinforce your child for making small changes in the direction of more desirable behavior, you will promote movement toward the final goal.

Six-year-old Polly had never before attempted to make her own bed. One day she pulled up the blanket on the bed. Her mother told her that her bed looked nice. The next day Polly pulled up the blanket and also straightened her pillow. Again her mother noticed the improvement. On successive days Polly began pulling up the sheet along with the blanket and finally the bedspread. Although the bed would not pass military inspection, it represented a substantial improvement for Polly, and her mother expressed her appreciation.[35]

Unacceptable behavior can be weakened by strengthening its opposite. A child cannot simultaneously yell and talk quietly; if talking quietly is reinforced, yelling will be less likely to occur. A child cannot simultaneously walk and run; if walking is reinforced, running will be less likely to occur.

Robin had the bad habit of interrupting her parents whenever she wanted to say something or ask a question. When her mother was talking on the phone, Robin would run in and ask where her slippers were. When her parents were talking with friends, Robin would break into the conversation in the middle of a sentence and report that she had learned a new song.

Robin's parents decided to adopt a twofold program to break the bad habit: (1) they agreed to completely ignore Robin's interruptions by not responding to them at all, and (2) they decided to reinforce her whenever she waited until someone was through talking before asking her question. The purpose of the second strategy was to strengthen a response (waiting) that was incompatible with the bad habit (interrupting).

At first, they found few opportunities to support Robin for waiting, but whenever an occasion did occur, they would thank her for waiting, then give her request their close attention. Gradually, Robin began to interrupt less and less often.

Applying the Reinforcement Method

Step 1. Weaken misbehavior by removing its reinforcement — e.g., withhold such favorable consequences as parental attention following some unacceptable action.

Step 2. Weaken misbehavior by reinforcing its opposite — e.g., by rewarding honesty, you will weaken dishonesty.

Step 3. Shape good behavior through gradual approximation; by rewarding small improvements, behavior will gradually improve.

Step 4. Strengthen good behavior by reinforcing it; since behavior that is not reinforced will diminish, you should provide favorable consequences for good behavior in order to maintain it.

Communication Method

The communication method is a way of promoting socially acceptable behavior by improving the pattern of communication within the family. It is based on principles of client-centered therapy, a form of psychotherapy initially developed by Carl Rogers. Families often do not communicate very well. Parents often do not listen to their children and do not understand how they feel. Children often do not understand how their behavior affects their parents. The goal of this method is to open up the lines of communication. When children feel understood by their parents, they do not want to make their parents feel bad — at least, not very often.

Active listening is a special way of listening to children that opens the door to the flow of communication. In active listening, the parent tries to figure out exactly what the child is feeling or what he or she wants and then reflects that feeling back to the child. You try to understand the message that the child is sending and state it back so that it can be confirmed or disconfirmed. You try to serve as a mirror to the child, reflecting not the exact words of the child but their underlying meaning. For example,

Child: (crying) Jimmy took my truck away from me.

Parent: You sure feel bad about that — you don't like it when he does that.

Child: That's right.[21]

Notice that the parent's response concerns itself with the feeling that the child is communicating, and the child confirms that the parent understands. Sometimes you will misunderstand:

Child: I hate school. It's stupid! I don't see why I have to go, anyway.

Parent: Sounds like you're pretty upset about the whole thing.

Child: No . . . It's the other kids — they keep picking on me.[21]

When you actively listen, the child feels understood; and you have the opportunity to be corrected if your understanding is faulty. Through providing the child with your reflection or feedback, you check your understanding and give the child a chance to correct it. When children have the benefit of active listening — and the corresponding freedom from negative judgment — they often feel freer from frustration and tension and the need to act out their angers.

Sending "I" messages is a special way of communicating how you feel to your child. With "I" messages — instead of telling your child what to do or what not to do — you tell your child how his or her behavior makes you feel. You disclose your feelings to the child.

Mrs. H. reported an incident during their family vacation. Their small children had been very loud and boisterous in the back of the station wagon. Mrs. H. and her husband had been resentfully enduring the racket, but finally Mr. H. could stand no more. He braked the car abruptly, pulled off the road and announced, "I just can't stand all this noise and jumping around in the back. I want to enjoy my vacation and I want to have fun when I'm driving. But damn it, when there is noise back there, I get nervous and I hate to drive. I feel I have a right to enjoy this vacation, too."[21]

Rather than name-calling, bossing, threatening, or moralizing, Mr. H. simply revealed exactly how his children's behavior made him feel. Rather than responding with resentment, retaliation, or rebellion, his children quieted down and became more considerate; they had not realized how their father was feeling. Consider the alternative to sending "I" messages: Mr. H., in the example above, could have reacted in the following way.

"Shut up back there!" (ordering). "You're acting like spoiled brats" (name-calling). "You're just trying to annoy me" (interpreting). "You never think of others" (accusing). "If you don't stop, you'll get a good spanking!" (threatening).

Instead of saying what's wrong with someone else, "I" messages say how you feel; instead of insults, you gain understanding.

When you actively listen, you gain understanding of how your children feel. When you send "I" messages, your children gain understanding of how you feel. With increased understanding and improved communication, family relationships often dramatically improve.

Applying the Communication Method

Step 1. Listen "actively" by understanding the feelings of your children and reflecting these feelings back to them.

Step 2. Send "I" messages by telling your children how their behavior makes you feel. Stop threatening, ordering, and insulting them.

Summary

Learning and intelligence develop rapidly during childhood. However, children not only see things differently, they think less abstractly than adults.

Piaget has developed a theory of intellectual development, which states that children pass through a fixed sequence of four stages. During these stages, children begin to think more abstractly. The environment contributes greatly to mental growth, and new inventions, such as the talking typewriter, have also aided this process. Unfortunately, sexism is one way to discourage this intellectual growth. However, although there are differences in intellectual development between boys and girls, there are methods for promoting intellectual growth in any child.

When a child misbehaves, you can choose to change either the child's behavior or your reaction to the child's behavior. In order to teach children values, we have to be good models. Freud believed that early childhood experiences affect our adult personality. For example, physical and verbal abuse of children by parents is not uncommon and can lead to serious adult disorders. Two constructive approaches to dealing with children's behavior are the reinforcement and communication methods.

Notes

1. Fraiberg, S. H. *The magic years.* New York: Scribner's, 1959.

2. Bloom, B. S. *Stability and change in human characteristics.* New York: Wiley, 1964.

3. Watson, J. B. *Psychological care of infant and child.* New York: Norton, 1928.

4. *Newsweek,* May 22, 1972, p. 93.

5. Pick, H. I., Jr., and Pick, A. D. Sensory and perceptual development. In P. H. Mussen (ed.), *Carmichael's manual of child psychology, Vol. 1.* New York: Wiley, 1970.

6. Milne, A. A. *Winnie-the-Pooh.* New York: Dutton, 1926.

7. Phillips, J. L., Jr. *The origins of intellect: Piaget's theory.* San Francisco: W. H. Freeman, 1969.

8. Hunt, J. McV. *Intelligence and experience.* New York: Ronald Press, 1961.

9. Pines, M. *Revolution in learning: The years from birth to six.* New York: Harper & Row, 1966.

10. Kagan, J., and Klein, R. E. Cross-cultural perspectives on early development. *American Psychologist,* 1973, **28,** 947–961.

11. Bloom, B. S., Davis, A., and Hess, R. *Compensatory education for cultural deprivation.* New York: Holt, Rinehart, and Winston, 1965.

12. Bardwick, J. M., and Douvan, E. Ambivalence: The socialization of women. In V. Gornick and B. K. Moran (eds.), *Woman in sexist society.* New York: Basic Books, 1971.

13. Rossi, A. S. Barriers to career choice of engineering, medicine, or science among American women. In J. A. Nattfold and C. G. Van Aken (eds.), *Women and the scientific professions.* Cambridge, Mass.: M.I.T. Press, 1965.

14. Mencken, H. L. *In defense of woman.* New York: Knopf, 1922.

15. Macooby, E. E. Sex differences in intellectual functioning. In J. M. Bardwick (ed.), *Readings on the psychology of women.* New York: Harper & Row, 1972.

16. Tyler, L. Sex differences. In *International encyclopedia of the social sciences, Vol. 7.* New York: Macmillan, 1968.

17. Maslow, A. H. *The psychology of science.* Chicago: Henry Regnery, 1969.

18. Freeman, J. The social construction of the second sex. In M. H. Garskof (ed.), *Roles women play: Readings toward women's liberation.* Belmont, Calif.: Brooks/Cole, 1971.

19. Weisstein, N. Psychology constructs the female, or the fantasy life of the male psychologist. In M. H. Garskof (ed.), *Roles women play: Readings toward women's liberation.* Belmont, Calif.: Brooks/Cole, 1971.

20. Ginott, H. G. *Between parent and child.* New York: Avon Books, 1965.

21. Gordon, T. *P.E.T. Parent effectiveness training: A tested new way to raise responsible children.* New York: Peter H. Wyden, 1970.

22. Beloff, H. The structure and origin of the anal character. *Genetic Psychology Monographs,* 1957, **55,** 141–172.

23. Huschka, M. The child's response to coercive bowel training. *Psychosomatic Medicine,* 1942, **4,** 301–308.

24. Wittenborn, J. R. A study of adoptive children. *Psychological Monographs,* 1956, **70,** 1–115.

25. Adorno, T. W., Frenkel-Brunswik, E., Levinson, D. J., and Sanford, N. R. *The authoritarian personality.* New York: Harper & Row, 1950.

26. Glueck, S., and Glueck, E. *Unraveling juvenile delinquency.* New York: Commonwealth Fund, 1950.

27. Arieti, S. Schizophrenia. In S. Arieti (ed.), *American handbook of psychiatry, Vol. 1.* New York: Basic Books, 1959.

28. Wilkinson, R. *The broken rebel.* New York: Harper & Row, 1972.

29. *New York Times,* June 27, 1969.

30. Bakan, D. *Slaughter of the innocents: A study of the battered child phenomenon.* Boston: Beacon Press, 1971.

31. Curtis, G. C. Violence breeds violence — perhaps? *American Journal of Psychiatry,* 1963, **120,** 386–387.

32. Bateson, G., Jackson, D. D., Haley, J., and Weakland, J. Toward a theory of schizophrenia. *Behavioral Science,* 1956, **1,** 251–264.

33. Laing, R. D. *Self and others.* Baltimore: Penguin Books, 1969.

34. Laing, R. D., and Esterson, A. *Sanity, madness, and the family.* Baltimore: Penguin Books, 1970.

35. Krumboltz, J. D., and Krumboltz, H. B. *Changing children's behavior.* Englewood Cliffs, N.J.: Prentice-Hall, 1972.

Suggested Readings

Ginott, H. G. *Between parent and child.* New York: Avon Books, 1965.

Gordon, T. *P.E.T. Parent effectiveness training: A tested new way to raise responsible children.* New York: Peter H. Wyden, 1970.

Krumboltz, J. D., and Krumboltz, H. B. *Changing children's behavior.* Englewood Cliffs, N.J.: Prentice-Hall, 1972.

Mussen, P. H., Conger, J. J., and Kagan, J. *Child development and personality* (Fourth edition). New York: Harper & Row, 1974.

Patterson, G. R. *Living with children.* Champaign, Ill.: Research Press, 1976.

Piaget, J. *The origins of intelligence in children.* New York: International Universities Press, 1952.

Singer, D. G., and Revson, T. A. *A Piaget primer: How a child thinks.* New York: International Universities Press, 1978.

Chapter Ten

Written by Stephanie Crane/Drawn by Ben Black

Improving Personal Relationships

Dave had been deeply hurt once by a close friend, and he swore it would never happen to him again. In high school he had met and slowly grown to love a girl in his class. One afternoon he opened up and revealed to her some of his deepest, most private desires and fears; he was later embarrassed to learn that she had told others at school what he had said. After this experience, Dave kept his feelings to himself; he never let anybody know when he was angry, when he was pleased, or when his feelings were hurt. But his coolness was costly; he had no one he could truly call a friend. Determined finally to remedy this, he began one day, quite deliberately, to reach out to others, to reveal his feelings, and to take risks—by actually disclosing to some of his classmates that he liked them. He was applying certain principles of interpersonal effectiveness. His problems of loneliness gradually vanished.

We are consumed with working out our complex relations with others. Human relationship, its joy and frustrations, is the basis of novels, plays, poems, songs, and movies. We can't quite understand it; we can't quite get it straight; we struggle endlessly to unravel the threads tying us together, in the hope of knowing, for once, how we fit in.

"Hell is other people," said Sartre.

If so, heaven is other people, too.

Friendship

Who are your friends? Why are they your friends, and not others? You like some people, you get along well with them, you enjoy seeing them — but why? Friendship patterns are not random; to some degree, they can be predicted.

Physical proximity is one factor contributing to the formation of friendship. People who never meet don't have the opportunity to be friends; people whom you can't help bumping into now and then are at least potential friends (or enemies). One study of friendship patterns in a large married-student housing project found that friendships were much more likely between next-door neighbors even though the students did not know each other before moving into the project. The author concluded:

> The two major factors affecting the friendships which developed were (1) sheer distance between houses and (2) the direction in which a house faced. Friendships developed more frequently between next-door neighbors, less frequently between people whose houses were separated by another house, and so on. As the distance between houses increased, the number of friendships fell off so rapidly that it was rare to find a friendship between persons who lived in houses that were separated by more than four or five other houses.[1]

The study showed that students living in houses that faced each other were more likely to be friends than students living in houses not facing each other. Apparently it is not the case, after all, that familiarity breeds contempt.

Marriage is more likely, too, between persons who live in the same neighborhood. Marrying the kid next door is more than a cliché. One study of 5,000 marriages in Philadelphia found that 12 percent of the couples were living at the same address before marriage — but that, of course, is another story; what is interesting in this case is the remaining 88 percent. Of the remainder, one third lived within five or fewer blocks of each other; as the distance between couples increased, the likelihood of marriage decreased.[2]

A second factor contributing to the formation of friendships is shared experiences. People with shared experiences have memories in common, and — to the extent that interests and skills derive from experience — they have common interests and skills. People without shared experiences have little to talk about. Students tend to make friends with those who share their classes or their dorms. Workers tend to make friends with those who work with them. Sometimes a dramatic experience — such as being caught in an elevator — provides a sufficient common base to facilitate strangers becoming instant friends.

A third factor contributing to the formation of friendships is similarity in attitudes. In general, the more a person expresses points of view that correspond to your own, the more you will like the person.[3] When we share the same point of view we are more likely to validate and support each other in our interactions. Similar attitudes also serve as a cue, indicating similarity in background, geography, education, or family experience; they may serve as a cue signifying your future behavior and the extent to which it would please or displease someone you meet.

A fourth factor contributing to the formation of friendship is the extent to which you meet each other's needs. We are social creatures. We all have important needs that can be met only by other people — the need to be liked, accepted, respected; the need for feedback and help; the need for companionship. Some people — in general, those who are accepting and supportive — meet these needs for us and others don't.

What Are Your Communication Problems?

Before continuing, try to identify your communication problems by using the following checklist:

_____ People don't listen to what I have to say.

_____ I don't listen to what other people say.

_____ I can't really tell people how I am feeling.

_____ I am not honest when I communicate.

_____ I can't seem to accept other people for what they are.

_____ I have a hard time praising other people.

_____ My body sometimes sends out a different message than what I am saying.

Communication

Friendship rests on accurate communication. We relate to each other by communicating how we feel and what we know. Communicating is not limited to talking: it involves both sending and receiving, and talking is but one form of sending. Facial expression, body posture, hands and legs, all send messages; often these nonverbal channels of communication are at least as important to understanding as the verbal channels.

Communication has three components: (1) an intended message, (2) a sent message, and (3) a received message. Communication skill involves the ability to send the message that you intend; listening skills involve the sensitivity to interpret the sent message properly so as to understand what was intended. Relationship problems develop from miscommunication and misunderstandings. Often the intended message and the sent message are not the same.

One of the problems in sending messages effectively is knowing your own intentions — getting straight exactly what you mean to communicate. You have seen other people talking to you in one way and communicating something else entirely with their body or the inflections of their voice. Perhaps you have walked up to talk with someone who says, "I'm really glad to see you again!" — while looking tense and impatient, and glancing furtively at the clock every few seconds. Is he or she glad to see you, or irritated because of the interruption? What is the intended message? It may be that the person does not know for sure. Do you understand your own intended messages? Are you sending the same message with your mouth that you are with your body?

One of the problems in accurately receiving messages is your own tendency to judge and evaluate. Many people seem to be waiting for a break in the flow of conversation just so they can make their own personal statement; they really are not listening at all to what is being said. Others are so quick to judge and criticize that they rarely understand in depth what is being said. This leads to misunderstandings and feelings of invalidation. Relationships are nourished by understanding; but understanding is a skill, dependent upon you. One way to increase your understanding is to "actively listen" — to paraphrase the meaning of the messages as you understand them, giving the sender the opportunity to confirm or reject your understanding.

The way in which you listen and respond to another person is crucial for building a fulfilling relationship. You can either listen and respond in ways that make the relationship more distant and impersonal, or you can listen and respond in ways that bring you and the sender into a closer, more personal relationship. It is crucial in a close relationship for you to communicate that you have clearly heard and understood the sender. . . . When you listen accurately and respond relevantly, you communicate to the sender, "I care about what you are saying, and I want to understand it."[4]

Listening is a skill, and the techniques for listening to adults are the same as those for children (see "Relating to Children," Chapter Nine).

Self-Disclosure

To be liked or loved, you must be known. If other people do not know who you are, how you feel, what you think, what your hopes and fears are, they do not at all have the opportunity to have a relationship with you. You must disclose yourself; you must take the risk, as Dave did, of revealing who you are.

Self-disclosure, unveiling your feelings and thoughts to others, is the basis of authenticity — being real instead of being phony. Many people hide their feelings behind a mask for fear of ridicule or rejection; but the price they pay for safety is high — they cannot be real.

If you and I can honestly tell each other who we are, that is, what we think, judge, feel, value, love, honor and esteem, hate, fear, desire, hope for, believe in and are committed to, then and then only can each of us grow. Then and then alone can each of us be what he really is, say what he really thinks, tell what he really feels, express what he really loves. This is the real meaning of authenticity as a person, that my exterior truly reflects my interior.[5]

When my exterior reflects my interior — that is, when I stop hiding my intentions, feelings, and thoughts — then you can experience me as I really am, instead of experiencing the facade, the mask that I wear in public. When my exterior reflects my interior, then I can learn about myself, too; by revealing my feelings to you, I become more aware of how I feel; by allowing you to see me unveiled, I am able to see myself through you. As Emerson wrote, "Other men are lenses through which we read our own minds."

When you disclose your feelings and thoughts to others, you display your trust of them; and they, in turn, are encouraged to disclose their feelings and thoughts to you. You make a small disclosure; the other person makes a small disclosure. You then make a more personal disclosure; the other person often will reciprocate. In as little as an hour, two strangers can become intimate friends. The idea that disclosure begets disclosure is called *the dyadic effect: self-disclosure is usually reciprocated.*

Most of us have learned to be closed, to keep our armor up, to show little of the intensity of feeling that goes on inside, because open people are more vulnerable to hurt. But open people are also more vulnerable to love. As Sidney Jourard said:

Self-disclosure follows an attitude of love and trust. If I love someone, not only do I strive to know him; I also display my love by letting him know me. At the same time, by so doing, I permit him to love me.

Loving is scary, because when you permit yourself to be known, you expose yourself not only to a lover's balm, but also to a hater's bombs!

When he knows you, he knows just where to plant them for maximum effect.[6]

What happens if you begin to disclose yourself and the other person does not reciprocate? If you stop, you have risked little; if you continue, you may threaten the other person. Feeling the urge to reciprocate, but being afraid to do so, the other person may change the subject, ridicule you, or leave.

The dyadic effect: Self-disclosure is usually reciprocated.

When you reveal your experiences and feelings to other people, they in turn tend to disclose themselves to you. Powell (cited in Jourard, 1968) conducted interviews with college students and asked them to disclose themselves to him as fully as they wished. Part of the time he responded to the students by restating what they said to him; the rest of the time, he responded by disclosing himself to the students. He found that his disclosures resulted in greater disclosure (both positive and negative) on the part of the students than did his restating responses.

Jourard, S. M. *Disclosing Man to Himself.* Princeton, N.J.: Van Nostrand, 1968.
Jourard, S. M. *Self-Disclosure: An Experimental Analysis of the Transparent Self.* New York: Wiley, 1971.

Risk nothing, gain nothing. You have a choice: to withdraw from honest encounters, to hide your feelings, to falsify your intentions — or to be transparent, open and real through self-disclosure.

Exercise—Communication: Getting in Touch with Feelings

To gain some experience in expressing feelings, try to recall a time when you experienced each of the emotional states listed below. Try to imagine yourself in a situation where you have felt afraid, angry, bored, and so on. Try to describe in as much detail as possible how you felt at these times. Be specific; think about your physical and psychological reactions as they actually occurred.

1. Afraid
2. Angry
3. Bored

4. Confused
5. Happy
6. Hurt

7. Lonely	9. Sad
8. Loving	10. Satisfied

How did you describe your feelings? Did you use behavioral statements that indicated what you did or felt like doing? Or, did you describe your feelings experientially, in terms of your inner experiences at the time you felt different emotions? How easy is it for you to describe your feelings? Can you verbalize your feelings easily, or is it difficult to tell someone else how you feel?

Acceptance

Think of when you have felt most put off by someone else. Chances are, you felt you were not accepted for who you are. Think of when you have felt most close in your relations with others. Chances are, you felt totally acceptable and unjudged in that situation.

The lack of acceptance is a major blocking force, a distancing force, in interpersonal relations. To judge, criticize, or reject other people is to push them away; to accept others is to draw them closer and encourage them to be real.

How can you communicate acceptance in your interpersonal relations? The attitude of acceptance is expressed in three main ways: through warmth — expressing caring; through genuineness — trusting the person enough to be real and open yourself; and through empathy — understanding how the person feels and letting him or her know that you understand. These three ingredients have been found to characterize great teachers, great therapists, and healthy personal relationships. Psychologist Carl Rogers has studied the effect of these attributes and shown that personal growth is facilitated by such accepting relationships. According to *the Rogerian principle of personal growth, relationships characterized by warmth, genuineness, and empathy tend to produce positive personality change.*

Steps toward Better Relationships

Step 1. Disclosing feelings. You build trust in your relationships when you disclose your feelings in a straightforward way. Try to identify your feelings and name them: "I feel angry," or "I feel embarrassed." Take responsibility for the way you feel: rather than saying, "You make me angry," say "I feel angry with you." Try to express the way you feel in the present — now — rather than dwell on the past.

Step 2. Expressing acceptance. The second step to building trust in your relationships is to communicate acceptance when the other person

The Rogerian principle of personal growth: Relationships characterized by warmth, genuineness, and empathy tend to produce positive personality change.

Rogers reports a number of studies that evaluated the client-therapist relationship in psychotherapy and its relationship to the client's personality change. Positive personality change was regarded as a move away from rigid, impersonal functioning toward an open, changing way of behaving. Using the ratings of independent judges who listened to portions of tape-recorded therapy sessions, they found that relationships in which clients perceived therapists as genuine, as empathic, and as having unconditional regard for them were associated with positive personality change.

Bergin, A. E., and Solomon, S. Personality and performance correlates of empathetic understanding in psychotherapy. In J. T. Hart and T. M. Tomlinson (eds.), *New Directions in Client Centered Therapy.* Boston: Houghton Mifflin, 1970.

Rogers, C. The process equation of psychotherapy. *American Journal of Psychotherapy,* 1961, **15,** 27–45.

Tomlinson, T. M. and Hart, J. T. A validation study of the process scale. *Journal of Consulting Psychology,* 1962, **26,** 74–78.

discloses personal thoughts or feelings. To like and accept the other person is not the same as approving of everything the other person does. You can accept the person while rejecting one of his or her actions. Acceptance is communicated through warmth, empathic understanding, and genuineness. You express warmth by expressing liking. You express empathic understanding by listening actively to the other person and displaying your understanding through feedback. You express genuineness by being real and open yourself.

Step 3. Avoiding problems. There are some common difficulties in interpersonal relations that can be avoided when they are made conscious and recognized. Some of these problems appear below.[7]

(*a*) Unrealistic expectations — expecting a paragon instead of a human being; for example, expecting a loved one to be always attentive, patient, thoughtful and objective.

(*b*) Hostility — a tendency, usually associated with authority problems, to be antagonistic and suspicious toward other people.

(*c*) Overdependency — a tendency to lean excessively upon others for either material aid or emotional support and to rely upon them for making decisions.

(d) "I-it" orientation — a tendency to regard other people as objects rather than as other feeling, striving beings (I am an "I"; you are an "it").

(e) Emotional insulation — an inability to make the necessary emotional investment in a relationship, for fear of being hurt.

(f) Inferiority feelings — a basic lack of self-confidence or self-esteem which may be expressed either in oversensitivity to threat or in exaggerated efforts to prove one's own adequacy and worth by such techniques as boasting, showing off, and being hypercritical of other people.

Summary

Human relationships are complex and can be happy or frustrating. Friendship is a relationship dependent on physical proximity, shared experiences, similarity of attitudes, and the extent to which each person's needs are met. Good communication is also important to friendship. Effective communication involves the ability to send the message you want as well as the ability to listen to other people's messages. Disclosing your feelings is the basis of an honest relationship and is usually reciprocated. Acceptance of others is also necessary and can be expressed through warmth, trust, and empathy. Communication can play an important part in other problems such as shyness, anger, and relating to children.

Notes

1. Festinger, L. Architecture and group membership. *Journal of Social Issues,* 1951, **1,** 152–163.

2. Bossard, J. H. S. Residential propinquity as a factor in mate selection. *American Journal of Sociology,* 1932, **38,** 219–224.

3. Byrne, D., and Clore, G. L., Jr. Predicting interpersonal attraction toward strangers presented in three different stimulus modes. *Psychonomic Science,* 1966, **4,** 239–240.

4. Johnson, D. W. *Reaching out: Interpersonal effectiveness and self-actualization.* Englewood Cliffs, N.J.: Prentice-Hall, 1972.

5. Powell, J. *Why am I afraid to tell you who I am?* Chicago: Argus Communications, 1969.

6. Jourard, S. M. *The transparent self* (Revised edition). New York: Van Nostrand Reinhold, 1971.

7. Coleman, J. C. *Psychology and effective behavior.* Glenview, Ill.: Scott, Foresman, 1969.

Suggested Readings

Bach, G., and Deutsh, R. *Pairing.* New York: Avon Books, 1970.

Berne, E. *Games people play: The psychology of human relationships.* New York: Grove Press, 1964.

Buber, M. *I and thou.* New York: Scribner's, 1970.

Johnson, D. W. *Reaching Out: Interpersonal effectiveness and self-actualization.* Englewood Cliffs, N.J.: Prentice-Hall, 1972.

Jourard, S. M. *The transparent self* (Revised edition). New York: Van Nostrand Reinhold, 1971.

McCroskey, J. C., Larson, C. E., and Knapp, M. L. *Introduction to interpersonal communication.* Englewood Cliffs, N.J.: Prentice-Hall, 1971.

Wood, J. (ed.). *How do you feel?* Englewood Cliffs, N.J.: Prentice-Hall, 1974.

Chapter Eleven

Written by Stephanie Crane/Drawn by Ben Black

Coping with Shyness

When I was very young my parents often had relatives and friends visit our house. I never wanted to say hello to them and I tried hiding in my room, the closet, or the basement. When I had to sit down at meals with these people I would be polite, but I would have very little to say.

As I grew up I avoided parties and gatherings unless I knew most of the people. I was afraid to talk to girls and never did have a date until I was a senior in high school. I remember how embarrassed I used to become when I went out on a date. If there was any talk of sex I started blushing and could not look the other person in the eye.

In college I spent many nights alone in my dorm room. It was depressing, but it was easier than going out and facing the world. I used that time to study my music. I became an excellent flautist and started performing for larger and larger audiences. I wonder if the people listening to me would believe that I am shy?

Shyness is universal. It affects the young and the old, men and women, celebrities and ordinary people, and even college students. Shyness affects the way we act and communicate with other people. It involves a lack of social skills combined with a high level of anxiety. The lack of social skills usually includes a negative self-image (low self-esteem) and problems in interpersonal relations (listening, self-disclosure, expression of feelings, trust, and social attractiveness). Nonassertiveness, or not standing up for your own rights, is also a contributor to the syndrome we call shyness.

Before continuing, it may be interesting to determine your own level of shyness. Answer each of the following questions either true or false.

1. I feel relaxed even in unfamiliar social situations. F
2. I try to avoid situations which force me to be very sociable. F

165

3. It is easy for me to relax when I am with strangers. F
4. I have no particular desire to avoid people. T
5. I often find social occasions upsetting. F
6. I usually feel calm and comfortable at social occasions. T
7. I am usually at ease when talking to someone of the opposite sex. T
8. I try to avoid talking to people unless I know them well. F
9. If the chance comes to meet new people, I often take it. T
10. I often feel nervous or tense in casual get-togethers in which both sexes are present. F
11. I am usually nervous with people unless I know them well. T
12. I usually feel relaxed when I am with a group of people. T
13. I often want to get away from people. F
14. I usually feel uncomfortable when I am in a group of people I don't know. F
15. I usually feel relaxed when I meet someone for the first time. F
16. Being introduced to people makes me tense and nervous. T
17. Even though a room is full of strangers, I may enter it anyway. F
18. I would avoid walking up and joining a large group of people. F
19. When my superiors want to talk with me, I talk willingly. T
20. I often feel on edge when I am with a group of people. F
21. I tend to withdraw from people. F
22. I don't mind talking to people at parties or social gatherings. T
23. I am seldom at ease in a large group of people. F
24. I often think of excuses in order to avoid social engagements.
25. I sometimes take the responsibility for introducing people to each other. F
26. I try to avoid formal social occasions. F
27. I usually go to whatever social engagements I have. T
28. I find it easy to relax with other people. F

The above scale is called the social avoidance and distress (SAD) scale and was developed by David Watson and Ronald Friend.[1] In order to obtain your score, determine how many of your answers agree with the following answers: 1 F, 2 T, 3 F, 4 F, 5 T, 6 F, 7 F, 8 T, 9 F, 10 T, 11 T, 12 F, 13 T, 14 T, 15 F, 16 T, 17 F, 18 T, 19 T, 20 T, 21 T, 22 F, 23 T, 24 T, 25 F, 26 T, 27 F, 28 F. The mean, or average, score for males is approximately eleven and for females, approximately eight. People with high scores tend to avoid social interactions, prefer to work alone, talk less, and are more worried and less confident about social relationships.

Most people are shy in specific circumstances. This is called situational shyness. Many people, like the flautist at the beginning of the chapter, don't have confidence in their own social skills to comfortably interact with other people. They have trouble starting conversations, speaking up for their rights, saying "no," or disagreeing with other people. It may be certain people, or certain places, that leads to this situational shyness.

Susan had been in college for three years. She dated frequently, had many friends, and a variety of interests. She never considered herself a shy person. She enjoyed going to movies, concerts, parties, or just sitting around talking with her friends. As a student, Susan had maintained a B average, but many people who knew her felt she could do better. Susan's problem in school was that she was afraid to ask questions in large lecture classes. If she missed an important point or didn't understand the professor, she would just sit back and hope that someone else would ask the question she was thinking about. A friend who had seen Susan ask many intelligent questions in smaller classes asked her why she didn't raise her hand and ask questions in the larger classes. Susan would explain: "I wasn't sure my question was important," or "I didn't want to look foolish."

Susan was only shy in large lecture classes. This is an example of situational shyness. Some people are shy in almost all social situations. It is painful for them to meet strangers, to ask a question in class, and to participate in conversations. Because they avoid social interactions, they have few friends and are often lonely.

David was doing well enough in school but couldn't seem to manage his social life. He could not initiate a conversation or ask a girl for a date. He desperately wanted to have friends, but was so uncomfortable around other people that he avoided them whenever possible. One day, shortly after he first came to campus, he had to use the library but did not know where it was. It took him two hours to find it because he was too shy to stop someone to ask for directions.

How can shyness be overcome? The problem is complex and involves a number of steps.

The Need to Relax

One major contributor to shyness is anxiety; reducing shyness involves reducing anxiety. You may be unable to cope with shyness if you are constantly anxious when you are around other people. This fear may have developed in a number of ways. You may have had a bad social experience in the past that now makes you feel anxious. For example, if you had to make a speech in school and forgot what you were going to say and were laughed at by your schoolmates, you may now associate speech making with this negative consequence. You may also have developed your anxiety by watching and listening to another person who had a bad experience in a similar social situation.

As stated in Chapter Seven, anxiety that has been learned can be unlearned. One way to do this is through the use of relaxation exercises that are incompatible with anxiety. Joseph Wolpe described this incompatibility as the principle of *reciprocal inhibition.*

The principle of reciprocal inhibition: If a response that inhibits anxiety can be made to occur in the presence of an anxiety-evoking stimulus, it will weaken the connection between the stimulus and the anxiety.

The principle is based on a classic study of children's fears by Mary Clover Jones, in which a child was given attractive foods while a feared object was progressively brought closer and closer to the child. The object soon became associated with the food and the child's anxiety was reduced.

Currently, two common types of behaviors have been used by therapists to inhibit anxiety: relaxation and assertiveness. Each act of assertion or relaxation in a situation will weaken the relationship between the situation and anxiety. The technique of desensitization (see Chapter Seven) is based on the principle of reciprocal inhibition.

Hain, J. D., Butcher, H. G., and Stevenson, I. Systematic desensitization therapy: An analysis of results in twenty-seven patients. *British Journal of Psychiatry,* 1966, **112,** 295–307.

Jones, M. C. A laboratory study of fear: The case of Peter. *Pedagogical Seminary,* 1924, **31,** 308–315.

Wolpe, J. *Psychotherapy By Reciprocal Inhibition.* Stanford, Calif.: Stanford University Press, 1958.

If shyness is a problem for you, you might want to begin solving the problem by mastering progressive relaxation, a technique for reducing anxiety discussed in Chapter Six.

Social Attractiveness

Increasing your social attractiveness will help you cope with shyness. Few of us look like movie stars, but there are always ways to maximize your appearance. By keeping your hair clean and combed and wearing clothes that look good on you, you may be able to improve your social attractiveness. Getting feedback from your friends about your grooming and appearance is helpful.

But social attractiveness is more than just physical appearance. Going to different activities is part of social attractiveness. At first, you may just want to go somewhere that is familiar and comfortable, but eventually you should attempt to go to other places that interest you. The first time you might want to try going with a friend.

Once you meet people, you should be prepared to have something to talk about. If you are worried that you will have nothing to say, you will feel anxious and withdraw. If you prepare yourself, you will feel less anxious and have more rewarding social encounters. Reading books and newspapers, going to concerts, movies, and various sporting events, or even being able to tell stories or jokes will make you more socially attractive.

Becoming socially attractive requires that you develop and refine your social skills. Whenever you interact with others, you will need the skills that were discussed in Chapter Ten. You must be able to listen, express your feelings, disclose information about yourself, and trust other people.

Meeting many different types of people also increases social attractiveness. Try to introduce yourself to a few new people each week. Join in on informal group discussions with other friends. Just being out and participating in activities will lead to new and varied social contacts.

Being socially attractive takes patience and effort. You are not born socially attractive. Increasing your social attractiveness will help you cope with shyness.

Improving Your Self-Image

Reducing shyness involves improving your self-image. Your self-image (or self-esteem) is your evaluation of your self-worth. People with a good self-image appear confident and satisfied. People with a poor self-image appear overly sensitive and are often shy.

Your self-image is largely determined by comparing yourself to other people. Whom do you compare yourself to? It is important to choose appropriate models for comparison. A female choosing a beautiful actress as a model will probably feel physically inferior. When people have poor self-images, it is usually the result of their own evaluation of themselves. You can improve your self-image by changing some of the negative thoughts you have about yourself.

First, it is necessary to start thinking positively about yourself. List your strengths and set goals that realistically reflect these strengths. Try to find something you really excel in, and emphasize it. Start with some small tasks and build up to more important major objectives.

Try to eliminate negative self-statements like "I'm a failure." Don't say bad things about yourself or allow other people to attack you as a person. If people or activities lower your self-image, either change or eliminate the source of these bad feelings.

Even if you are shy only in specific situations, your overall self-image generally suffers. This happens because you tend to focus only on your problem instead of on your areas of strength or your personality as a whole. Try to keep the many aspects of your personality in mind when you evaluate yourself. Accentuating the positive and downplaying the negative will start you on the road to a better self-image.

Asserting Yourself

Alex really enjoyed going to movies and plays and would often wait in line for hours to get student price tickets. Yesterday, he had been waiting in line for concert tickets when he saw a person cutting in line in front of him. He didn't say anything, figuring others would not allow line cutting and would kick the person out of the line. Besides, it would only mean waiting a few minutes longer and he really didn't feel like bothering anybody.

Alex was not assertive. Reducing shyness involves becoming more assertive. Assertive behavior has been defined as "behavior which enables a person to act in his own best interests, to stand up for himself without undue anxiety, to express honest feelings comfortably or to exercise his own rights without denying the rights of others."[2] The line-cutting incident is a classic example of nonassertive behavior. Nonassertive people allow others to take advantage of them; they do not stick up for their own rights. This generally leads to frustration, unhappiness, or anxiety.

Alex could have been assertive by calmly approaching the person who had cut in line and simply stating: "I saw you cut in line. The line forms at the rear. People have been waiting here for hours. Please go to the end of the line." The response is direct, nonaggressive, and allows Alex to stick up for his own interests.

Certain nonverbal communications skills are essential to becoming assertive. You must have good eye contact with the person you are talking to; staring at someone, or never looking at them, leads to communication problems. Your facial expression must be consistent with the message you are trying to send; you can't express dissatisfaction while smiling. Nervous hand gestures and constant movement also distract from your intended message. Don't stand too close or too far away from the recipient; inappropriate body positioning and posturing can indicate a tentativeness in communicating your thoughts. In fact, you must use your body posture to emphasize important points.

How you verbalize your message may be as important as what you say. The message should be presented with a loudness that is appropriate to the circumstances and at a rate of speech that is not too fast or too slow. Try to avoid distracting verbal habits like "um" or "you know." Emotional tones should also be consistent with the emotion being expressed.

Mastering the basic communication skills will allow you to concentrate on what you want to say. Knowing that your message has been successfully communicated helps to overcome shyness.

Exercises—Assertiveness

To become more attuned to the way that your message is communicated, you can try one of the following exercises during a casual conversation with a friend.

1. Intentionally raise or lower your voice during part of your conversation.
2. Experiment with the amount of eye contact you have during a conversation. Try staring at the person as well as making no eye contact at all.
3. Vary your rate of speech from very fast to very slow.

What is the reaction of the other person? At what points do you feel comfortable? How do these variables affect the message you are trying to send?

A common assertive problem is initiating conversations. You may want to start a conversation by mentioning a common experience that you share with another person. Paying a complement or requesting information are other methods of initiating a conversation. Choose one or more of the following exercises in order to get some practice at initiating conversations.

1. Call a radio talk show and ask a question.
2. While standing in a long line, start a conversation with a stranger.
3. Before a movie, concert, or lecture, talk to the person sitting next to you.

Which technique of starting a conversation did you choose? Can you think of other general techniques that could be used to start a conversation?

Many assertive individuals have a hard time understanding what it feels like to be nonassertive. The following exercises might help the assertive person understand the feelings of nonassertiveness.

1. Go into a bar and ask for a glass of water.
2. Try to get a Mercedes-Benz dealer to let you test drive one of the cars.
3. Drive into a gas station and ask to have your windshield cleaned without buying any gas.

Step-by-Step Approach to Overcome Shyness

Step 1. To reduce anxiety and body tension, practice the progressive relaxation exercises in Chapter Six. Try to be fully relaxed in social situations.

Step 2. Practice the skills of interpersonal relations (listening, expression of feelings, self-disclosure, and trust) discussed in Chapter Ten.

Step 3. Begin to build your self-image by recognizing your strengths and by emphasizing past and current successes. Start with easy tasks and build up to major ones.

Step 4. De-emphasize negative statements or thoughts about yourself like "I am stupid." When you find yourself saying negative things about yourself, say "Stop."

Step 5. Keep a record of situations in which you feel shy. Try to write down where the situation took place, who was present, your behavior, and the consequences of your behavior. This will enable you to pinpoint recurring patterns of shyness and typical reactions to shyness.

Step 6. Take each situation in your journal and try to imagine how you would behave if you were not shy. If you are not sure of the correct behavior, try to imagine what the reaction would be of someone you know who is not shy.

Step 7. Consider different alternatives. There may be many ways to act assertively. Try to pick an alternative that makes you feel comfortable.

Step 8. Practice the appropriate behavior with a friend who is willing to act the part of another person.

Step 9. Get feedback from your friend regarding strengths and weaknesses of your behavior. Include nonverbal and verbal aspects of communication.

Step 10. Repeat the situation a few times, developing each time the weak areas that are observed by your friend.

Step 11. Apply the new behaviors to the "real life" situation as soon as possible. You should get feedback from the people involved in the situation as to whether your communication was assertive or nonassertive.

Step 12. Repeat steps 7 through 11 if you still find your behavior to be nonassertive.

Summary

Shyness is a common problem that may include anxiety, low self-esteem, poor interpersonal relations, a lack of social attractiveness, and nonassertiveness. Most people feel shy in specific situations or with specific people. In order to cope with shyness, you may have to deal with many different problems. You may have to learn to inhibit anxiety by using progressive relaxation. Improving the interpersonal skills of listening, expressing your feelings, self-disclosure, and trust will help you reduce feelings of shyness. Becoming socially attractive by improving your physical appearance, expanding your areas of interest, and increasing your social contacts may also be necessary. Your self-image can be improved by increasing positive thoughts, and decreasing negative thoughts, about yourself. Assertiveness, or standing up for your rights, is an essential component of overcoming shyness. Both nonverbal and verbal behaviors make up an assertive communication. Increasing assertiveness means practicing the appropriate responses and receiving feedback about your behavior.

Notes

1. Watson, D., and Friend, R. Measurement of social-evaluative anxiety. *Journal of Consulting and Clinical Psychology,* 1969, **33,** 448–457.

2. Alberti, R. E., and Emmons, M. L. *Your perfect right.* San Luis Obispo, Calif.: Impact, 1970.

Suggested Readings

Adler, R. B. *Confidence in communication: A guide to assertive and social skills.* New York: Holt, Rinehart and Winston, 1977.

Alberti, R. E., and Emmons, M. L. *Your perfect right.* San Luis Obispo, Calif.: Impact, 1978.

Smith, M. J. *When I say no, I feel guilty.* New York: Dial Press, 1975.

Zimbardo, P. G. *Shyness, what it is, what to do about it.* Reading, Mass.: Addison-Wesley, 1977.

Chapter Twelve

BATACAS ARE REALLY A GOOD WAY TO GET OUT YOUR ANGER.

I KNOW. I USED THAT PRINCIPLE LAST WEEK. I HIT TEN PEOPLE AND PRETENDED THEY WERE MY COUCH.

YOU'VE GOT IT IN REVERSE. YOU SHOULD HIT YOUR COUCH AND PRETEND IT IS THE PERSON YOU ARE ANGRY WITH.

WELL, WHAT DO YOU SUGGEST, BECAUSE I HATE MY COUCH?

Written by Stephanie Crane/Drawn by Ben Black

Dealing with Anger

Daniel James White was a 32-year-old former police officer who was described by most acquaintances as a handsome, athletic, ever achieving all-American boy. He had been captain of both the baseball and football teams and a Golden Gloves boxer while attending San Francisco's Woodrow Wilson High School. Son of a San Francisco fireman, he served in Vietnam, then worked three and one-half years as a policeman. He somehow managed to buy first an $8,000 Jaguar and a $15,000 Porsche, before taking leave of absence to hitchhike through the United States. After joining the Fire Department in 1973, he was cited for heroism for rescuing a mother and her child from the 17th floor of a burning building.

White had recently resigned as a member of the Board of Supervisors in San Francisco. On the morning of December 1, 1978, White entered the office of San Francisco mayor George Moscone and shot him in the right lung and the liver, and then twice in the head at extremely close range. He then reloaded his revolver, walked to the office of Supervisor Harvey Milk, and shot him three times in the body and twice in the head at close range. No one could believe that the man who did the killing was capable of such a deed.[1]

We all have different ways of expressing our anger. Daniel White's anger turned into homicide. Anger is perhaps the least accepted emotion that we have. It is a social emotion in that another person is usually involved. The emotion of anger may lead to aggression depending on the type of provocation, the situation, and an individual's method of coping. Before continuing, determine which of the following situations would anger or provoke you:[2]

_____ 1. On your way to go somewhere, you discover you have lost the keys to your car.

_____ 2. Going for a haircut and getting more cut off than you wanted.

_____ 3. You are walking along, minding your own business, when someone comes rushing past, knocking you out of his way.

_____ 4. Being called a liar.

_____ 5. You are in the midst of a dispute, and the other person calls you a stupid jerk.

_____ 6. Someone borrows your car, consumes one-third of a tank of gas, and doesn't replace it or compensate you for it.

_____ 7. You are waiting to be served at a restaurant. Fifteen minutes have gone by, and you still haven't received a glass of water.

_____ 8. Struggling to carry four cups of coffee to your table at a cafeteria, someone bumps into you, spilling the coffee.

_____ 9. You are typing a term paper, hurrying to make the deadline, and the typewriter jams.

_____ 10. Professors who refuse to listen to your point of view.

_____ 11. Being stood up for a date.

_____ 12. You are driving to pick up a friend at the airport and are forced to wait for a long freight train.

_____ 13. You are talking to someone and she doesn't answer you.

_____ 14. You have made arrangements to go somewhere with a person who backs off at the last minute and leaves you hanging.

_____ 15. Your car is stalled at a traffic light, and the guy behind you keeps blowing his horn.

_____ 16. Working hard on a project and getting a poor grade.

_____ 17. Someone makes a mistake and blames it on you.

_____ 18. You lend someone an important book and she fails to return it.

_____ 19. You are sitting next to someone who is smoking and he is letting the smoke drift right into your face.

_____ 20. Being told to go to hell.

_____ 21. Someone making fun of the clothes that you are wearing.

_____ 22. You use your last 10¢ to make a phone call, and you are disconnected before you finish dialing.

_____ 23. In a hurry to get somewhere, you tear a good pair of slacks on a sharp object.

_____ 24. While washing your favorite cup, you drop it and it breaks.

_____ 25. Being falsely accused of cheating.

Becoming Educated about Anger

What happens when you are angry? There are often biological, behavioral, and cognitive changes. Your muscles may become tense, blood pressure may rise, your heart may beat faster, and you may start grinding your teeth. Behaviorally, your voice may rise, or you may kick something, slam doors, or throw furniture. Cognitively, anger is a function of how you appraise a situation, what you expect, and then what you say to yourself. Many people say things to themselves that reflect a lack of tolerance for other people's mistakes (e.g., "that stupid jerk, he doesn't know what he is doing"), unreasonable expectations ("Why can't he drive as well as I do?"), or a necessity for retaliation ("she thinks she can take advantage of me; I'll get even with her"). Often these statements serve to escalate anger, especially when they are combined with physiological arousal. Beliefs, interpretations, self-statements, and other cognitions combine with physiological arousal to produce anger.

Anger produces many different effects. You become physically angry because the arousal of anger increases or energizes your behavior. Being highly aroused usually interferes with performing tasks. You start to act impulsively without thinking. Anger also serves to instigate aggressive actions. You learn to associate the arousal of anger with aggression.[3]

Exercise—Determining Your Angry Responses

As stated earlier, there are many different ways of responding to a provoking situation. Return to the list of situations at the beginning of the chapter and choose the response you would probably make from the following list:

1. I would curse or yell.
2. I would want to hit the person.
3. I would stay composed and try to hold back any angry feelings.
4. I would want to pound or kick something.
5. I would start an argument and tell the person off.
6. I would try to understand the situation, but would not feel angry.
7. I would feel angry, but would remain concerned with the task at hand and not express my anger.

8. I would feel angry and would try to express my anger appropriately.
9. I would have no reaction.

Do you inhibit your anger, try to deal with it constructively, or express it destructively? In situations that involve another person, would your response be different if his or her behavior were accidental rather than deliberate? What if the other person apologizes? What if it were a relative or friend rather than a stranger? A very big, strong person? A celebrity?

The cognitive physiological principle of emotion: Emotion depends upon your physiological arousal and your interpretation of the social situation.

You are usually aware of the fact that something is going on inside of you when you are angry, afraid, or sad. However, different emotions are associated with almost the same physiological changes — a state of general arousal. Usually when you tell someone you are angry, it is because of your appraisal of the social situation after you feel aroused. Schacter and Singer conducted an experiment where they injected some subjects (Group 1) with the drug epinephrine and told them (correctly) that it would produce such signs of physiological arousal as increased heartbeat and tremors of the hands and legs. Another group was injected with epinephrine and told nothing about the drug (Group 2). And a third group was injected with a neutral solution that had no effect. All subjects were then placed in a social situation that was either happy or angry. The results showed that Groups 1 and 3 did not experience strong emotional feelings. However, Group 2 subjects did feel either happy or sad, depending upon the particular social situation. The research concluded that you must have both physiological arousal and a cognitive explanation in order to experience an emotion. Knowing that your arousal is caused by a drug alone will not produce a strong emotional reaction. However, when you are physiologically aroused and have no explanation for your feelings, you label the emotion according to the emotions of people around you, and then behave accordingly.

Schacter, S. *Emotion, Obesity and Crime.* New York: Academic Press, 1971.
Schacter, S. and Singer, J. E. Cognitive, social and physiological determinants of emotional state. *Phychological Review,* 1962, **69,** 379–399.
Zillman, D. Excitation transfer in communication — Mediated aggressive behavior. *Journal of Experimental Social Psychology,* 1971, **7,** 419–434.

Consequences of Anger

Positive

Mental health workers know that anger can be used positively. The ability to express negative feelings or disappointments is necessary for a healthy relationship. If angry feelings are not expressed directly to the intended persons, the feelings are often discussed with a third party or in front of groups. This type of expression of feelings can only have negative consequences on a relationship. If you can express anger effectively, in nondestructive ways, you may be able to eliminate aggressive acts.

Expressing anger in a positive manner is usually an indication to the other person that you care enough about the relationship to want to make some changes. It shows respect for the other person by demonstrating that you are sharing your emotions. Positively expressing your anger demonstrates confidence in a relationship — confidence that the relationship can withstand turmoil and be strengthened. By experiencing anger constructively, you will experience increased feelings of relating; at the same time you make the other person aware of the need for greater understanding.

Perhaps the most important aspect of expressing anger positively is that it prevents the buildup of anger and negative pressures that are bad for both mental and physical health.

Negative

There are basically two ways of dealing with anger that has not been expressed appropriately: inhibiting anger and releasing aggression. Many people inhibit their anger and fail to express it. The type of people who don't want to make waves and just want to mind their own business most likely inhibit their angry feelings. Some people work very hard in not becoming angry. Other people think that if they forget about their angry feelings, the anger will go away. Inhibiting anger can also occur when a person tries to intellectually justify his or her feelings. The man who says to himself "I am angry at her, but I know she doesn't mean it and she will probably apologize tomorrow" is trying to weaken his angry feelings intellectually. His cognitions, what he is saying to himself, are inappropriate.

The extreme form of inhibiting anger is repression. The anger becomes unconscious and the person is not even aware that he or she is angry.

What happens when anger becomes inhibited? Anxiety, depression, guilt, sleep problems, overwork, and other symptoms may be related to this stored-up reservoir of anger. Additionally, many psychologists believe that psychosomatic disorders, such as headaches, high blood pressure, and asthma may arise from inhibited angry emotions.

The second negative consequence of anger is aggression. Aggression is the extreme form of self-assertion. But, unlike an assertive person, aggressive people get what they want at the expense of other people. They usually hurt other people and often humiliate them. This may lead to hatred and retaliation by the other people.

Aggression may be released both physically, as in Daniel White's case, and verbally. Screaming, swearing, having temper tantrums, throwing objects, and engaging in fist fights can all be considered aggressive acts.

What causes a person to become aggressive? Frustration is one cause that has been studied extensively.

John had been waiting in line for three hours for concert tickets. When the window opened at 10:00 A.M. an announcement was made that there were only 100 tickets available. Since there were about 200 people in front of him, John left the line to go home. He cursed at the person behind the ticket window who had made the announcement and was angry that there wasn't an earlier announcement. As he started to leave the parking lot, he backed into the car behind him, causing about $200 worth of damage.

John was frustrated, which made him angry and finally aggressive. If you are prevented from getting something you want, you are likely to feel angry and then to express that anger aggressively or destructively. But John did not express his anger directly at the people who frustrated him. Instead, his anger was displaced, or transferred, to a safe object that would not retaliate. Most of the time anger is displaced onto another person that resembles the frustrating person in some manner. If you become angry at your teacher (an authority figure) you may go home and displace the anger on your father.

If the aggression cannot be displaced, it may be turned inward and result in self-punishment. This may occur in many ways. Adults become self-punitive when they overeat, take dangerous drugs, or drink heavily.

Perhaps the most widely accepted theory of aggression states that aggression results from imitation and reinforcement. Proponents of this theory believe that children learn to express anger through aggression by observing it in society, in their parents, and in the media. Laboratory studies by Albert Bandura and his associates have supported this theory.[4] Children also learn that aggression is often rewarded. A young boy is often praised for fighting. Delinquent children and adults sometimes find that they get what they want by being aggressive. In this way, aggression replaces other, more appropriate ways of dealing with anger. Children who have been rewarded for being aggressive may fail to learn constructive ways of managing anger.

Managing Anger and Aggression

To manage anger you first must be able to accept angry feelings and then to express the anger appropriately. The first step, therefore, is to try to prevent a buildup of hostility by recognizing your anger and then verbally expressing it at the time you feel angry. An appropriate way to do this is to tell the other person that you are angry and also why you feel that way. Some common, constructive, verbal expressions of anger are: "I get very mad when you do that," or "That bothers me, stop doing it." Disclosing your feelings — by expressing your anger — need not hurt or provoke other people. Making the other person angry won't get you what you want. Learning to be assertive means expressing anger as well as other emotions (see Chapter Eleven).

Expressing Inhibited Anger

Anger that cannot be expressed accumulates to form a reservoir of angry emotions. This anger may then be released in unpredictable outbursts such as temper tantrums. A number of techniques have been developed to release these feelings of anger in less destructive ways.

Physical Releases

The physical release of anger has been called *catharsis*. There is still a controversy regarding the effectiveness of catharsis. One study showed that catharsis was effective in reducing subsequent aggression if it was expressed directly toward the person who made you angry.[5] One common form of constructive physical release is the bataca fight. A bataca is a foam bat with which people can hit each other at will without much pain. A good soft pillow can be used instead of batacas. A bataca fight must be agreed upon by both parties, and usually some handicap should be given to balance out physical inequities. For example, the stronger person may be only allowed to use the nondominant arm. Rules must be made as to what parts of the body can and cannot be hit, and there must be an agreed-upon time limit. This type of physical release of anger is helpful for many people who are not physically aggressive or who are frightened by physical aggression.

At times, a bataca spanking may be an appropriate physical release. The spanking is used when one person acknowledges a wrongdoing and allows the offended person to physically release feelings of hostility. Rules and time limits are negotiated as in the bataca fight. The offender is required to stand still and erect so that the other person can hit cleanly.

The final type of physical release involves the situation where the person at whom you are angry is not available. In this case, if you wanted to physically release your anger, you could start hitting a pillow as if it were the person you were angry at. Other techniques of individually releasing anger include trying to paint or draw your anger and expressing your anger in a physical activity such as running or pulling out weeds in your garden. Sports that involve hitting a ball, such as tennis, handball, or raquetball, can also be helpful in releasing anger.

Verbal Releases

Another class of cathartic releases of anger involves verbal outbursts. Angry verbal outbursts, reactions completely out of proportion to their provoking incidents, usually have a destructive effect on a relationship. This type of anger often occurs after a minor incident and may be the result of a pool of inhibited anger that has never been released. Verbal release techniques allow for these feelings to be expressed in a safe and structured situation.

A specific time each day should be mutually established for these verbal releases. At that time, the angry individual can yell, scream, and complain about all minor irritations and resentments. It is only a one-way explosion of anger, and the other person must listen and not respond to the anger.

An expansion of this technique involves two people verbally expressing their anger at each other at the same time without really listening to each other's comments. George Bach has appropriately termed this technique the "Virginia Woolf."[6] These angry outbursts are gross exaggerations of feelings using facial expressions, gestures, insults, and sarcasm. It is important to remember that a prior agreement on the rules of such an exchange is essential.

Controlling Aggression

People often become aggressive in an effort to take control of a situation in which their security is threatened. Changing self-statements is a method that enables you to gain control of the situation. Self-statements are what you say to yourself preceding, during, and following the event that "an-gers" you. They are important cognitive components to anger and aggression.

Susan often produced negative self-statements when she was put in an anger-provoking situation. One evening, she had been expecting her boyfriend at 6:00 P.M. and it already was 6:20 P.M. While she was waiting she told herself how mad she was that anyone could make her wait 20 minutes. She thought, "I am really going to let him have it if he ever gets here." When her boyfriend arrived at 6:30 P.M., she started to yell at him and would not listen to his explanations for being late. She would say to herself, "No excuse is going to make me feel any better," and "If he wants to fight, I'll fight him." After her boyfriend abruptly left her apartment Susan continued to produce negative self-statements such as "I am still angry and upset, I'm not even through telling him off."

In order to change self-statements it is necessary first to become aware of the statements you make during anger situations. If possible, you should record these statements in diary form for a two-week period. When reviewing the diary, try to pick out statements that are self-defeating or statements that increase feelings of anger. Try to come up with new self-statements for each part of your internal dialogue. For example, before the provocation you might want to say to yourself "I can do something to handle this situation," or "I don't have to get into an argument." These statements take the place of negative self-statements like, "I know I am going to fight with her."

When you are about to confront a situation try statements like "Stay relaxed and calm," or "It won't do any good to get mad." If you become more aroused and agitated try some similar statements like "It's not worth it to get upset," or "I think we should try to cooperate." If neces-sary, try to back off from the situation and analyze it as an outside ob-server might.

If these self-statements are successful you might want to try some self-reward statements like "I made it through without losing my temper," or "I'm really doing this well."

All these self-statements help to reduce the sense of a personal threat and allow you to focus in on the content of the task at hand.

Learning to Fight Fair

Once your anger is expressed, you will usually need a method of resolving interpersonal conflicts in a constructive manner. Using some of the methods previously discussed in this chapter, George Bach has developed a fair fight technique that is used only after the expression and reduction of less rational aspects of anger. This fair fight technique involves a verbal rather than a physical fight.

The fair fight allows both parties involved to totally air the issue. Bach states that "the only kinds of specific issues that are not negotiable under the fair fight format are disputes over behaviors that are beyond wilful control and therefore not open to change by an act of will. . . . These include smoking, alcoholism, and problems of temperament, such as tendencies to extreme mood swings, depression, and withdrawal."[6]

The fair fight involves techniques that emphasize how a conflict is resolved rather than the content of the dispute.

Steps in a Fair Fight

Step 1. The person with a complaint requests the other person to engage in a fair fight. If the other person agrees, a time and place for the fight is set.

Step 2. Fair fights should be carried out with other, neutral people present. Before initiating the fair fight, each person should have a strategy session with a neutral observer to help define the complaint and to develop a demand for change or resistance to the demand. The strategy session should be open so that everyone involved can listen.

Step 3. The initiator of the fight states his or her complaint and how the complaint affects the other person.

Step 4. The other person must repeat the complaint, not word for word but accurately reflecting its essence and the feelings of the initiator. From this point on in the fight, each participant must repeat every statement made by the other during the fight.

Step 5. The initiator states a "demand for change." This must be a change in behavior, not attitude.

Step 6. The other person responds to the complaint and the demand for change.

Step 7. The fair fight alternates back and forth with direct, simple statements.

Step 8. The fight is ended when there is an agreement for change, total rejection by one party, or the establishment of specific conditions for partial change.

Step 9. At a future meeting the success or failure of the agreement is discussed.

Summary

When you become angry, there are biological, behavioral, and cognitive changes. Anger serves many purposes and can have positive and negative consequences. Anger can be used positively to help solve problems in a relationship. Negative consequences of anger include inhibited or repressed anger and aggression. One cause of aggression may be frustration. Other explanations of aggression that are well supported by laboratory studies are imitation and reinforcement.

Physical and verbal cathartic techniques have been used to release inhibited anger. Altering what you say to yourself before, during, and after a provocation is an effective method of managing aggression. Learning fair fight techniques will allow you to manage interpersonal conflicts and to avoid angry outbursts. Managing your anger will take some work, but it should lead to better interpersonal relationships.

Notes

1. *Time,* December 11, 1978, pp. 24–26.

2. Novaco, R. W. *Anger control.* Lexington, Mass.: Lexington Books, 1975.

3. Bastiaans, J. The role of aggression in the genesis of psychosomatic disease. *Journal of Psychosomatic Research,* 1969, **13,** 311.

4. Bandura, A. *Aggression, a social learning analysis.* Englewood Cliffs, N.J.: Prentice-Hall, 1973.

5. Doob, A. N., and Wood, L. E. Catharsis and aggression: Effects of annoyance and retaliation on aggressive behavior. *Journal of Personality and Social Psychology,* 1972, **22,** 156–162.

6. Bach, G. B., and Goldberg, H. *Creative aggression, the art of assertive living.* New York: Avon, 1974.

Suggested Readings

Bach, G. R., and Goldberg, H. *Creative aggression, the art of assertive living.* New York: Avon, 1974.

Bandura, Albert. *Aggression, a social learning analysis.* Englewood Cliffs, N.J.: Prentice-Hall, 1973.

Lorenz, K. *On aggression.* New York: Bantam Books, 1966.

Novaco, R. W. *Anger control.* Lexington, Mass.: Lexington Books, 1975.

Rubin, T. I. *The angry book.* New York: Collier Books, 1969.

Schree, K. R., Abeles, R. P., and Fischer, C. S. *Human aggression and conflict: Interdisciplinary perspectives.* Englewood Cliffs, N.J.: Prentice-Hall, 1975.

Chapter Thirteen

Written by Stephanie Crane/Drawn by Ben Black

Relieving Depression

Alice has been feeling low for about eight months now. Like everyone else, she has had "down" periods before, but they have usually not lasted this long. She doesn't feel like doing much, has had trouble sleeping and eating, has lost her sense of humor, and is starting to wonder whether she is ever going to feel better.

Her relationship with her family has her worried. She feels that she is a burden on them and that her gloominess is affecting her husband and teenage children. Her job responsibilities are also a source of concern. As a real estate agent, her pace is generally quite fast. But in the last few months, she has slowed down considerably. She is just not functioning as efficiently as she used to. And though she has tried, she can't get herself motivated.

Alice is tired of feeling sad and blue. But even worse, she is afraid that there may be something seriously wrong with her. At times she's even wondered whether she might be losing control, having a "mental break-down," or even going crazy. She just doesn't understand what is happening to her and doesn't know how to overcome her distress. Yet her doctor tells her that there is nothing physically wrong with her.[1]

Almost everyone feels down or sad at one time or another and most people describe these feelings as "depression." Depression is one of the most common psychological problems. It consists of a number of behaviors and feelings that are present in different combinations in different people.

Depressed people, like Alice, often have a reduced activity level and are not motivated to participate in activities. Often the depressed person has trouble relating to others and as a result withdraws from social contact. Some depressed people feel guilty because they believe they are failures, and others feel weighed down by demands that are made upon them.

191

Perhaps the most common feeling of depression is dysphoria, or a sad-feeling state, characterized by crying spells.

Physical problems are common among depressed people. Fatigue, sleep problems, loss of appetite, and reduced sexual interest are frequent complaints.

At this point it may be helpful for you to determine your own level of depression. Complete the following questionnaire before continuing the chapter.

Beck Depression Inventory[1]

Read the entire group of statements in each category. Then pick out the one statement in the group which best describes the way you feel *today,* that is, *right now.* Circle the number beside the statement you have chosen. If several statements in the group seem to apply equally well, circle each one.

Be sure to read all the statements in the group before making your choice.

Sadness
0   I do not feel sad
1   I feel blue or sad
2a   I am blue or sad all the time and I can't snap out of it
2b   I am so sad or unhappy that it is quite painful
3   I am so sad or unhappy that I can't stand it

Pessimism
0   I am not particularly pessimistic or discouraged about the future
1   I feel discouraged about the future
2a   I feel I have nothing to look forward to
2b   I feel that I won't ever get over my troubles
3   I feel that the future is hopeless and that things cannot improve

Sense of failure
0   I do not feel like a failure
1   I feel I have failed more than the average person
2a   I feel I have accomplished very little that is worthwhile or that means anything
2b   As I look back on my life all I can see is a lot of failure
3   I feel I am a complete failure as a person (parent, spouse)

Dissatisfaction
0   I am not particularly dissatisfied
1   I feel bored most of the time

2a I don't enjoy things the way I used to
2b I don't get satisfaction out of anything any more
3   I am dissatisfied with everything

Guilt
0   I don't feel particularly guilty
1   I feel bad or unworthy a good part of the time
2a I feel quite guilty
2b I feel bad or unworthy practically all the time now
3   I feel as though I am very bad or worthless

Expectation of punishment
0   I don't feel I am being punished
1   I have a feeling that something bad may happen to me
2   I feel I am being punished or will be punished
3a I feel I deserve to be punished
3b I want to be punished

Self-dislike
0   I don't feel disappointed in myself
1a I am disappointed in myself
1b I don't like myself
2   I am disgusted with myself
3   I hate myself

Self-accusations
0   I don't feel I am worse than anybody else
1   I am critical of myself for my weaknesses or mistakes
2   I blame myself for my faults
3   I blame myself for everything that happens

Suicidal ideas
0   I don't have any thoughts of harming myself
1   I have thoughs of harming myself but I would not carry them out
2a I feel I would be better off dead
2b I feel my family would be better off if I were dead
3a I have definite plans about committing suicide
3b I would kill myself if I could

Crying
0   I don't cry any more than usual
1   I cry more than I used to
2   I cry all the time now. I can't stop it
3   I used to be able to cry but now I can't cry at all even though I want
    to

Irritability
0   I am no more irritated now than I ever am
1   I get annoyed or irritated more easily than I used to
2   I feel irritated all the time
3   I don't get irritated at all at things that used to irritate me

Social withdrawal
0   I have not lost interest in other people
1   I am less interested in other people now than I used to be
2   I have lost most of my interest in other people and have little
     feeling for them
3   I have lost all my interest in other people and don't care about them
     at all

Indecisiveness
0   I make decisions about as well as ever
1   I try to put off making decisions
2   I have great difficulty in making decisions
3   I can't make any decisions at all anymore

Body image change
0   I don't feel I look any worse than I used to
1   I am worried that I am looking old or unattractive
2   I feel that there are permanent changes in my appearance and they
     make me look unattractive
3   I feel that I am ugly or repulsive looking

Work retardation
0   I can work as well as before
1a   It takes extra effort to get started doing something
1b   I don't work as well as I used to
2   I have to push myself very hard to do anything
3   I can't do any work at all

Insomnia
0   I can sleep as well as usual
1   I wake up more tired in the morning than I used to
2   I wake up 2–3 hours earlier than usual and find it hard to get back
     to sleep
3   I wake up early every day and can't get more than 5 hours sleep

Fatigability
0   I don't get any more tired than usual
1   I get tired more easily than I used to
2   I get tired from doing nothing
3   I get too tired to do anything

Anorexia
0   My appetite is not worse than usual
1   My appetite is not as good as it used to be
2   My appetite is much worse now
3   I have no appetite at all

Weight loss
0   I haven't lost much weight, if any, lately
1   I have lost more than 5 pounds
2   I have lost more than 10 pounds
3   I have lost more than 15 pounds

Somatic preoccupation
0   I am no more concerned about my health than usual
1   I am concerned about aches and pains or upset stomach or consti-
     pation
2   I am so concerned with how I feel or what I feel that it's hard to
     think of much else
3   I am completely absorbed in what I feel

Loss of libido
0   I have not noticed any recent change in my interest in sex
1   I am less interested in sex than I used to be
2   I am much less interested in sex now
3   I have lost interest in sex completely

To score the questionnaire, add up the points you receive from your responses to each item. If you circled more than one response for an item, add only the points for the highest numbered response.

If your score is between 0 and 4 you are probably not depressed. If your score is between 5 and 15 you may be mildly to moderately depressed and may benefit by utilizing some of the techniques in this chapter. If your score is 16 or higher, you may try to use the techniques in this chapter but may also want to consider obtaining professional assistance as recommended in Chapter Two. Regardless of your score on this questionnaire, if you find yourself seriously thinking about suicide, you should seek professional assistance.

Theories of Depression

In ancient times, depression was called melancholia. Theories of depression date back to Hippocrates in 400 B.C. He felt that depression was caused by an excess of black bile in the body. Many subsequent theories stressed a biological cause for depression, and some current theorists still believe that depression may have a physiological base.[3]

Psychodynamic Theory

The psychodynamic theory of depression emphasizes the importance of internal psychological processes. Freud and his followers argued that certain early childhood experiences predisposed individuals to become depressed and that depression resulted when these people encountered frustration or loss later in life.

According to this theory, these predisposing experiences occur when the infant's needs are not satisfactorily met during the oral stage of personality development: the first year of life, when the infant is completely dependent upon parents for food and protection. According to Freud, insufficient gratification of needs during this first year of life is regarded by infants as a lack of love and as proof that they are not worthy of love. This leads to such personality traits as low self-esteem, reliance on external definitions of self-worth, and high dependency needs.

The psychodynamic theory assumes that depression results when a person having such predisposing traits experiences certain frustrations: the real or imagined loss of a love relationship, personal or economic failure, loss of health or power, or other setbacks. Such frustrations lead to a partial regression to the oral stage of development, the arousal of heightened dependency needs, and hostility toward those who could gratify dependency needs. The inability to express this hostility leads to the turning of anger against the self. Anger turned inward results in self-hatred and depression.

Reinforcement Theory

The reinforcement theory assumes that depression results from a reduction of positively reinforced behavior. Peter Lewinsohn believes that people become depressed when interactions with other people and the environment are not rewarded.[2] Sometimes these interactions become associated with unpleasant or punishing consequences that will discourage people from repeating the interaction in the future.

There are many different ways that interactions can lose their reinforcing value. When you have to produce a great deal of work to receive a reinforcement, you may lose interest in working. A good example is working on a term paper. You may put in many hours of work on the paper and never receive any reinforcement until your grade comes back one month later or you receive feedback from your professor. Behavior can also be reduced, or weakened, by punishment, such as criticism, or by withdrawal of rewards. For example, you studied three hours a night during high school and received straight A's and you are now studying the same amount of time in college and receiving C's. Your behaviors that were once rewarded are now no longer rewarded. With the loss of these important rewards, you may become depressed.

Behavior can be weakened by a sudden change in the environment. This may happen when someone you know dies.[4] Many of your behaviors may have been reinforced by, or associated with, the person who died. Eliminating that reinforcement and interaction may lower your activity level and leave you depressed.

Lewinsohn and his colleagues have extended the reinforcement theory of depression to include social learning theory, a process of learning through observation and imitation. In their view, not only environmental events but poor social skills can lead to reduced reinforcement and then depression. Social learning may also contribute to maintaining depression. Receiving sympathy, attention, and concern from others when you are depressed may reinforce depressive behaviors.

Learned Helplessness

People often become depressed after a particularly stressful life event (e.g., failure in school, a death in the family, or rejection from a spouse or lover). Some people are able to cope with stress while others feel helpless. The concept of learned helplessness states that depressed people learn, or believe, that they have no control over the stresses of life; they feel unable to relieve their suffering and to increase their gratification.

How does the experience of traumatic events lead to learned helplessness? It is not the traumatic event that interferes with effective responses, but the fact that the individual does not have control over the traumatic event. The individual learns that his or her responding does not produce the desired outcome. In essence, you learn that your behavior and reinforcement are independent.

If learned helplessness in animals is similar to depression in people, how is it overcome? In experiments with animals, Seligman found that it was necessary to forceably drag the animal to the side of the cage that would terminate the electric shock. After this was done many times the animal completely recovered from helplessness.[5] Extending this concept to humans, it would be necessary to show the depressed person that his or her responding does produce the gratification desired. Aaron Beck has

The principle of learned helplessness: An inability to control a trau-matic experience will lead to a loss of motivation, a powerless and hopeless attitude, and a poor outlook on the future.

The concept of learned helplessness was originally observed in laboratory animals. A typical experiment to demonstrate learned helplessness first places an animal in a situation where it is unable to avoid or escape serious electric shocks. The next day the animal is placed back in the same situation, except that it is now able to escape the shock by jumping over a barrier into the next compartment. Animals that were originally unable to escape the shock are slower to escape than animals that were never exposed to the original shocks.

Other effects that were noticed with experimental animals included the fact that learned helplessness is associated with reduced aggression and with less social and sexual behavior.

Overmier, J. B. and Seligman, M. E. P. Effects of inescapable shock upon subsequent escape in avoidance learning. *Journal of Comparative and Physiological Psychology,* 1967, **63,** 23–33.

Seligman, M. E. P. Depression in learned helplessness. In R. J. Friedman and M. M. Katz (eds.), *The Psychology of Depression: Contemporary Theory and Research.* Washington, D.C.: Winston-Wiley, 1974.

Seligman, M. E. P. and Maier, S. F. Failure to escape traumatic shock. *Journal of Experimental Psychology,* 1967, **74,** 1–9.

successfully used this type of technique in his work with depressed patients.[6]

What Keeps You Depressed

When you have few positive interactions and an increase in negative interactions you start feeling depressed. When you start feeling depressed you generally participate in fewer activities, which makes you feel more depressed. This type of cycle ·continues until you feel very depressed and are very inactive.

If this depression continues for a long time you start to become pessimistic. You expect negative interactions. You lose interest and motivation and you start to feel guilty that you are letting other people down.

Many people try to talk about their depression to friends and family. Often, the sympathy and attention given to the depression will act as a reinforcer of the depressive behavior; since reinforcement strengthens behavior, the person's depressive behavior is maintained.

Techniques have been developed that enable the depressed person to break the downward cycle of depression and to change depressive thought patterns.

Reducing Depression

People who are depressed frequently experience anxiety or tension in social situations. This anxiety may lead to physical symptoms, such as headaches or sleeping problems, which may lead to stronger feelings of depression. One way to break this chain of events is to relieve the anxiety. Learning and using progressive relaxation techniques (discussed in Chapter Six) should help reduce tension.

Once you feel relaxed you still may have problems with interpersonal relations that would make you feel depressed. Depressed people generally feel uncomfortable in social situations, are unassertive, and are unable to appropriately express anger. Mastery of many of the techniques discussed in Chapters Ten, Eleven, and Twelve may be needed by some depressed people to reduce depression.

Pleasant Activities

When you are not depressed you usually engage in activities that are enjoyable. Since depression is often associated with a decrease in your participation of the enjoyable activities, to relieve depression you should increase your participation. Different types of activities are enjoyable for different people. Researchers have found that the following three types are important in the relief of depression:[2] (1) friendly and meaningful interactions with other people; (2) activities that make you feel competent, adequate, and independent (e.g., completing a successful project); and (3) activities associated with emotions that are incompatible with depression (e.g., relaxation or laughter). For many people, jogging or physical exercise helps to relieve their depression.

Exercise—Discovering Pleasant Activities

Before continuing, try to develop your own list of 15 pleasant activities. Some examples are: being with friends, pleasure reading, going to a party, eating a good meal, going on a date, laughing.

How often have your 15 activities occurred in the previous month? Try to keep an accurate record of these pleasant activities during the next one or two weeks. Do you feel that most people become depressed because they do not participate in pleasant activities or that once you are depressed, you do not participate in pleasant activities?

Why do people reduce their participation in pleasant activities? For many people there is a pressure to perform unpleasant and everyday types of activities. Having three final exams and two papers due in one week might lead to reduction in your pleasant activities. Other people have a hard time choosing what activities are pleasurable.

If you have major changes in your life, such as an illness, moving away from friends, or losing a loved one, some of the pleasant activities that were formerly enjoyed may now be unavailable. The person who exercises every day and then breaks his leg and is unable to exercise may become depressed.

Finally, if you experience anxiety and tension during your pleasant activities it will detract from your enjoyment of them.

Reducing Depressive Thoughts

Jack tried to pull himself out of his depression by going out with his friends and participating in many of his pleasant activities. However, each time he went to a party he would tell himself, "I'm not going to enjoy this party," or "No one wants to meet a failure." He would come home feeling more depressed than when he left. Jack tried to keep busy all day but was constantly worried and thinking negative thoughts.

Many people participate in pleasant activities but still feel depressed. Most likely they are producing a large number of negative thoughts. Common depressive thoughts are "I am worthless," "Nobody cares about me," or "I am sick." If these negative thoughts can be decreased and replaced by positive thoughts (e.g., "I really enjoy my job," or "I am bright"), it will aid in reducing depression.

But how do you eliminate the negative thoughts? One technique, mentioned in Chapter Eleven, is called *thought stopping.* Each time you find yourself thinking a negative thought shout "stop!" and then redirect your thinking to positive thoughts. A gentler method to reduce negative thoughts is to tell yourself calmly to stop thinking about the thought and to allow your thinking to move back to other, nonnegative thoughts.

Many people need time during the day to purge themselves of negative thoughts. If this is true for you, establish a set time every day for "worrying."

Once negative thoughts have been reduced they should be replaced by positive thoughts.

Exercise—Identifying Positive Thoughts

The purpose of this exercise is to generate a list of five positive thoughts. One of the best ways to establish this list is to observe closely what you accomplished during the day. Many depressed people do not feel they have accomplished anything when, in fact, their day has been productive. Examples of everyday activities and the corresponding positive thoughts are: (1) Having a pleasant talk with friends (I really enjoy talking with people); (2) Scheduling your time for the day (I am good at scheduling my day); (3) Finishing a task (It's great that I am able to follow through on a project).

Use your daily activities to help you generate a list of five positive thoughts. Having this reserve of positive thoughts will enable you to substitute each of these thoughts for a negative thought that has been eliminated.

Why is it important to replace negative thoughts with positive thoughts? How do other people influence your positive and negative thoughts?

A Step-by-Step Program to Relieve Depression

Step 1. Determine your level of depression by completing the Beck Depression Inventory. Generally, if your score is in the 5–15 range this program may be helpful.

Step 2. Keep track of your mood by rating it at the end of each day (1 = very depressed, 9 = very happy). Keep a record throughout the entire program.

Step 3. If anxiety and tension are contributing to your depression, try learning the progressive relaxation techniques discussed in Chapter Six.

Step 4. If inappropriate or poor social skills are contributing to your depression, you may want to review the techniques discussed in Chapters Ten, Eleven, and Twelve.

Step 5. Based on your past records of pleasant activities, set a goal for a modest increase in the number of pleasant activities you will participate in during the next week. Gradually increase this goal each week until you're satisfied with the number of pleasant activities you are doing each week. Try to be consistent each day of the week. Participating in four pleasant activities each on Monday and Tuesday is much better than two on Monday and six on Tuesday.

Step 6. Reward yourself each week you attain your goal of pleasant activities. Buy yourself small presents or treat yourself to a good meal each week that you are successful.

Step 7. Reduce the number of negative thoughts you produce by using the thought-stopping techniques discussed in this chapter.

Step 8. Increase use of the list of positive thoughts you developed earlier in this chapter. It may be helpful if you write the thoughts down on 3 × 5 index cards and pull out individual cards randomly during the day and read them. You can use certain times of the day (e.g., meals or driving time) as reminders to use these positive thoughts.

Step 9. Evaluate the program by comparing your current mood scores and Beck Depression Inventory score to your earlier scores for both.

Remember: It is normal to feel sad and depressed at times. But when depression leads to a loss of hope and to a negative outlook on life, you should try actively to change that feeling state.

Summary

Depression is a very common feeling and a common psychological problem. Many different symptoms are part of the depression syndrome. Several different theories of depression have been formulated. Psychodynamic theory assumes that early childhood experiences predispose you to becoming depressed. Reinforcement theory assumes that depression results from a reduction of reinforcements. The learned helplessness theory of depression is derived from experiments with laboratory animals and states that people become depressed over an inability to control traumatic events.

Depressive behavior often leads to more depression. Other people also may inadvertently reinforce depression. To reduce depression it first is necessary to eliminate tension and anxiety, to become comfortable in social situations, and to act assertively. Increasing pleasant activities and positive thoughts and decreasing negative, depressive thoughts are techniques that have been used successfully with many depressed people.

Notes

1. Beck, A. T. *Depression.* New York: Harper & Row, 1967.

2. Lewinsohn, P. M., Munoz, R. F., Youngren, M. A., and Zeiss, A. M. *Control your depression.* Englewood Cliffs, N.J.: Prentice-Hall, 1978.

3. Akiskal, H. S., and McKinney, W. T. Depressive disorders: Towards a unified hypothesis. *Science,* 1973, **182,** 20–29.

4. Ferster, C. B. Animal behavior in mental illness. *Psychological Record,* 1966, **16,** 345–356.

5. Seligman, M. E. P. Chronic fear produced by unpredictable shock. *Journal of Comparative and Physiological Psychology,* 1968, **65,** 402–411.

6. Beck, A. T. Cognitive therapy: Nature and Relation to behavior therapy. *Behavior Therapy,* 1970, **1,** 184–200.

Suggested Readings

Friedman, R. J., and Katz, M. M. (eds.). *The psychology of depression: Contemporary theory and research.* Washington, D.C.: Winston-Wiley, 1974.

Kline, N. S. *From sad to glad.* New York: Ballantine Books, 1975.

Lewinsohn, P. M., Munoz, R. F., Youngren, M. A., and Zeiss, A. M. *Control your depression.* Englewood Cliffs, N.J.: Prentice-Hall, 1978.

Seligman, M. E. P. *Helplessness.* San Francisco: W. H. Freeman, 1975.

Chapter Fourteen

Written by Stephanie Crane/Drawn by Ben Black

Influencing Others

Even in a business that isn't noted for the subtlety of its sales pitch, Detroit auto salesman Joe Girard is something special. If you admire his flashy sport shirt, the fast-talking Girard will take it off and hand it to you right there in his office. If you want a drink, he will pop open the bar he keeps there. If somebody else offers you a better deal, Girard will undercut him every time. "I'll do anything to make a sale," Girard boasts. "I'll kiss the baby. I'll hug the wife. It's nothing but an act." The act has made Joe Girard, who is rather ordinary in most respects, the world's champion automobile salesman. Girard sold an astounding total of 1,208 Chevrolets to individual customers last year alone—and that was the seventh straight year in which he ranked No. 1.

"I don't even know nothing about a car," Girard concedes.[1]

How can Girard sell something that he knows nothing about? If selling were primarily the communication of product information, Girard would sell nothing; but selling is rarely based on information — or when it is, the information is often exaggerated or false. Centuries ago, advertisements primarily served to convey information about the availability of products. One of the earliest examples of an advertisement in a periodical stated:

That excellent, and by all physicians approved *China* drink, called by the Chinese *Tcha,* by other nations *Tay* alias *Tee,* is sold at the Sultaness Head Cophee-House, in Sweeting's Rents, by the Royal Exchange, London.[2]

Today, there is so much competition for the consumer dollar that mere facts will rarely sell. A review of a decade of studies of advertising effectiveness concluded that while consumers learn new information from advertisements in the mass media, the information they acquire has little effect on their attitudes or behavior. The review found "no relationship

205

between what a person learned, knew, or recalled on the one hand, and what he did or how he felt on the other."[3]

Modern advertisements do not convey much information. They feed on fear, insecurity, and self-doubt; and they appeal to sexual and achievement needs. In one author's opinion, the women in TV ads are all paranoid:

They believe they will lose love, respect, friendship, everything that makes life tolerable, if their coffee is judged to be under par. One bride who's just moved into a neighborhood is convinced that nobody in the precinct will give her a second chance, if she lays a rotten cup of coffee on them. Another cringes when her mother-in-law sneers at her coffee. . . .

Out-of-work movie stars are involved in some of the most ludicrous commercials aimed at women. Like the one featuring the pretentious lovely who, Barrymore throb in voice, explains how passionate she is when her children's welfare is at issue. She doesn't permit them to chunk just any old garbage down their precious throats. Spinach, you figure she's selling. Or grapefruit. Forget it. She's pushing cupcakes.[4]

Advertisers have learned an elementary psychological fact: the most important influence on people is other people. People move people.

Some people are able to influence others easily. Take the following quiz to determine your attitude about influencing others; check the point on the scale that most closely represents your attitude.

	Disagree a lot	Disagree a little	Neutral	Agree a little	Agree a lot
1. The best way to handle people is to tell them what they want to hear.	1	2	3	4	5
2. When you ask someone to do something for you, it is best to give the real reasons for wanting it rather than giving reasons which might carry more weight.	1	2	3	4	5
3. Anyone who completely trusts anyone else is asking for trouble.	1	2	3	4	5

	Disagree			Agree	
	a lot	a little	Neutral	a little	a lot
4. It is hard to get ahead without cutting corners here and there.	1	2	3	4	5
5. It is safest to assume that all people have a vicious streak and it will come out when they are given a chance.	1	2	3	4	5
6. One should take action only when sure it is morally right.	1	2	3	4	5
7. Most people are basically good and kind.	1	2	3	4	5
8. There is no excuse for lying to someone else.	1	2	3	4	5
9. Most men forget more easily the death of their father than the loss of their property.	1	2	3	4	5
10. Generally speaking, men won't work hard unless they're forced to do so.	1	2	3	4	5

To find your score, add the numbers you have checked on questions 1, 3, 4, 5, 9 and 10. For the other four questions, reverse the numbers you checked — 5 becomes 1, 4 is 2, 2 is 4, 1 is 5. Total your 10 numbers. This is your score. The higher your score, the more effective you probably are in manipulating others. The National Opinion Research Center used this form in a random sample of American adults and found that the national average was 25.[5]

The Salesperson

Good salespeople have also made an art of interpersonal influence. The characteristics of the salesperson — as the source of influence and persuasion — make an important difference in the effectiveness of selling.

Some people are more believable, or credible, than others; and the most credible are the most persuasive. People tend to believe those whom they respect or admire. This effect is demonstrated in the following example:

At the beginning of class the professor introduces a "Dr. Hans Schmidt" to the students, informing them that the guest is a "research chemist of international renown currently employed by the U.S. Government to study the properties of gas diffusion." Dr. Schmidt, clad in a full length white lab coat and sporting a well-tended goatee, then steps forward and, in a heavy German accent, tells the class he wishes to test the properties of a new chemical vapor he has developed. "Specifically," he says, "I wish to determine how quickly the vapor diffuses throughout the room and how readily people can detect it." Pointing to a small glass beaker the doctor continues: "Therefore I would ask your cooperation in a little experiment. I am going to pull this stopper and release the vapor. It is completely harmless but purposely treated to smell like gas—the kind you smell around a stove when the burner doesn't ignite. This particular sample is highly odorous so no one should have any trouble detecting its presence. What I want you to do is raise your hand as soon as you smell the vapor. Are there any questions?" At this point the "chemist" pulls the stopper and releases the "vapor." Very soon, and in a very orderly manner, hands begin going up—first in the front rows and then on back—like a wave rolling through the lecture hall.[6]

The beaker contains only water and the "chemist" is an instructor in the German department. People believe those whom they perceive as authorities. People also tend to believe those who appear to have nothing to gain by the interchange; some of the highest-paid actresses in TV commercials are those who act like the next-door neighbor and appear to be offering a free testimonial. In the long run, however, it makes little difference whether the salesperson is credible or not; over time, people tend to forget the sources of their ideas; even if the idea was planted by a TV commercial of which they were highly skeptical, later the idea will become dissociated from the untrustworthy source and stand alone.

If you are trying to make a sale today, however, what happens in the long run may not interest you. You are interested in the effectiveness of your persuasion now, not later. Under these conditions, your credibility does make a difference. What can you do if you are not a particularly credible source? Should you let this be known before you make your sales pitch or afterwards? Comparative studies show that your message will be more persuasive if you delay identifying your lack of authority until afterwards.[7]

Likability as well as credibility is an important characteristic of the effective salesperson. A salesperson is more likely to be persuasive if he or she initially expresses views shared by the buyer.[8] One study compared an individual's persuasiveness following a period of contrived friendly or unfriendly interaction with the audience.[9] Friendliness gave him a stronger influence. The experimenter concluded: "Make sure the person you are trying to persuade likes you in the first place, or your efforts are likely to be in vain."[9]

A structural engineer who was friendly and persuasive might make a good salesperson for the Brooklyn Bridge.

The Buyer

The appeal once made by the Red Cross to the patriotism of potential donors proved to be a dismal failure. This was because abstract, ideological principles rarely motivate immediate, concrete action. Using the skillful techniques of motivation research, it was determined that giving blood arouses many unconscious anxieties, especially with men, by whom it is equated with giving away part of their virility and strength. . . .

To get a man to give blood, then, it is vital to make him feel more masculine, to prove that he has so much virility he can afford to give away a little, and to make him personally proud of any suffering (for example, by giving him a pin in the form of a white drop of blood, the equivalent of a wounded soldier's Purple Heart Medal). . . .

In this particular instance, the recommended persuasive tactics did, in fact, result in a sudden, dramatic increase in blood donations to the Red Cross.[10]

The attitudes of consumers influence their needs, perceptions of products, their preferences, and their buying habits. Understanding the underlying attitudes and motives of consumers is the aim of those psychologists who work in motivational research for industry. They are especially concerned with identifying and manipulating what they believe are unconscious determinants of consumer attitudes and behavior.

One airline company advertised their new jets and emphasized how fast passengers could travel from their homes to another city; sales declined. The airline utilized motivational research to determine the problem. The researchers discovered that potential passengers felt guilty about leaving home for business trips. The airline subsequently began advertising how fast their new jets could bring passengers back home again, after a business trip; sales increased dramatically.[10]

The effective salesperson must consider who the potential buyer is and why he or she might buy the product or service. The "why" here involves more than rational reasons; most consumption is irrational — the choice between most products is an illusory choice, there often being essentially no difference between competing brands.

The Sale

Selling is persuading people to decide to buy your product. Deciding to buy many things today involves fairly heavy decisions. One way salespeople overcome resistance to making large decisions is to induce people first to make small decisions. This technique is called the "foot-in-the-door technique."

The foot-in-the-door technique has probably been used on you. A salesperson calls and asks you to answer a few questions for a "survey." An advertisement in the paper invites you to return a coupon for a free booklet. You are asked to accept a free sample. Or a car dealer asks you to come down to the showroom for a party. Once you have taken a small step, a larger step is more likely; once a salesperson has a "foot" in your door, you are more likely to open the door all the way.

In one study, a group of women was contacted by experimenters who explained that they were working for the Committee for Safe Driving.[11] They asked the women to sign petitions urging the legislature to give more attention to driving safety; most of the women signed the petition. Later, the experimenters called again on these women — and another group who had not been previously contacted — and asked each of them to permit the committee to put in their front yards a large, unattractive sign reading "Drive Carefully." The women who had previously been requested to sign the petition reacted much differently from the women who had not been approached. Over half of the women previously approached agreed to have the sign in their front yards, while less than a fifth of the women who had not been approached agreed to the request. Once a small favor (signing a petition) was granted, a much larger favor (displaying a large sign) was more likely to be granted.

The foot-in-the-door technique also was applied in a sales program aimed at selling a large inventory of curtains and upholstery material to retail shops:

The salesman visited the store of the retailer (the target audience) and asked for a small favor: whether he would display a small sign which simply said, "Coming soon, Pronti-Cort." Since nothing further was explained to the storekeeper, his curiosity was piqued, and it was maintained by customers who asked him what the sign meant.

A week later, the salesman returned and asked those retailers who did the small favor to do a larger one—to come with him to the wholesaler's showroom, at which time the meaning of the sign would be made clear. Most of the storekeepers agreed.[10]

The larger favor (coming to the showroom) was granted more easily after the smaller favor (displaying a small sign) was granted. At the showroom, the storekeepers were shown the products and a sales pitch was made; the sales volume was three times the initial forecast. The foot-in-the-door technique had been successful.

Why should the foot-in-the-door technique work? How does agreeing to a small request make you more vulnerable to a large request? You might think that after you've done someone a favor, you'd be less likely to do them another; in fact, the opposite is the case—you are more likely to do it. One explanation of this effect is that people are motivated to be consistent in thought and action. Consider the three possible thoughts:

(a) I like you.
(b) I dislike you.
(c) I have just done a favor for you.

Now, *a* and *c* are consistent, but *b* and *c* are inconsistent—it is not consistent for me to do you a favor if I don't like you. If I am motivated to be consistent, and if I have just done a favor for you, I am motivated to like you. In fact, I will probably like you more after I have done a favor for you than I did before the favor, because of my need for internal consistency between feeling and action. Because of my need to avoid cognitive inconsistency, or *cognitive dissonance,* I also tend to avoid reading things that are incompatible with my beliefs; I selectively expose myself to information supporting my existing belief system.

Belief follows action: what you do affects what you believe. Remarkably enough, if you say things that you don't believe you may begin to believe them. People who have been paid small sums to make public speeches arguing for positions contrary to their private beliefs wind up having beliefs more consonant with their public statements.[10] This evidence supports *the principle of cognitive dissonance: when actions are not consistent with underlying attitudes, the attitudes tend to change so as to become more consistent with the actions.* That is, your actions change your beliefs.

The principle of cognitive dissonance: When actions are not consistent with underlying attitudes, the attitudes tend to change so as to become more consistent with the actions.

When you do something at odds with what you believe, you are faced with a problem; you have acted inconsistently, not in keeping with your underlying attitudes and beliefs. You usually resolve this by changing what you believe to reflect what you have done. Subjects in an experiment by Festinger and Carlsmith performed a number of very dull tasks. Later, at the experimenter's request, they lied and told a prospective subject that the tasks were actually very interesting. Some subjects were paid one dollar to do this and some were paid twenty dollars. Subjects paid twenty dollars to lie had some justification for their actions (it paid off). Subjects paid only one dollar had little justification to lie about how interesting the tasks were. They were faced with the inconsistency of their actions and their attitudes about the tasks. One way to resolve this inconsistency and justify their actions would be to decide that the tasks were not so bad after all. That is apparently what happened. These subjects later reported the tasks to be more enjoyable than did the subjects with substantial monetary justification for their actions. Thus, their attitudes had changed to become more consistent with their actions.

Aronson, E. Dissonance theory: progress and problems. In R. P. Abelson, E. Aronson, W. S. McGuire, T. M. Newcombe, M. J. Rosenberg, and P. H. Tannenbaum (eds.), *Theories of Cognitive Consistency: a Sourcebook.* Chicago: Rand-McNally, 1968.

Carlsmith, J. M., Collins, B. E., and Helmreich, R. L. Studies in forced compliance on attitude change produced by face-to-face role playing and anonymous essay writing. *Journal of Personality and Social Psychology,* 1966, **4,** 1–13.

Festinger, L. and Carlsmith, J. M. Cognitive consequences of forced compliance. *Journal of Abnormal and Social Psychology,* 1959, **58,** 203–210.

One way to apply the cognitive dissonance principle in selling is to use the foot-in-the-door technique. A second application is to observe the effect of your sales pitch on your prospective buyers, and invite them to express their views only when you judge them to be relatively positive about your product; their positive pronouncements should lead them to have even more positive attitudes about your product, and ultimately lead to a higher probability of making a sale.

Exercise—Determining Selling Techniques

Television advertising is a multimillion-dollar business. A tremendous amount of research time and money are spent to sell products. The purpose of this exercise is to see if you can determine the techniques that major advertisers use to sell you their products. During the next week, look for commercials advertising the following products:

1. A major food chain (e.g., Kentucky Fried Chicken or McDonald's)
2. A major tire manufacturer (e.g., Goodyear or Firestone)
3. A cosmetic company (e.g., Chanel or Avon)
4. Clothes (e.g., Levi's or Arrow)
5. Television sets (e.g., RCA or Sony)

Whom did the commercials try to appeal to? How did they get your attention? How did they try to make the sale? What is the most effective technique to get *you* to buy a product advertised on TV?

Staying Sold

After you make your sale you still have to worry; your job is not yet finished—you must concern yourself with the problems of "post-decision regret" and the influence of competitors. You want your buyer, in essence, to stay sold. If you have sold a car to a man, you don't want him to change his mind and return it after his friend questions his judgment. If you have sold a TV to a man, you don't want to lose the sale before delivery because he has met another salesperson. If you have sold the Brooklyn Bridge, you don't want your buyer to renege before you can complete the contract. After you have persuaded your buyer, how do you induce resistance to counter-persuasion by competitors? How do you keep them sold?

One approach to this problem is *inoculation*. People can be made resistant to disease by deliberately exposing them to a weakened form of the disease: this method of producing immunity is called inoculation. By the same method people can be made resistant to a particular line of argument by deliberately exposing them to a weakened form of the argument, and then vigorously destroying it. After people have decided to buy your product, you can strengthen that decision and make them less likely to change their minds by suggesting a counter-argument and then rebutting it. For example, after you've sold a person the Brooklyn Bridge, you might say:

Now, some people—who don't understand the business world—might see your purchase as extravagant. What they don't know is that you were smart enough to buy the bridge when it was on special, and so you actually saved several million dollars; furthermore, its value is bound to go up, so it's a terrific investment and a great hedge against inflation.

This method for inducing resistance to persuasion by others is discussed by the well-known trial lawyer, Louis Nizer, in his book *My Life in Court*:

When I am required to sum up first, I endeavor to prepare the jury so that it will not yield to the blandishments of my adversary. I remind the jury that he will have the last word and that I will not be permitted to correct any misstatement of fact which my opponent, who follows me, may make. I must rely on their discriminating judgment to reject any false arguments. Then, as I proceed to build my own case, I anticipate the contentions of my adversary. I announce his slogans and attempt to destroy them, asking the jurors to become my watchmen when they hear such sophistry, and reject it as an insult to their intelligence.[12]

An Ethical Question:
Should You Use These Techniques?

Selling is an attempt to control the behavior of another person; the science of psychology offers some tools to make that control more effective, and more certain. Is this kind of control good or bad?

Each person must decide such ethical questions alone. Persuading people to read books, take vitamin pills, or brush their teeth seems to be a problem different from persuading people to apply deodorants, eat cupcakes, or use hair coloring. Selling life insurance seems to be different from Joe Girard's selling of used cars. But ultimately, these distinctions are a matter of personal values; how you stand must depend upon your particular values.

You use selling techniques now, either directly or indirectly. If you don't explicitly sell products or services, you nevertheless attempt to sell your ideas and your choices to your friends, family, and associates. You attempt to influence other people daily, and you will continue to do so. Should you improve your persuasiveness by using psychological tools? Or is it more ethical to be a less effective salesperson?

Whether you choose to use these techniques or not, there is not the slightest doubt that others are now using them on you. There is some reason to believe that your resistance to the persuasive manipulation of others depends upon your knowledge of the methods being used. If you don't know what is being done to you, your power to resist is lessened. Thus, even if you do not use the techniques yourself, you should become acquainted with the psychology of selling.

How to Make a Sale

Step 1. You are what you are: if your credibility is high (you have status, authority, or credentials), use it by mentioning it early; if you have low credibility, don't mention it; or if you must, mention it after the sale.

Step 2. Find out who your potential customers are. What are their attitudes toward the product? What psychological needs might your product fulfill?

Step 3. Get your "foot in the door." Encourage people to do you a favor in your job of selling the product. Get them to make a public statement expressing a favorable attitude toward the product; get them to commit themselves, even if on a minor point.

Step 4. Actively involve the potential customers. Get them to talk — especially when it's a point that they might agree with. Get them to take some positive action toward the product.

Step 5. Following a commitment to buy, "sew up the deal" by knocking minor arguments against the product. Invite the customer to make a strong commitment and endorsement of the product before leaving.

Leading and Influencing Groups

Groups have never thirsted after truth. They demand illusions, and cannot do without them. They constantly give what is unreal precedence over what is real. . . . A group is an obedient herd, which could never live without a master. It has such a thirst for obedience that it submits instinctively to anyone who appoints himself as its master.

—Sigmund Freud[13]

I *must* follow the people. Am I not their leader?

—Disraeli

Whether as a master or as an instrument of the people, an effective leader can turn a mob into a superbly functioning group, and can organize the independent parts into a dynamic whole. How is a leader able to effect this magical transformation? What does it mean to be a leader?

A leader is a person who is influential in assisting the group to achieve its goals. Leaders by their actions influence other people to reach common ends. Everybody is to some degree a leader, since everybody influences the groups to which they belong. This influence is stronger in certain groups than in others, and is more evident at certain times than at others; thus, being a leader is different at different times and places.

What Do Leaders Do?

How do leaders lead? What do they actually do? The following questionnaire is adapted from one actually used by researchers to assess the qualities of leadership behavior in a wide variety of situations.[14] You can use the questionnaire either to describe your behavior as a leader or to predict how you would behave in a position of leadership in a group. Answer each statement true or false to show whether it does or does not apply to you.

_____ 1. Makes attitudes clear to other members.

_____ 2. Does personal favors for members.

_____ 3. Tries out new ideas with members.

_____ 4. Does little things to make it pleasant to be a member.

_____ 5. Does not rule with an iron hand.

_____ 6. Is easy to understand.

_____ 7. Criticizes poor work.

_____ 8. Finds time to listen to members.

_____ 9. Speaks in a manner not to be questioned.

_____ 10. Freely associates with other members.

_____ 11. Assigns members to particular tasks.

_____ 12. Looks out for the personal welfare of individual members.

_____ 13. Works with a plan.

_____ 14. Explains actions taken as leader.

_____ 15. Maintains definite standards of performance.

_____ 16. Consults members before acting.

_____ 17. Emphasizes the meeting of deadlines.

_____ 18. Accepts new ideas easily.

_____ 19. Encourages the use of uniform procedures.

_____ 20. Treats self and members as equals.

_____ 21. Asks members to follow standard rules and regulations.

_____ 22. Is willing to make changes.

_____ 23. Lets members know what is expected of them.

_____ 24. Is friendly and approachable.

_____ 25. Sees to it that members are working up to capacity.

_____ 26. Makes members feel at ease when talking with them.

_____ 27. Sees to it that the work of members is coordinated.

_____ 28. Puts suggestions made by members into operation.

Although there are 28 different descriptions listed in the questionnaire, there are only two different dimensions of leadership behavior sampled in the list: _task orientation_ and _group-maintenance orientation._ The odd-numbered statements reflect task orientation and even-numbered statements reflect group-maintenance orientation. Task orientation refers to the leader's attempt to get the job done, to structure the group efficiently, clear up channels of communication, establish methods of procedure, and organize resources. Group-maintenance orientation refers to the leader's awareness of the needs of the members of the group, to efforts to establish group cohesiveness and trust, and to attempts to facilitate the interpersonal relations among group members. Few leaders are able to perform effectively both the task and the group orientations; most are mainly one or the other. You can compute your task and group orientation score by adding up the number of times you answered "true" for the two sets of items, odd and even.

There are no right answers to the leadership questionnaire. No one style of leadership is best for all people and all situations. A leader who is effective in one situation may not be in another. Many different factors seem to be involved.

The extent to which a leader should show a task orientation depends upon how well he or she is liked by the group and how structured is the task of the group. When the leader either is well liked or strongly disliked, a task orientation seems to be most appropriate:

When the group backs the leader and the task is straightforward, the leader is expected to give clear direction and orders. The leader who under these conditions acts in a passive, nondirective manner will tend to lose the esteem of his group. We do not want the pilot of an airliner to strive for consensus on landing procedures while he is making his final approach. Similarly, when the task is confused, when the leader has little power, and when he is disliked, he would be better off paying attention to the task than waiting until he can get better interpersonal relations with his group. In fact, unless the leader takes charge of the task under these unfavorable conditions, his group is likely to fall apart. This is reflected in the old army advice that the leader in an emergency is better off giving wrong orders than no orders.

The considerate, human relations oriented approach seems most appropriate when the liked leader deals with a group engaged in a highly unstructured task such as a committee engaged in creative work or in decision-making and problem-solving tasks. Here the leader must be considerate of the feelings and opinions of his members.[15]

Another factor which affects the choice of leadership style is the time-table for the group's operation. Which is more important, the group's short-term goals or the group's long-term effectiveness? In the short run, a leader may not have time to attend to such group-maintenance functions as being considerate of the feelings of group members, encouraging open and friendly communication, and striving for group cohesiveness; such concerns become much more significant if the group must work together over an extended period of time. Thomas Gordon refers to the group-maintenance orientation as "group-centered leadership":

Group-centered leadership is an approach in which the leader places value on two goals: the ultimate development of the group's independence and self-responsibility, and the release of the group's potential capacities. . . . The group-centered leader chooses to adopt goals which are long-range rather than immediate. He is confident that the group will solve its immediate problems, yet he helps the group become more capable of solving future problems. . . . The group-centered leader believes in the worth of the members of the group and respects them as individuals different from himself. They are not persons to be used, influenced, or directed in order to accomplish the leader's aims. They are not people to be "led" by someone who has "superior" qualities or more important values. . . . He believes in the group's fundamental right to self-direction and to self-actualization on its own terms.[16]

Participation

The pajama factory in Marion, Virginia, was having problems. Productivity was low and there were high rates of resignations whenever workers had to shift jobs because of style changes. Psychologist Coch and Personnel Manager French wanted to find out why.[17]

The two men set up an experiment comparing three different methods of shifting jobs: (1) for one group the change was simply announced and explained; (2) for a second group of workers a number of worker representatives met and participated in laying out the details for the new job; (3) for the third group, each worker participated in planning for the new job. Following the job shift, worker productivity was examined and the three groups were compared. The results were dramatic.

Productivity was highest in the total-participation group, intermediate in the group with participation through representation, and lowest in the no-participation group. Productivity in the no-participation group dropped 20 percent and stayed low; morale fell sharply and complaints and slowdowns occurred. None of the group which participated through representation quit; productivity dropped, but returned to normal within two weeks. The total-participation group regained normal productivity within two days and output continued to increase until it reached a level 14 percent higher than normal; no one quit and morale was high.

When group members participate in making choices affecting the group and in setting goals for the group, the choices and the goals are more acceptable to the individuals involved. Participation in decision-making is the essence of democracy. It is possible to lead either in a democratic or authoritarian manner, depending upon the extent to which participation is allowed.

Authoritarian and Democratic Leaders

In an early study of leadership style, small groups of children were led by adults who adopted one of three different modes of leadership: authoritarian, democratic, or laissez-faire.[18] The most interesting differences occurred between the authoritarian and democratic styles. Those adult leaders using the authoritarian style of leadership made all determination of policy, dictated the goals and the work for the members, and remained aloof from group members. Those adult leaders using the democratic style of leadership tried to be regular group members, encouraged the members to come to a joint decision concerning policies and goals, and allowed members to divide up the work themselves.

There were striking differences between the behavior of the children under these two types of leadership. Group morale and unity was higher in the democratic groups. Authoritarian groups were more aggressive, particularly when the leader was temporarily absent. Work done in the authoritarian groups depended upon the presence of the leader; when the leader was away, the group became unproductive.

A problem in interpreting this study is that the authoritarian and democratic leaders differed in several ways, and it is not clear which of these differences were responsible for the different reactions of the two types of groups. Authoritarian leaders tend to be more cold, aloof, and task oriented than democratic leaders. It is possible that simply the warmth of the leaders could produce the different member attitudes.

Cooperation and Competition

Shannon was appointed for a group project. Weekly meetings throughout the term and a written report were required. He was pleased to be chosen the leader but was also somewhat nervous about taking on the responsibility. He decided that the way to get the most work out of the group was to encourage rivalry among group members. The first day the group met he announced, "Let's see who can come up with the most ideas." He maintained a spirit of individual competition throughout the term; as a consequence, the group was never able to work together effectively. At the end of the term they turned in a project paper that was long but disjointed. It lacked any sense of unity or integration.

The leader is able to create different climates in a group: trust or suspicion; acceptance or rejection; optimism or pessimism; and cooperation or competition. "Rugged individualism" has its place; but when people come together in a group, they do so to work together toward common goals. Working together means cooperating: helping each other, sharing ideas and resources, abandoning individual glory for group success.

Although we tend to value cooperation among people, we also value individual achievement and the competitive spirit. In terms of effective group functioning, cooperation is often the most important factor, but not always so. When the group's task involves individual and independent work from each member, then an atmosphere of individual competition seems to be more effective; however, when the task requires shared information or resources from group members, a cooperative spirit is more productive.[19] The combination of individual cooperation among group members plus competition between different groups tends to promote strong group cohesiveness and feelings of intragroup dependency.

Cooperative groups show better communication, increased cohesiveness, and greater friendliness.[20] In a study comparing individual cooperation and competition within groups, Deutsch found that cooperative groups showed more diversity of contributions from individual members, more achievement pressure, more attentiveness to fellow members, more productivity per unit time, a higher quality of product, and more liking for the group.[21]

Leading a Group

Step 1. Spend some time getting to know each other. Strengthening interpersonal relations in the group and opening up channels of communication between group members will build group cohesiveness. As a leader you can facilitate an atmosphere of trust by being sensitive to the feelings of others and by openly disclosing your own thoughts and feelings. Acceptance of the thoughts and feelings of others will be promoted if you yourself are accepting.

Step 2. Help organize the decision-making process, the means by which procedures and goals will be established, identifying choices and clarifying the positions and feelings of other members.

Step 3. Encourage cooperation among group members and discourage competition within the group. Comparisons among group members about quality of performance or amount of work should be avoided.

Step 4. Encourage member participation in decisions by asking for input, listening, and accepting. How dominant your role should be in the process depends upon the nature of the group. If your group is temporary, with short-term goals only, it will probably pay off for you to take a relatively directive and active stance; if your group must continue to function for a prolonged period and you have some long-term goals, it will probably pay off for you to focus on building effective communication and interpersonal relations within the group, and to encourage group members to become active and take responsibility for the future of the group.

Summary

Selling products involves the ability to influence others. Credibility and likability are two important characteristics of effective salespeople. Knowing what motivates the buyer is also important in making a sale. The foot-in-the-door technique, or asking prospective buyers to agree to a small request before agreeing to a larger one, takes advantage of the psychological principle of cognitive dissonance to influence people. Once the sale has been made, inoculation is a method commonly used to convince buyers that they have made a wise choice.

Like a salesperson, a leader has the ability to influence others. A leader influences a group in achieving its goals. Leaders can run their group in a task oriented or group-maintenance oriented approach. Allowing participation in group decision-making leads to high morale and productivity. Leadership styles can be authoritarian, democratic, or laissez-faire. The leader can create a climate of cooperation, competition, or both within the group.

Notes

1. *Newsweek,* July 2, 1973, pp. 62–64.

2. Brown, J. A. C. *Techniques of persuasion: From propaganda to brainwashing.* Baltimore: Penguin Books, 1963.

3. Haskins, J. Factual recall as a measure of advertising effectiveness. *Journal of Advertising Research,* 1966, **6,** 2–8.

4. Chase, C. "And now a few words from our sponsor . . ." *Good Housekeeping,* 1973, **177,** 90–91.

5. Christie, R. The Machiavelli among us. *Psychology Today,* 1970, **4** (6), 82–86.

6. Karlins, M., and Abelson, H. I. *Persuasion: How opinions and attitudes are changed.* New York: Springer, 1970.

7. Greenberg, B., and Miller, G. The effects of low-credible sources on message acceptance. *Speech Monographs,* 1966, **33,** 127–136.

8. Weiss, W. Opinion congruence with a negative source on one issue as a factor influencing agreement on another issue. *Journal of Abnormal and Social Psychology,* 1957, **54,** 180–186.

9. Wright, P. Attitude change under direct and indirect interpersonal influence. *Human Relations,* 1966, **19,** 199–211.

10. Zimbardo, P., and Ebbesen, E. B. *Influencing attitudes and changing behavior.* Reading, Mass.: Addison-Wesley, 1969.

11. Freedman, J. L., and Fraser, S. C. Compliance without pressure: The foot-in-the-door technique. *Journal of Personality and Social Psychology,* 1966, **4,** 195–202.

12. Nizer, L. *My life in court.* New York: Pyramid, 1961.

13. Freud, S. *Group psychology and the analysis of the ego.* London: Hogarth Press, 1948.

14. Halpin, A. W. *Theory and research in administration.* New York: Macmillan, 1966.

15. Fiedler, F. E. Personality and situational determinants of leadership effectiveness. In D. Cartwright and A. Zander (eds.), *Group dynamics: Research and theory.* New York: Harper & Row, 1968.

16. Gordon, T. Group-centered leadership and administration. In C. R. Rogers (ed.), *Client-centered therapy: Its current practice, implications, and theory.* Boston: Houghton Mifflin, 1965.

17. Coch, L., and French, J. R. P., Jr. Overcoming resistance to change. *Human Relations,* 1948, **1,** 41–53.

18. Lewin, K., Lippitt, R., and White, R. K. Patterns of aggressive behavior in experimentally created "social climates." *Journal of Social Psychology,* 1939, **10,** 271–299.

19. Miller, L. K., and Hamblin, R. L. Interdependence, differential rewarding, and productivity. *American Sociological Review,* 1963, **28,** 768–778.

20. Crombag, H. F. Cooperation and competition in means-independent triads. *Journal of Personality and Social Psychology,* 1966, **4,** 692–695.

21. Deutsch, M. The effects of cooperation and competition upon group process. In D. Cartwright and A. Zander (eds.), *Group dynamics: Research and theory.* New York: Harper & Row, 1968.

Suggested Readings

Bem, D. *Beliefs, attitudes and human affairs.* Belmont, Calif.: Brooks/Cole, 1970.

Davis, J. H. *Group performance.* Reading, Mass.: Addison-Wesley, 1969.

Janis, I. L., *Victims of group think: A psychological study of foreign policy decisions in finances.* Boston: Houghton Mifflin, 1973.

Karlins, M., and Abelson, H. I. *Persuasion: How opinions and attitudes are changed.* New York: Springer, 1970.

Key, W. B. *Subliminal seduction.* New York: Signet Books, 1974.

Zimbardo, P., and Ebbesen, E. B. *Influencing attitudes and changing behavior.* Reading, Mass.: Addison-Wesley, 1969.

Chapter Fifteen

Written by Gerald Tarlow/Drawn by Ben Black

Abusing
Psychology

Jim Jones was a 47-year-old preacher. He founded the Peoples Temple in Indianapolis, and then moved it out to California. Jones turned each service into a performance in itself, using all forms of ritual and music and appealing to large numbers of people. Among his parishioners he required total immersion and support of the liberal causes and politicians he favored.

In 1974 Jones moved his Peoples Temple and his followers to a 27,000 acre plantation in Guyana. The membership continued to grow, reaching 20,000, according to Jones. Yet Jones's behavior was becoming less stable with each day. He brought forth "cancers" from sickly parishioners, simulated by bloody chicken gizzards. Jones went from calling himself the reincarnation of Jesus straight to self-appointed God, claiming to be responsible for all creation. He forced his followers to sell to the public small pictures of himself, said to ward off evil. Jones amassed each member's earnings and savings into the temple's main fund, which one member guessed to be close to $15,000,000. Discipline was replaced by the disorder of brutal punishment. At times, Jones would initiate "white night" exercises where all residents of Jonestown were summoned at a late hour to the central pavilion while Jones would speak to them on "the beauty of dying." The members would line up, taking a drink which Jones claimed was poison. Expecting to die, each member unquestionably drank this "poison." Then Jones would admit the liquid was not really poison but part of his "loyalty test," which all had passed. He emphasized that if Jonestown were ever threatened from the outer world, "revolutionary suicide" would be necessary to dramatize their dedication to their unique calling.

On November 26, 1978, after members of the Peoples Temple had ambushed and murdered California Congressman Leo Ryan and three newsmen, Jones ordered preparation for a mass suicide. Many took their lives willingly. Some mothers fed their children the poison, then took it themselves. Jones sat above the crowd in the high wicker chair that served as his throne, encouraging the group and speaking of the time when they would all "meet in another place." Many of the cultists ended their lives in groups, with their arms entwined about each other. When it was all over, about 900 people had taken their own lives.

Knowledge is power. Knowing how to influence and control other people is a power of great human consequence. People have always been manipulated and manipulating; you frequently try to exercise personal influence when you are with people. In recent decades scientific psychology has offered a new understanding of this interpersonal influence and has developed more effective techniques for manipulating people. These techniques are used in politics, advertising, business, and education.

Advertisers, politicians, nutritionists, and ecologists all try to manipulate attitudes and behavior. Millions of dollars are spent daily to alter our beliefs and feelings so that we will buy another brand of toothpaste or vote for a different candidate. Social psychology has investigated ways of changing beliefs and attitudes and has developed a body of principles upon which advertising companies — and others dedicated to changing the minds of people — base their campaigns.

Many examples of psychological manipulation can be found. Parents, teachers, and psychotherapists modify children. Prisons attempt to modify criminals. You attempt to influence your friends, and sometimes you are successful.

The technology of psychology, like any tools, can be used for or against people. What is a "good use" of psychology? What constitutes an "abuse"? These are questions of human values, of ethics; and ethical issues are complex. Your values may differ from those of others.

Is all manipulation bad? Is it bad to manipulate someone without his or her knowledge and consent? If you think it is, what about people who are so young or so disturbed that communication is impossible, and thus neither their understanding nor their approval of your plan to "help" is possible? For example, should you attempt to influence and change the behavior of someone who is suicidal? Should a political administration secretly use psychological techniques to modify the attitudes of their opponents? When do you think psychological manipulation is good and when bad?

In this concluding chapter we will discuss certain forms of interpersonal influence that we will call abuses because they seem uniquely devoid of respect for the other person's rationality and freedom of choice. Note that this is a value judgment on our part.

You Are in My Power

Those who understand human behavior have learned that people are particularly vulnerable to coercion through the orders of an "authority," through group pressure, and through conditioning procedures. When ordered to do so, some people do terrible things. In Nazi Germany one group of people, when ordered to, tortured and killed others. We judge such people guilty, both legally and morally, because we believe they could have done otherwise; we think that we might have resisted the inhuman commands.

Hypnosis is a procedure which weakens resistance to the orders of others. The hypnotist tells the subject to sleep and he cannot help sleeping; the hypnotist tells the subject that he is a dog and he starts barking. Perhaps you have heard that people under hypnosis cannot be induced to do anything that they would find repugnant in their waking state; for example, that they cannot be hypnotized into harming themselves or others. This is not so.

In one study by Orne, undergraduate college students volunteered to participate in an investigation of hypnosis and suggestibility. Of those who volunteered, six were finally selected who "could readily achieve deep somnambulistic hypnosis manifesting such typical phenomena as catalepsy and rigidities, positive and negative hallucinations, posthypnotic suggestions, and complete posthypnotic amnesia."[1] The students were hypnotized one at a time, and were led into a special testing room where they were seated and told that they would have an irresistible urge to do whatever the hypnotist instructed. The hypnotist told them to pick up a highly poisonous snake with their bare hands. They attempted to do so — and were stopped at the last moment. The hypnotist told them to place their hands in a beaker of concentrated nitric acid — they attempted to comply. The hypnotist told them to throw the acid into the face of a nearby student, and they obeyed — but the student was prevented from being harmed by a change in the liquid. People can be hypnotized to perform dangerous and deadly acts.

But Orne's study of hypnosis led to an even more frightening finding. In addition to ordering hypnotized volunteers to perform the three dangerous acts, he also asked a number of unhypnotized volunteers to perform the acts of picking up the deadly snake, dunking their hands in acid, and throwing acid in the face of another person. Most of them followed orders.[1]

In studying obedience, psychologists have asked student volunteers to do strange, boring, meaningless, or dangerous acts. It is almost impossible to devise a task that people will not agree to do. In one series of experiments, subjects were asked to add pages full of random numbers and, after each page, to tear it up into no less than 32 pieces.[1] In another study, subjects were asked to eat dry soda crackers and to balance a marble on a steel ball — one a disagreeable task and the other impossible.[2] One experimenter asked subjects to sort through garbage.[3] In all cases, most of the subjects performed without complaint. Apparently, people do what they are told to do by those in positions of authority. Further, when they are following orders, they no longer feel much personal responsibility for their actions.

Obedience

In 1971 Lt. William Calley was brought to trial for the massacre of unarmed civilians in the Vietnamese hamlet of My Lai 4. Calley was accused of the premeditated murder of 109 innocent men, women, and children. One observer at My Lai described a particularly brutal incident:

Someone hollered, "there's a child." You know, it was running back toward the village. I don't know whether it was a girl or a boy. It was a little baby. Lt. Calley grabbed it by the arm and threw it into the ditch and fired.[4]

Of course, Calley was not alone at My Lai 4; he was leading a company of soldiers. Most of them followed his orders in the killing. One of his men was questioned at the trial and reported that Calley ordered his men to shove the villagers into a ditch and then to shoot them. Many of the Vietnamese who were killed were women with babies in their arms. Calley started shooting them in the ravine; his men followed his orders. One of his men could not stomach it:

Calley told us to start putting people into the ditch. We moved the people into the ditch with our rifles at a point arms' position. Some started crying and they were yelling. I was ordered to shoot.

Q. By whom?

A. Lt. Calley.

Q. What did he say?

A. I can't remember the exact wording. . . . Then Lt. Calley and Meadlo started firing into the ditch. Meadlo turned to me shortly after the shooting began and said, Shoot! Why don't you fire? He was crying and yelling. I just said, I can't, I won't, and looked down at the ground. . . .

Q. Lt. Calley ordered you to fire?

A. Yes sir.

Q. Why did you not fire?

A. I couldn't go through with it—these defenseless men, women, kids.[4]

At the trial, Calley based his defense on the contention that he had been ordered to do what he did, that the orders came from his superiors, and that he therefore had no choice but to do what he did. The judges disagreed, and he was convicted.

Calley's conviction triggered a wave of protest across the country. Many citizens believed that he should not have been found guilty, that he was a man who was simply doing his duty and doing the job he was sent there to do. Others argued that an order to kill children was illegal and should not have been obeyed.

When are people responsible for what they do and when not?

Following the Second World War, the United States Government cooperated with the International Tribunal in the trials of 19 German leaders for war crimes. The Nazis based their defense on the argument that they were only following the orders of their superiors when they tortured and murdered several million innocent civilians. They were convicted and sentenced to life imprisonment and death.

Both Calley and the Nazis implied that they had no choice but to follow their orders. How does an order produce such obedience? Why are dangerous and immoral orders obeyed? This might be a product of the strains and crises of war—something which, in ordinary times, would never occur.

Stanley Milgram disagrees. He points out that whenever people live together there are those who command and those who obey:

Obedience is as basic an element in the structure of social life as one can point to. Some system of authority is a requirement of all communal living, and it is only the person dwelling in isolation who is not forced to respond, with defiance or submission, to the commands of others. For many people, obedience is a deeply ingrained behavior tendency, indeed a potent impulse overriding training in ethics, sympathy, and moral conduct.[5]

Electrocuting a Stranger

Stanley Milgram, an experimental psychologist, has been concerned with the study of obedience and its implications. He writes:

Obedience, as a determinant of behavior, is of particular relevance to our time. It has been reliably established that from 1933–45 millions of innocent persons were systematically slaughtered on command. Gas chambers were built, death camps were guarded, daily quotas of corpses were produced with the same efficiency as the manufacture of appliances. These inhuman policies may have originated in the mind of a single person, but they could only be carried out on a massive scale if a very large number of persons obeyed orders.[6]

Puzzled by what leads people to follow orders, Milgram conducted a series of laboratory investigations in which the consequences of extraordinary commands could be studied. He decided to order people to electrocute a stranger. Would they obey such an order?

The procedure involved ordering a subject to administer electric shock to a victim. The "victim" was actually an accomplice of the experimenter, and the cover story was that the study was to determine the effect of punishment (shock) on learning. The subject was to be a "teacher" who read a series of word pairs to a "learner," who sat in a modified electric chair, strapped down and wired for shock. After a time, the "teacher" would read the first word of a pair to the "learner" and the "learner" would have to recognize the second word of the pair, a classic word-associate task. Whenever the "learner" made a mistake, the "teacher" was ordered to administer electric shock as punishment. Each time the "learner" made a mistake, the "teacher" was supposed to move a lever to increase the voltage of the shock being given. The range of possible shock was 15 to 450 volts. In fact, unknown to the "teacher," the "learner" was an actor working for the experimenter and was never actually given the electric shock.

The subjects in this experiment, the "teachers," could refuse to administer shock to the "learner" whenever they decided to do so. Or, they could give what they thought was an increasingly powerful electric shock trial after trial until they were administering a level of voltage labeled: "Danger: Severe Shock." If they chose to, they could continue increasing the voltage beyond that, to 450 volts, labeled simply: "XXX." In order to increase their conflict about continuing to give the shock, the victim — the "learner" — followed a script in which he groaned, screamed, and complained about his dangerous "heart condition" at different points along the way.

The question for Milgram was, would anybody actually give the highest level of shock to the victim? Milgram predicted that at least a select few would administer the shock regardless of the screams of the victim; they would obediently follow their orders — and not in the context of war, but in a scientific laboratory.

What would you predict? Would you administer shock to the victim?

The results of Milgram's study were depressing. Everybody shocked the victim. In fact, between 60 and 85 percent of the subjects in different investigations obeyed the experimenter and continued giving the electric shock until they reached the most dangerous level — 450 volts. The following excerpt from one of their testing sessions shows what it was like:

Fred Prozi's reactions, if more dramatic than most, illuminate the conflicts experienced by others in less visible form. About fifty years old and unemployed at the time of the experiment, he has a good-natured, if slightly dissolute, appearance, and he strikes people as a rather ordinary fellow. He begins the session calmly but becomes tense as it proceeds. After delivering the 180-volt shock, he pivots around in his chair and, shaking his head, addresses the experimenter in agitated tones:

Prozi: I can't stand it. I'm not going to kill that man in there. You hear him hollering? . . .

Experimenter: It's absolutely essential that you continue, Prozi. . . .

Prozi: Who's going to take the responsibility if anything happens to that gentleman?

Experimenter: I'm responsible for anything that happens to him. Continue please.

Prozi: All right (Consults list of words.) The next one's "Slow—walk, truck, dance, music." Answer, please. (A buzzing sound indicates the learner has signaled his answer.) Wrong. A hundred and ninety-five volts. "Dance." (Zzumph!)

Learner (yelling): Let me out of here! My heart's bothering me! (Teacher looks at the experimenter.)

Experimenter: Continue, please.

Learner (screaming): Let me out of here! You have no right to keep me here! Let me out of here, my heart's bothering me, let me out! . . .

Experimenter: Continue. The next word is "Green," please.

Prozi: "Green—grass, hat, ink, apple." (Nothing happens. No answering buzz. Just gloomy silence.) [Experiment continues, with learner groaning once or twice, but otherwise not answering; the shock level continues to increase.]

Prozi: Something's happened to that man in there. You better check in on him, sir. He won't answer or nothing.

Experimenter: Continue. Go on please.

Prozi: You accept all responsibility?

Experimenter: The responsibility is mine. Correct. Please go on. (Subject returns to his list, starts running through words as rapidly as he can read them, works through to 450 volts.)

Prozi: That's that.[6]

Studies of obedience by Milgram and Orne show that ordinary people such as you and I may obey orders from a person in authority and no longer feel responsibility for our actions. The conflict between moral beliefs, on the one hand, and obedience, on the other, is often resolved by temporarily abandoning moral responsibility.

Group Pressure

Once the mass suicide in Jonestown was underway, people followed orders and simply did what everyone else was doing. Why should "everyone else is doing it" make so much of a difference? We are all profoundly affected by what other people do and what they think. It is easy to conform and difficult to go against the crowd. To conform is to yield to group pressure.

The power of group pressure to produce conformity was shown dramatically in a classic study by Asch.[7] Subjects were given the task of discriminating differences in the lengths of lines presented on cards. Six confederates of the experimenter, according to a prepared plan, all gave false answers on certain predetermined trials. The seventh subject to answer faced a conflict: go along with the (false) judgments of the majority or rely on his own independent judgment. Conform or stand alone. Even though the line discrimination was so easy that almost no errors were made by people judging it alone, when the majority gave a false answer subjects conformed to the majority judgment about one-third of the time. Rather than trust their own eyes, people were led to trust the judgments of the crowd.

Using the line judgment technique to study conformity to group pressure, scientists have found that (1) up to a point, the larger the group, the more intense the pressure to conform; (2) if one person goes against the majority view, it is far easier for others to do so; and (3) conformity to group pressure increases when people are anxious or afraid.[8] These studies support *the group pressure principle: people tend to conform to group pressure; the more unanimous the group and, up to a point, the larger the group, the greater the pressure to conform.*

The group pressure principle: People tend to conform to group pressure; the more unanimous the group and, up to a point, the larger the group, the greater the pressure to conform.

People act differently in a group than when they are alone; groups pressure their members to conform. Sherif used the autokinetic illusion to observe the effect of group pressure. In this illusion, a stationary point of light in a dark room appears to move. Subjects estimated the amount of perceived movement when alone and when they were in a group. Subjects' estimates made while they were alone varied considerably. When they were in a group, however, their estimates tended to be very similar. Asch confirmed that many individuals in a group tend to give up their independent judgment and yield to the view of the majority.

Asch, S. A. Effects of group pressure upon modification and distribution of judgments. In E. E. Macoby, T. M. Newcomb, and E. L. Hartley (eds.), *Readings in Social Psychology.* New York: Holt, 1958.

Kiesler, C. A. Group pressure and conformity. In J. Mills (ed.), *Experimental Social Psychology,* New York: Macmillan, 1969.

Sherif, M. A study of some social factors in perception. *Archives of Psychology,* 1935, **27,** No. 187.

Group pressure operates in a variety of contexts, from the determination of clothing fashions to the craze of the lynch mob. "Going along with the crowd" means giving up your own unique inclinations; this produces both the benefit of cooperation and the tragic consequences of mindless conformity. Group pressure provides the urge to accept ethical principles as well as, at times, the urge to abandon them.

Abusing Conditioning Techniques

Some of the oldest forms of human control are based on the brute use of physical force: with enough power over people, with a large enough club, you can force them to do, or not to do, many different things. . . . Of course, you can't then turn your back on them safely.

A more powerful and permanent method for manipulating people is the use of psychological principles for mind control. The human will can be conditioned, so that people want to do what you want them to do — even in your absence. This powerful technology of human control can, of course, be used either for evil or humanitarian ends. Conditioning methods can help you break a bad habit, can eliminate a crippling phobia, and can help you acquire new skills and competencies; conditioning methods can also be used to teach fear, to brainwash, and to force conformity to the whims of the state. You can be conditioned either with, or without, your consent. One scientist described the power of conditioning as follows:

People can be conditioned to blush or otherwise react emotionally to meaningless words or phrases; to respond impassively to outrageous epithets; to hallucinate to signals; to feel fear, revulsion, embarrassment, or arousal upon demand; to feel cold when they are being warmed or warm when being chilled; to become ill when lights are flashed; to feel like urinating with an empty bladder or not feel the need with a full one; to establish habits and mannerisms they had never known before; and to break free forever from lifelong patterns of activity they thought could never be forgotten.[9]

The Law of Contiguity Applied:
How to Teach Fear

According to *the law of contiguity,* a stimulus that repeatedly occurs at about the same time as a response may acquire the power to elicit that response (see Chapter Seven). This law—the basis for classical (Pavlovian conditioning—can be applied to change feelings and attitudes. Most often the technique is used for humanitarian purposes — but it can be otherwise. For example, a rat that was repeatedly accompanied by a frightening noise would soon elicit fear. A book that was repeatedly accompanied by a painful electric shock would soon elicit anxiety and terror.

Aldous Huxley, in his novel of the future, *Brave New World,* described how this conditioning method could be used to train future citizens to conform to an authoritarian political regime. In one episode, Huxley reveals how babies chosen by the state to be "workers" are taught through classical conditioning to dislike books and nature, so that they will not be distracted from their labor in the future:

Infant Nurseries, Neo-Pavlovian Conditioning Rooms, announced the notice board.

The Director opened a door. They were in a large bare room, very bright and sunny; for the whole of the southern wall was a single window. Half a dozen nurses, trousered and jacketed in the regulation white viscose-linen uniform, their hair aseptically hidden under white caps, were engaged in setting out bowls of roses in a long row across the floor . . .

"Set out the books," he said curtly.

In silence the nurses obeyed his command. Between the rose bowls the books were duly set out — a row of nursery quartos opened invitingly each at some gaily colored image of beast or fish or bird.

"Now bring the children."

They hurried out of the room and returned in a minute or two, each pushing a kind of tall dumb-waiter laden, on all its four wire-netted shelves, with eight-month-old babies, all exactly alike (a Bokanovsky Group, it was evident) and all (since their caste was Delta) dressed in khaki.

"Put them down on the floor."

The infants were unloaded.

"Now turn them so that they can see the flowers and books."

From the ranks of the crawling babies came little squeals of excitement, gurgles and twitterings of pleasure . . .

The swiftest crawlers were already at their goal. Small hands reached out uncertainly, touched, grasped, unpetaling the transfigured roses, crumpling the illuminated pages of the books. The Director waited until all were happily busy. Then, "Watch carefully," he said. And lifting his hand, he gave the signal.

The Head Nurse, who was standing by a switchboard at the other end of the room, pressed down a little lever.

There was a violent explosion. Shriller and even shriller, a siren shrieked. Alarm bells maddeningly sounded.

The children started, screamed; their faces were distorted with terror.

"And now," the Director shouted (for the noise was deafening), "now we proceed to rub in the lesson with a mild electric shock."

He waved his hand again, and the Head Nurse pressed a second lever. The screaming of the babies suddenly changed its tone . . . Their little bodies twitched and stiffened; their limbs moved jerkily as if to the tug of unseen wires . . .

"Offer them the flowers and the books again."

The nurses obeyed; but at the approach of the roses, at the mere sight of those gaily-colored images of pussy and cock-a-doodle-doo and baa-baa black sheep, the infants shrank away in horror; the volume of their howling suddenly increased.

"Observe," said the Director triumphantly, "observe."

Books and loud noises, flowers and electric shocks—already in the infant mind these couples were compromisingly linked; and after two hundred repetitions of the same or a similar lesson would be webbed indissolubly. What man has joined, nature is powerless to put asunder.

"They'll grow up with what the psychologists used to call an 'instinctive' hatred of books and flowers. Reflexes unalterably conditioned. They'll be safe from books and botany all their lives." The Director turned to his nurses. "Take them away again."

Still yelling, the khaki babies were loaded on to their dumb-waiters and wheeled out, leaving behind them the smell of sour milk and a most welcome silence.[10]

A dozen years before Huxley published *Brave New World,* John B. Watson actually conducted a similar experiment.[11] The unfortunate subject of Watson's experiment was a nine-month-old boy named Albert. Before his experience in Watson's laboratory, Albert was described as a healthy, alert, and unemotional baby. Watson's first step was to discover what could be used to frighten the child. Albert was afraid of very little, it turned out, except one thing: loud noises made unexpectedly behind his head. They startled him and made him cry. With this discovery, Professor Watson was ready to begin Albert's "lessons."

The object of the lessons was fear — in particular, fear of white rats, an animal that, at first, little Albert was fond of. Watson wanted to prove that Albert could be taught to be terrified of rats. The procedure he used in the lessons was classical conditioning, based on *the law of contiguity,* a procedure very similar to the one Huxley described in *Brave New World.*

First, the white rat was presented to Albert. Then, just as Albert reached for it, a loud gong was struck just behind his head. The lesson was repeated several times. How did it work? Watson reported what happened afterwards, when the rat was shown to Albert without the loud noise:

The instant the rat was shown the baby began to cry. Almost instantly he turned sharply to the left, fell over on [his] left side, raised himself on all fours and began to crawl away so rapidly that [he] was caught with difficulty before reaching the edge of the table.[11]

Albert had learned to fear rats. Later tests indicated that Albert's fear had generalized to many different white furry objects, such as rabbits, fur coats, and beards. At this point, Albert's mother removed him from the experiment.

A few years later, Professor Watson boasted of his great power to manipulate people through the principles of conditioning:

Give me a dozen healthy infants, well formed, and my own specified world to bring them up in and I'll guarantee to take any one at random and train him to become any type of specialist I might select—doctor, lawyer, artist, merchant-chief, and, yes, even beggarman and thief, regardless of his talents, penchants, tendencies, abilities, vocations, and race of his ancestors.[12]

This exaggerated claim has, of course, never been shown to be true. The technology of conditioning can modify people, but only in limited ways. Most human learning is based on far more complex processes than simple conditioning.

The Law of Effect: How to Be a Rewarding Manipulator

Acts with favorable consequences tend to be repeated, according to *the law of effect* — the principle underlying operant conditioning. In order to control people using this principle, you must control their access to what they want: when they do what you want, you give them something they want (a favorable consequence for them). Using this operant conditioning procedure, you can manipulate people by controlling their rewards.

Two college students wanted to change their roommate into an art lover. The first step involved hanging pictures on the walls of their apartment. They decided that the only effective reward that they had control over was *attention;* so they withheld attention from their roommate whenever possible, except when he was looking at or commenting on the art pictures hanging on the wall. Although he was unaware of it, his "reward" for noticing the pictures was the attention of his roommates. He began to be more and more interested in the pictures on the wall (*the law of effect* was working); soon he was talking about the pictures all the time. One day he said, "Hey, fellows, how about going to the museum?"[13]

Prisons, schools, mental hospitals, and other institutions often use the principles of operant conditioning to control the behavior of their "inmates"; this type of control is particularly effective in custodial institutions which are able to control all aspects of the individuals' environment. Manipulation is not difficult when it is possible to deprive individuals of what they want (food, comfort, or attention), and to "reward" them for appropriate behavior by reinstating what was taken away.

Controlling Consequences

"After this, if you don't work, you don't eat. Who is ready to start work immediately rather than miss any meals?"[14]

The American psychiatrist who made this announcement was in charge of a Vietnamese mental hospital. He believed in the efficacy of work; the patients either felt otherwise or were too ill to comply. In order to press his point of view, the psychiatrist instituted a program of operant conditioning based on *the law of effect* — manipulating behavior by controlling consequences. He made eating contingent on working. Given the choice of working or starving, some patients chose to work. He writes:

About twelve patients made this choice. After one day without food, ten more patients volunteered for work and after two days without food, ten more. After three days without food, all the remaining patients volunteered for work. As has been repeatedly demonstrated, when the subject is hungry food is one of the strongest and most useful of positive reinforcements. . . . The fear expressed by hospital personnel that some . . . patients would starve to death was not borne out by our experience.[14]

The conditioning program for another group of patients at the hospital involved electroconvulsive shock treatment (ECT). For ECT, patients are strapped down and a high-voltage current is passed through their brains.

The procedure causes convulsions and unconsciousness; some temporary memory problems are also common. The psychiatrist described this aspect of the program:

. . . we announced, "People who are too sick to work need treatment. Treatment starts tomorrow—electroconvulsive treatment. It is not painful and is nothing to be afraid of. When you are well enough to work, let us know."

The next day we gave 120 unmodified electroconvulsive treatments. . . . Perhaps because of the smaller size and musculature of the Vietnamese people, no symptoms of compression fractures were reported at any time. The treatments were continued on a three-times-a-week schedule.[14]

Gradually, more and more patients decided to "volunteer" for work. Going to work was reinforced with favorable consequences—the end of the feared ECT treatments.

Token Economies

Programs in prisons have been set up using operant conditioning to control the behavior of inmates. In 1974 the Federal Bureau of Prisons decided to dismantle its behavior modification program in the Springfield, Missouri, prison. The *New York Times* described the program as follows:

In the project, prison guards and doctors tried to alter the conduct of troublesome inmates by first locking them in cells for hours and depriving them of all their privileges, then rewarding them if they behaved properly by restoring their privileges. The project known as START had become an object of fear and hatred to inmates in federal prisons across the country. Some inmates, hearing of START in the prison grapevine, staged hunger strikes against the program. Inmates and former inmates wrote letters and articles describing START, an acronym for special treatment and rehabilitation training as "Pavlovian" and "Clockwork Orange."[15]

Other programs in mental hospitals have utilized operant conditioning techniques to control all aspects of the patients' lives. These programs, often termed token economies, have used operant conditioning techniques to make the hospital run smoother, to reduce custodial work, and to eliminate patient behaviors that are troublesome to the staff.

Many token economy systems have apparently been very successful in motivating mental patients to care for themselves and to learn to behave in more socially acceptable ways. Some applications of token economies, however, seem to be aimed primarily at solving custodial and administrative problems. In one such system, for example, patients can earn 6 tokens for washing pots and pans, 4 tokens for cleaning up after other patients who are unable to control their bladder or bowels, 3 tokens for cleaning up the toilet, one token for making their beds, and tokens for many other similar custodial jobs. Patients can attend religious services for a cost of 10 tokens, can watch a movie for one token, can see the ward psychologist for 20 tokens, and can go for a 20-minute walk outside for 2 tokens.[16] The administrative and custodial work in the hospital is greatly reduced by the token economy system: patients conform much more readily to the rules and do much of the work themselves. One enthusiastic psychiatric nurse described the effects of one program as follows:

The project goes extremely well. We no longer have to call individuals for meals or coax them to go into the dining room. This used to require considerable time. Patients are taking the responsibility now of getting to the dining room on time. It sometimes seems to us today that this came about automatically with the use of tokens. Other by-products are that at mealtimes the general atmosphere seems more relaxed. There is no longer the mad rush to eat and get out. Patients get up without being called. Many of the patients we had to look out for in the beginning are now looking out for themselves. We hope this will continue. The night technician no longer has to go from bed to bed, calling the patients to get up for breakfast, get dressed for breakfast, and so on. She merely turns on the light and in 3 minutes goes back, and the patients who are up get their tokens. The ones who are not up get nothing. Very few are *not* up by then.[17]

One reason that the patients in this program got to the dining room on time is that otherwise they were not permitted to eat at all; furthermore, they could eat only if they had earned sufficient tokens through their behaving properly. The token economy resulted in patients taking more responsibility for their own care, and this is, in a limited sense, an improvement in their condition.

With the emphasis on patients' rights in the last few years many token economies have been eliminated from mental hospitals. It is no longer possible to deprive patients of certain basic rights (e.g., meals or a room) in order to manipulate them into behaving appropriately. The token economies that exist today are more individualized and integrate the patient's needs and treatment goals into the program.

Ethics

Psychologists as well as other mental health professionals operate under a code of ethics. One reason ethical guidelines exist is to protect society from psychologists who might use some of the techniques described in this chapter against other people.

The preamble to the ethical standards of the American Psychological Association reads:

Psychologists respect the dignity and worth of the individual and honor the preservation and protection of fundamental human rights. They are committed to increasing knowledge of human behavior and of people's understandings of themselves and others and to the utilization of such knowledge for the promotion of human welfare. While pursuing these endeavors, they make every effort to protect the welfare of those who seek their services or of any human being or animal that may be the object of study. They use their skills only for purposes consistent with these values and do not knowingly permit their misuse by others. While demanding for themselves freedom of inquiry and communication, psychologists accept the responsibility this freedom requires: competence, objectivity in the application of skills and concern for the best interests of clients, colleagues and society in general.[18]

Specific ethical guidelines have been developed to deal with responsibility, competence, moral and legal standards, public statements, confidentiality, welfare of the consumer, professional relationships, utilization of assessment techniques, and pursuit of research activities. However, oftentimes it is individuals who are not members of a mental health profession who abuse psychological techniques. When this happens it is up to you to fight back.

Resisting Manipulation

At present, the impressive power of the conditioning technology resides in a relatively few informed persons, who in certain circumstances could, if they chose to do so, manipulate others without their knowledge or consent. To some extent this is occurring now in institutions; advertising, too, is using the principles of conditioning as a "hidden persuader." Consent is crucial. When your behavior is manipulated, modified without your consent, your right to your own personality is violated. A professor of law comments:

Surely the right to live one's life free from bodily and psychological alteration is basic to our scheme of society. The ability to remain as you are is clearly a right suggested by the general pattern of the Bill of Rights. The First Amendment prohibitions . . . demonstrate that a man's thoughts, mind, conscience, and psychological processes are not to be manipulated or coerced by the state.[19]

The principles of conditioning, obedience, and group pressure provide the means for manipulation; but they need not be used against people. Psychological knowledge need not lead inevitably to the manipulation of the many by the few; an alternative is to become, through psychological understanding, less manipulative and less vulnerable to manipulation. When you know what you are doing and what others are trying to do to you, you strengthen your resistance to manipulation; you enhance your possibility for freedom.

These and other tools of psychology are now available to you; you can use them to change your life and to change your society. You face the difficult choice of how to use that power—for what ends and whose purposes. In your hands psychology offers the hope of a revolutionary advance in human potential and individual freedom.

Summary

It is possible to control and manipulate people using psychological principles. The use of these principles often involves value judgments. Psychologists have found that people can be easily manipulated by authority, group pressure, and conditioning procedures. These principles have been demonstrated in Nazi Germany, in Vietnam, and most recently in Jonestown.

Stanley Milgram's classic psychological experiment demonstrated that ordinary people would obey an authority figure and no longer feel responsible for their actions. Solomon Asch demonstrated that people conform to group pressure.

Conditioning techniques have also been abused. Pavlovian conditioning has been used to teach people fear, while operant conditioning techniques have been used to manipulate hospital patients and prisoners.

A code of ethics has been developed by psychologists that helps to guard the public against abuses. However, it is ultimately up to each of us to become informed about the abuses and uses of psychology in order to protect ourselves. Once we are informed, we can use psychology to improve our own life and society.

Notes

1. Orne, M. T., and Evans, F. J. Social control in the psychological experiment: Antisocial behavior and hypnosis. *Journal of Personality and Social Psychology,* 1965, **1,** 189–200.

2. Frank, J. Experimental studies of personal pressure and resistance. *Journal of General Psychology,* 1944, **30,** 23–64.

3. Gamson, W. *Power and discontent.* Homewood, Ill.: Dorsey Press, 1968.

4. Everett, A., Johnson, K., and Rosenthal, H. F. *Calley.* New York: Dell, 1971.

5. Milgram, S. The perils of obedience. *Harper's,* 1973, **247,** 62–77.

6. Milgram, S. Behavioral study of obedience. *Journal of Abnormal and Social Psychology,* 1963, **67,** 371–378.

7. Asch, S. E. Opinions and group pressure. *Scientific American,* 1955, **193,** 31–35.

8. Darley, J. M. Fear and social comparison as determinants of conformity behavior. *Journal of Personality and Social Psychology,* 1966, **4,** 73–78.

9. London, P. *Behavior control.* New York: Harper & Row, 1969.

10. Huxley, A. *Brave new world.* New York: Harper & Row, 1960.

11. Watson, J. B., and Rayner, R. Conditioned emotional reactions. *Journal of Experimental Psychology,* 1920, **3,** 1–14.

12. Watson, J. B. *Behaviorism.* New York: People's Institute, 1924.

13. Wald, G. Determinancy, individuality, and the problem of free will. In J. Platt (ed.), *New views of the nature of man.* Chicago: University of Chicago Press, 1965.

14. Cotter, L. H. Operant conditioning in a Vietnamese mental hospital. *American Journal of Psychiatry,* 1967, **124,** 23–28.

15. *New York Times,* February 7, 1974, p. 12.

16. Ayllon, T., and Azrin, N. *The token economy.* New York: Appleton-Century-Crofts, 1968.

17. Gericke, O. L. Practical use of operant conditioning in a mental hospital. *Psychiatric Studies and Projects,* 1965, **3,** 3–10.

18. American Psychological Association. *Ethical standards of psychologists.* Washington, D.C.: American Psychological Association, 1977.

19. Kittrie, N. N. *The right to be different: Deviance and enforced therapy.* Baltimore: Penguin Books, 1973.

Suggested Readings

Huxley, A. *Brave new world.* New York: Harper & Row, 1960.

Martin, R. *Legal challenges to behavior modification: Trends in schools, corrections, and mental health.* Champaign, Ill.: Research Press, 1975.

Orwell, G. *1984.* New York: Harcourt, Brace, 1949.

Skinner, B. F. *Beyond freedom and dignity.* New York: Knopf, 1971.

Index